# TAKING
# A STAND

# TAKING
# A STAND

### JANET LYNN MITCHELL

*"I will give you the treasures of darkness, riches stored in secret places,
so that you may know that  I am the LORD, the God of Israel,
who summons you by name."*
Isaiah 45:3, NIV

GREEN KEY BOOKS
Holiday, Florida

**Library of Congress Cataloging-in-Publication Data**

Mitchell, Janet Lynn.
  Taking a stand / by Janet Lynn Mitchell.
     p. cm.
  ISBN 1-60098-001-5
  1. Mitchell, Janet Lynn—Health. 2.
Knee—Surgery—Patients—California—Biography. 3. Medical
personnel—Malpractice—California. 4. Medical laws and
legislation—California. I. Title.
  RD561.M58 2006
  362.197'5820092—dc22
  [B]
                                     2006029454

## To Marjorie Day, Esq.

This book is dedicated to the life and memory of Marjorie Day, who practiced law for thirty-two years with integrity and style. Marjorie was the first female president of Western State University of Law and the first woman elected to the national executive board of ABOTA, American Board of Trial Advocates. Throughout Marjorie's career, she received many awards. Just before her death in 2002, she was honored by ABOTA and named "Trial Lawyer of the Year." Marjorie dedicated her life to helping those who had been harmed by medical mistakes. Her dream was that they would find the courage to face their situations and the ability to live their lives to the fullest. I am living Marjorie's dream.

## To Dr. Jack Hughston

This book is also dedicated to the life and memory of Dr. Jack C. Hughston, physician, educator, author, and founder of the Hughston Clinic in Columbus, Georgia. Dr. Hughston was a pioneer in the field of sports medicine and orthopedics, known worldwide for his knowledge in treating knee injuries. His life was devoted to education and research and to his patients, bringing hope and healing to many. I walk today because of Dr. Hughston's determination, skill, and wisdom.

# TABLE OF CONTENTS

# *Foreword*

## by H. Norman Wright

Sixteen-year-old Janet Mitchell trusted her orthopedic surgeons. Through ten surgeries she relied on her doctors. She believed them when they told her that her poor surgical outcome was "due to the way God had made her." Conquering seemingly impossible odds, she rose from her wheelchair, faced the parallel bars, and met her challenge—walking! It was not until fifteen years later that one of her doctors confessed—divulging the truth regarding the cause of her condition and the need for Janet's repeated surgeries. On the first surgery, the doctors had made a serious surgical error. In time, they altered and purged her medical records. X-rays were conveniently "missing" to cover up the mistake. Then they lied to her. Janet felt used and betrayed, and she was angry!

The experience of anger is normal and natural. As part of being made in God's image, humans have emotions, and one of those emotions is anger. Like all of God's gifts, anger has tremendous potential for good. We can choose to express our anger in ways that help or in ways that hinder, in ways that build or in ways that destroy. We can be irresponsible and allow the emotion of anger to control us, and we can express that anger in cruel and violent ways. Or we can be wise by choosing to express our anger in healthy and positive ways.

After a tremendous struggle, Janet admitted her anger, determined the causes, and committed the situation to the Lord. She discovered a healthy way to respond to that emotion—with positive action. Janet chose to take a stand for what she believed. She took her case from the state court to the appellate court to the federal court. Ultimately, she found herself on the steps of her state capitol, supporting a bill written specifically out of her experience. In September 2000, Assembly Bill AB 2571 was signed into law.

Janet's story is a true example of how one woman allowed God to heal her anger and then allowed Him to use her life's experience in making a difference for others.

# Acknowledgments

My precious husband, *Marty,* thank you for loving me, laughing with me, and sharing your life with me. Walking or not, you think I'm beautiful! *Dad and Mom* (George and Mary Lou Hepp), thanks for dreaming big dreams and reaching for the stars. Because you dared to dream, I walk today. *Jenna, Jason, and Joel,* my children, thanks for living your faith through this incredible time in our lives. And thank you for your encouragement, patience, and prayers through the writing of this manuscript. My sister, *Kathy,* thanks for being my legs when I couldn't walk and for being there for my kids—through it all. *Max and Agnes Mitchell,* my in-laws, thank you for our late-night chats and your constant prayers. And *Jane Hall,* thanks for being one of the best friends a gal could have.

*Bridget Halvorson, Esq.,* thank you for believing in me. Through your dedication, professionalism, and love I have learned to trust again. Bridget, you knew the odds and faced them head on. Without you, the secrets would have remained secrets. *H. Norman Wright,* Norm, thank you. For you challenged me to face my anger—then forgive. You showed me how to rise above my situation and move on triumphantly. Your wisdom, counsel, and support were life changing. And to *each nurse* who cared for me with excellence, thank you.

*Marcia Cooley,* thanks for your contributions to this book. Your red pen, wisdom, and love mark each page. Your dedication and encouragement gave this book life. My precious aunt, *Joyce Piper,* thank you for praying with me through my surgeries, for standing by my side as I "took a stand," and for poring over each page of this manuscript. *Bonnie Hanson and Kathy Ide,* my friends and mentors, thank you for your constant sharpening, counsel, and final touches to these pages. *Krissi Castor,* thank you for using your wisdom to make these pages shine. Lastly, I would like to thank the *many others* who helped to make this book possible. My life has been blessed because of you!

# Disclaimer

This story is my memoir and an account of God's faithfulness. All letters, records, depositions, and trial dialogue have been taken from actual trial-related correspondences and court records, including deposition and trial transcripts. Fictitious names have been given all doctors and medical staff, with the exception of Dr. Jack Hughston and Dr. Robert K. Kerlan. Fictitious names have also been given to the attorneys who represented the doctors I have called Dr. Albert Allgood and Dr. Ryan Ulid.

The names of H. Norman Wright, Bridget Halvorson, Esq., Lisa Neal, Esq., Matthew Ross, Esq., John Ball, Esq., Will Day, Esq., and Marjorie Day, Esq., have not been changed, as this is also a story of their professionalism and dedication.

*Chapter One*

# BETRAYED

I'D NEVER FELT SO SCARED.

My husband, Marty, and I sat in the Los Angeles International Airport, staring out the floor-to-ceiling window in shock. Planes sat on the tarmac—none landing, none taking off. Inside the terminal, silence reigned. The usual noisy, crowded, bustling airport stood empty, void of activity. Even the employees had abandoned their posts and fled.

We had come from Orange County intending to pick up Agnes, my mother-in-law. While we waited for her plane to arrive, airport officials informed us that a major riot had erupted on the streets nearby. Guns fired into the open sky. Looting, fires, and mayhem had exploded throughout the city. All outgoing flights had been canceled; all incoming flights were diverted.

I grabbed Marty's arm and hesitantly we headed through the long passageway leading out of the terminal. Our eyes darted from one abandoned shop to the next, wondering what or who we might find. I turned to Marty, my heart pounding. "I don't think it's safe to leave," I said more than once.

"We're not safe here either," Marty insisted. As he took my hand, I saw my own fear mirrored in his eyes.

"Wonder where your mom will land?" I asked, trying to lighten the moment.

"Don't know. But I know it won't be L.A. tonight."

I didn't see the melted ice cream until it was too late. In seconds my left foot slid across the tile floor. "No!" I screamed. I held tightly to Marty's arm, trying to prevent myself from going down. Despite my efforts, my right leg buckled beneath me. My greatest fear became reality—I fell on my right knee.

"Honey!" Marty shrieked. "Are you all right?"

Sprawled on the cold floor of the deserted airport, I clutched my throbbing leg. Chills seized my body. I squeezed my thigh, trying to prevent the pain from traveling farther. Marty squatted beside me. His frightened eyes met mine.

*This can't be happening. It just can't,* I thought.

"Marty, I hurt my right knee."

"Can you move it?"

"I'm afraid to try."

"Can you at least straighten your leg so I can take a look?"

"Aughhhhhh... don't touch it! Marty, be careful!"

"It's already so swollen, I can't get your pants rolled up to see it."

"Marty, I couldn't have..." I cried. "After all the surgeries I've been through to walk, it has to be okay. It just has to be."

"Janet Lynn, listen to me." Marty held my face with his hands. "You're going to be all right."

I closed my eyes and prayed, *God...oh, my God, please help me.*

"Help!" Marty shouted. "Somebody help us!" But all we heard was the echo of his voice. Reluctantly, Marty stood and started down the hall. As the sound of his footsteps diminished, I pulled myself across the floor and leaned against the wall.

Alone and scared, I thought about the anger and rage that had turned Los Angeles into a war zone. Earlier that day, April 29, 1992, Americans across the nation were stunned by the verdict of the Rodney King trial—four white police officers found innocent of beating an African-American man. Outraged mobs poured into the streets to protest, causing mass destruction and endangering lives. And now I sat in the midst of this turmoil, hoping to be found, yet afraid of who might find me.

Finally, in the distance, I saw a motorized cart heading my direction. For a second I panicked, not knowing if it was friend or foe who made the rapid approach. Then I saw Marty's wave and his smile of satisfaction at finding help.

A maintenance man who was still on the job was my rescuer. "Ma'am, I don't think my first-aid kit is gonna help you at all," he said. Without any further conversation, he yanked the plastic lid off his glass of soda and dumped the ice cubes into a small plastic trash can liner that hung on his cart. He tied a knot in the top of the bag and placed it on my knee.

Nodding to Marty, he said, "Let's lift her up on my cart. I'll drive you out to your car."

After a bumpy ride to the parking lot during which we insisted that I wanted to go home and not to the hospital, we thanked the kind man for his help. Minutes later Marty drove out of the airport, through the outskirts of L.A. The streets were eerily quiet.

It was almost daybreak when we arrived home to our three children. Exhausted, I crawled into bed. Marty packed my knee in ice and elevated my leg on pillows. Then he scrounged through the cupboards for pain pills.

As the medication took effect, I reflected on how odd it was that one afternoon could bring such unexpected events—L.A. a disaster zone, me getting injured, and Marty's mom being diverted, spending the night somewhere all alone.

Dozing off, I wondered what Rodney King was thinking. I wondered how his jurors were feeling. And I began to question the hows and whys of the legal system I had always thought to be fair.

The next morning Marty dusted off my crutches. We then went next door to see Dr. Adams, a neighbor who was chief of staff at Long

Beach Memorial Hospital. After examining my knee, he advised me to see an orthopedist. I agreed to call Dr. Jack Hughston in Georgia, the world-renowned specialist who had performed my last three surgeries. I also made an appointment with Dr. Ulid, a local orthopedic surgeon, who had looked after my family and me for many years.

"Janet Hepp Mitchell, you're back!" Dr. Ulid said when he saw me. One look at my swollen knee and he ordered an MRI. "Stay off that leg until we know what you've done," he advised.

At my next appointment days later, Dr. Ulid strolled into the examining room, studying my MRI report. He paused, lifted his eyes from the page, and greeted me.

"I brought you a surprise," I said with a smile. "A copy of my medical records from Dr. Hughston in Georgia."

Instantly Dr. Ulid dropped my MRI report on to the examining table, snatched the folder from my hand, and sat down. Clearly agitated, he thumbed through Dr. Hughston's records, page by page. Suddenly his eyes froze on the content before him. His finger followed the words across the page. Abruptly he closed the file and jumped to his feet. "Janet, we have a real problem," Dr. Ulid sighed. "It's time you know… "

*Know what?* I wondered as his eyes bored into mine.

"Janet, what has happened to you is *water under the bridge*. It doesn't make a d— of difference."

Head bowed, he avoided eye contact, crossed the room, and reached for the door. "Janet, I'm going to see my other patients, then I'll be back to meet with you. We need to talk."

Once the door closed behind him, I buried my face in my trembling hands. Fighting the desire to curl up into a ball on the examining table, I reached down to rub my leg. My heart pounded; I could hear each beat. I began to cry.

Dr. Ulid's stern voice echoed in my thoughts, "Janet, it's time you know…it's time you know." *What do I need to know? What does he need to tell me?* In the past fifteen years of our doctor-patient relationship, Dr. Ulid had never spoken to me like this before.

As quickly as he left, he returned, cracking the door just wide enough to pass me a box of tissues. Then he was gone, leaving me alone to agonize over what was yet to come.

My mind searched. I thought back to my last appointment with Dr. Ulid right after my fall. I recalled the look on his face when he saw my swollen knee. His cheeks puffed as if he were trying to swallow his words while his hands held my knee, sliding it back and forth into positions in which a knee shouldn't be able to move. He shook his head.

My thoughts flashed back to the many times I'd been in this office. When I was in high school, Doctor Ulid became one of my orthopedic surgeons. He had been my confidant through a difficult time in my life. He had followed me through ten surgeries performed within three and a half years. Dr. Ulid had helped me face the "poor outcomes" of my surgeries. He had encouraged me as I struggled with the subsequent therapy. Dr. Ulid had challenged me to walk. *Why today, fifteen years later, is he acting like a stranger? Why today am I afraid of him?*

I climbed down from the examining table, slipped off my gym shorts, and pulled on my blue jeans—not wanting to expose my scarred legs. I couldn't handle wandering around bare legged, even in a surgeon's office. Needing to call my father to tell him I'd be late picking up my children, I walked out to the reception area and asked to use the telephone.

Jenna, my seven-year-old at home, answered. After she passed the phone to her five-year-old brother, Jason, and I heard the latest funny sound my baby, Joel, was making, Grandpa finally took the phone.

"Dad," I whispered through the telephone receiver, "Dr. Ulid wants to talk with me. I don't know what about, but something is wrong. I'll be late."

"Janet, I can't imagine there being any problem too serious," my dad said. Like always, my dad tried his best to reassure me that everything was going to be all right. But this time, my intuition told me differently.

Walking back to the examining room, memories of 1980 flooded my mind. My medical condition and fight to walk had gone beyond the expertise of my Southern California doctors to Dr. Jack Hughston in Columbus, Georgia. At the time, I was barely twenty years old, alone in a hospital thousands of miles away from family or friends, having surgeries number nine and ten. Old thoughts and feelings, buried so deep they had not surfaced in years, crawled into my heart and mind: *At what point does one give up? Is there a time when the pain and suffering is so great that it's okay to quit the fight and resign myself to the reality that I might not walk again? All my dreams had come crashing down while my friends were across the country, going on with their lives. Did they remember where I was? Did they know that I was in the fight of my life?*

I gasped, startling myself. Refusing to let my mind continue on, I stepped back into my gym shorts, crawled back on to the examining table, and waited.

As I sat on the edge, I dangled my legs and then straightened my right knee. Holding it out in front of me, I counted the surgical scars—one, two, three, four, five. The sight of my leg repulsed me, so I rarely looked at it. Its disfigurement represented the wounds of my past.

I ran my finger along the two vertical lines, each about twenty inches long. Feeling every knot and groove along its path, I had to blink my eyes to shed the tears that had pooled. The scars had widened over the years from being opened more than once. Most had been cut into three or four times. If I looked closely, I could see the individual incisions that merged into thick pink scars. *Ugly! My legs are ugly. No one will ever be able to convince me differently.*

In an effort to refocus my thoughts, I looked around the examining room. Nothing new. The beige walls were still empty of decor except for a chart of the skeletal system and a gold-framed mirror. I watched the sun flicker through the slits in the blinds. To pass the time, I examined the skeleton poster, playing "name that bone" with myself. Once again, I studied my MRI report, but it made no more sense to me now than it had an hour ago. I thumbed through the medical records Dr. Hughston had mailed to me from Georgia after I'd phoned him about my accident. They didn't make any sense to me either.

Dr. Hughston was deeply concerned when he heard I'd fallen, twisting my right knee. Wondering if I'd caused "unwelcome complications," he suggested I see Dr. Ulid. "Let 'em take a good look at it." Along with a copy of my records, Dr. Hughston had included copies of a few x-rays in case Dr. Ulid needed to compare my past to the present. In the light coming through the blinds, I held up each of my six x-rays, all dated July 1980. "Yep, they look like bones to me."

At least an hour went by before Dr. Ulid returned and closed the door behind him. His mood was solemn as he took a seat across from me. Slouching in his chair, he reviewed my records. The room was silent except for his breathing and the turning of each page.

I watched his every move. His six-foot-plus "teddy bear" appearance seemed smaller than I remembered, yet his muscular form still revealed his strength. I noticed his shiny silver hair, which had once been a warm golden brown. Suddenly, I could see the signs of age, little things I had not noticed in the past years. Dr. Ulid's large, skilled fingers ran their way through Dr. Hughston's file. His face cringed as he studied its contents.

*God, Dr. Ulid is scaring me. Please help me,* I prayed silently.

"Janet," Dr. Ulid said in a firm yet hushed voice. "It's time you know." Pausing momentarily he cleared his throat. "I was there. I saw it happen. I was in on your first surgery." He broke eye contact with me. He folded his arms tightly over his chest and looked down with his head bowed as if he felt ashamed. Seconds later he continued, "Dr. Allgood cut your bone wrong, at the wrong angle, the wrong degree." Dr. Ulid's voice was charged with irritation and emotion as he stood up and confessed, "I tried to stop him, to tell him not to cut there. But Allgood goes too fast."

Immediately my stomach drew up into knots. I could hear myself screaming, yet my mouth had not moved. I was paralyzed by his words.

Uneasiness filled the room, as if neither of us knew what to say next. After a long, speechless moment, Dr. Ulid's authoritative voice broke through the silence. "The cut went diagonally, up to the joint space of your knee, cutting your ligaments and causing the instability. The rest of your surgeries were to try to fix this mistake."

*What did he say? No!*

"Janet, Dr. Allgood didn't intend for this to happen." Bringing his eyes back in line with mine he tried to assure me, "We had nothing against you. It was a mistake."

My thoughts raged, *Since 1977 you've told me that my problems were due to a "congenital complication," from the way God made me. You lied and had the nerve to blame my God!*

By now, my scarred legs stuck to the paper on the examining table. My hands trembled and a cold sweat covered my body. Dr. Ulid interrupted my horrifying thoughts by saying, "I suggest you go to Dr. Allgood and tell him that you know. See what he'll do for you.

Allgood won't have any of your medical records. I'm certain he's gotten rid of them."

Leaning back against the wall, Dr. Ulid cleared his throat and glared menacingly. "I need to make one thing clear to you, Janet. You're not to tell Dr. Allgood how you got this information. Under no circumstances are you to tell anyone whom you heard this from. Do you understand?"

I nodded yes and then tried to find some semblance of composure as I faced the reality of my doctors' secrets, mistakes, and lies. *Please tell me you're sorry!* I wanted to scream. *Why can't you say these two simple words? Aren't you sorry? "Water under the bridge," he says. How dare he!*

I studied this man I'd considered a hero. From his sun-bronzed skin to the thick gold chain around his neck, I didn't recognize him. A stranger stood before me. Fighting back my rage, I somehow found the courage to question him. Strangely, I wanted to be careful not to upset him.

I felt my bottom lip begin to curl as I held back my tears. "Dr. Ulid, why didn't anyone ever tell me this before? Why didn't you tell my parents?"

"Janet, we never thought it would come to this. We thought we could fix it!"

I had no idea what Dr. Ulid meant by "this," and I was too intimidated to ask. Instead, I listened carefully as a lump formed in my throat, making it difficult to swallow.

Our discussion continued; forty-five minutes or more passed. In the cold office with a man who had betrayed me, we now began to discuss my future. Dr. Ulid reviewed my options. The MRI I'd had a month earlier showed I had not reinjured my right knee in my fall. Unfortunately, it showed that I had degenerative arthritis in all compartments of my knee. Dr. Ulid said it best when he informed me, "Your knee is like that of an eighty-year-old woman."

*But I'm only thirty-two years old,* I wanted to yell back at him. Instead, stumbling for words, I said, "Dr. Ulid, I'm confused. You always told me that the reason I had the first corrective surgery was to prevent arthritis."

He ignored my comment, raising his eyebrows so that the wrinkles in his forehead merged into one. Folding his arms close to his chest, he blurted, "Your knee is like an old used tire. Eventually it will blow." Frightening words rebounded in my head: *fusion, cement, knee replacement, inability to walk, mistake.*

At Dr. Ulid's insistence, I promised I would return to his office in a couple of weeks. During that visit he planned to discuss my condition and treatment options with both my husband and me. At the conclusion of my appointment, Dr. Ulid stepped toward me, stretched out his arm, and authoritatively took the x-rays out of my hands.

*You can't have these. They're mine. Some go back in time to 1980, 1981; x-rays Dr. Hughston gave me in case...*But I didn't dare tell him that he couldn't have my x-rays. Afraid and shaken, I didn't say a word.

"I'll make sure you get these back. I want to evaluate them, compare them with the x-rays we took last month," Dr. Ulid said. Tucking the films tightly under his arm, he nodded goodbye and closed the door behind him.

Still sitting on the table, I drew my knees in and rocked back and forth. Muffling the sound of my cries, I wept uncontrollably. How could he do this to me? I trusted him! I relied on him, and he deceived me. I felt violated, betrayed, taken advantage of. My childlike faith and trust in people had, in a flash, been shaken to the core.

Finally I changed back into my jeans and grabbed my purse. At the front desk, I scribbled the check to pay for my appointment. As

I walked down the hall, I heard Dr. Ulid remark behind me, "You know, you walk with a limp."

Clenching my jaw I kept walking. Once outside, I forced back bitter thoughts and stumbled out to my car. I again began to sob. Scripture I'd memorized as a child came forth like a faithful friend. Through trembling lips I began to recite Psalm 121: "I lift up my eyes to the hills—where does my help come from? My help comes from the Lord, the Maker of heaven and earth. He will not let your foot slip" (NIV).

I choked on my tears, my knees buckled, and I leaned against the door of my car as I personalized the next verse: "He who watches over me will not slumber; indeed, he who watches over Israel will neither slumber nor sleep."

I crawled into my car and drove toward my parents' house. "Can this be true?" I cried aloud. "Have I really been lied to and deceived by my doctors all these years?" I drove in a daze and found myself shouting, "God, didn't you know about this? Why did you let them do this? Why did Dr. Ulid choose this time in my life to bare his soul? Is this his way of trying to cleanse his conscience?" I paused to take a breath, sobbing. I shouted, "Why did Dr. Ulid tell me this? It would have been less painful not to know the truth." My body shivered as I remembered the implacable way he had forbidden me to tell. I wept uncontrollably.

I drove up the driveway of my parents' home and parked behind several cars. Totally preoccupied with the last couple of hours, it suddenly occurred to me how many people would be there. Today was the day after the Tederman family reunion. Relatives from around the country were still visiting. I noticed that my husband's car had not yet arrived. Oh, how I longed for Marty to hold me in his arms and take me someplace to be alone—so I could scream.

I tried to compose myself before entering the home where I'd grown up, the place where I had struggled to recuperate from ten knee surgeries, but one look into my father's eyes, and I again burst into tears as I lunged into his open arms. Catching my breath, I told my parents of the mistakes and secrets. I explained to them about the condition of my knee and the questions about my future.

My mother called Dr. Ulid's office, outraged. "I need to speak with Dr. Ulid right away," she fumed.

"Dr. Ulid is in a meeting, and not available at this time," the nurse replied. "I'll take a message and have him return your call."

But he didn't.

After hearing about my day, the upbeat mood of the reunion-goers rapidly changed. People quietly gathered in the living room to discuss the "could bes" and the "what ifs." Could this really be true? What if it is true, what then? While they talked, I went outside and sat on the front steps to wait for Marty, my husband, my "knight in shining armor..."

Marty had come into my life toward the end of my knee surgeries. I met him the night of my tenth operation. Just hours from surgery, Terri, my hospital roommate, shook me to wake me up. When my eyes opened, three young guys stood over me, gazing at what they understood to be an authentic Los Angeles Rams cheerleader. I didn't recognize my "prince" when he appeared by my hospital bedside. Of course, I wasn't looking for, nor was I prepared for, his arrival. I'd never heard of hospitals being hot spots for matchmaking. Now, I'm told that Marty cannot honestly say that he immediately recognized me as his future princess either. At the time, I more closely resembled a damsel in distress.

Nevertheless, being married for eleven years, our lives had moved far from the circumstances of our dating years. We seldom talked about my past physical struggles, but often chuckled about the amazing odds of our lives crossing paths as they did. Now, sitting on the steps of my parents' home, twelve years later, I waited for my six-foot, gentle southern man, who loved me.

I saw his Volvo turn the corner and park. Peering out his window, Marty took one look at my puffed and swollen eyes and knew my appointment had not gone well. Emotionally exhausted, I could hardly repeat my story as I fell into his arms. We sat down on the front step, neither of us knowing what to say. Marty put his arms around me and let me cry.

*Chapter Two*

# INDISPUTABLE EVIDENCE

TWO DAYS AFTER MY WORLD WAS SHAKEN by Dr. Ulid's confession, my friend Shannon stopped by with a present. I carefully opened the package. My mouth fell open as I stood holding a replica of Dr. Ulid's office name plaque in one hand and a dart in the other. Then a tiny piece of paper floated to the floor. I picked it up and read, "It's OKAY to be angry."

Shannon had given me a priceless gift—permission to be angry. My friend knew I'd been wounded both physically and emotionally. She also knew that acknowledging and facing my anger would be a difficult challenge for me.

Before I could allow my anger to escalate, I had to do some research. I needed to know for sure that what Dr. Ulid had confessed to me was true. I decided to call Dr. Hughston in Georgia. He was world renowned for his knowledge of the human knee and his extraordinary skills in knee reconstruction and repair. He had pioneered sports medicine in the United States and had given fifty years to its study.

Dr. Hughston had performed my last three knee operations. He was a perfect southern gentleman, always wearing a colorful bow tie and wing-tipped shoes. Even though he was in his seventies, *retirement* was not in his vocabulary. He was still teaching, writing for professional journals, and seeing patients one day a week. It was obvious to everyone who knew him that his patients were his first concern and medicine was his calling.

As I sat down to call Dr. Hughston to tell him about my appointment with Dr. Ulid, so many questions ran through my mind: What if he confirms that Dr. Ulid's story is true? If so, why hadn't Dr. Hughston ever told me? What if he tells me that Dr. Ulid's story is only a fabricated tale? What then will all this mean?

Dr. Hughston was out of town. I briefed Wendy, his secretary, of my news, and she assured me that Dr. Hughston would call as soon as he got back into town.

Despite my anger, I decided to write Dr. Ulid to thank him for his honesty. I found a blank card with little ballerinas on the front. Oddly, I wanted to thank him for having *one* moment of integrity. But I fought those feelings back and began writing, repeating back to him word for word the statements he had made. I believed I had understood him accurately. Yet I wanted to provide him an opportunity to correct me if, by some chance, I had misunderstood. I wrote the following:

August 8, 1992

Dear Dr. Ulid,

I want to thank you for your honesty in telling me the truth about my right knee. No one has ever had the courage to tell me before. My family didn't even know. For the past fifteen years, I had understood that the deformity of my right leg was due to the congenital hip problem at birth. The statement is true, "Sometimes the truth hurts," and yet when one faces the truth, healing can happen. Since I have discovered the real reason that my knee is bowed and the need for the knee replacements to come, my entire body hurts. I wish I could make it all go away! I need time to work through my choices of a fusion or total knee replacement. When I asked you in your office why no one had ever told me that Dr. Allgood cut my bone in the wrong direction, you stated, "Janet, we never thought that it would come to this." Well, neither did I. I just wanted to have my feet straight.

My husband and I will be coming to see you in a few weeks. I'd like you to explain to him all my options and tell him that you said I can do all that I can now, ride a bike, walk, and swim. I have been afraid to go into the ocean for the past fifteen years. I thought it might twist my knee.... This next week I'm going to Mazatlan and I'm going swimming in the waves! I even bought shorts to wear!

Dr. Ulid, I know that this has been difficult for you, too. Thank you again for your honesty.

Sincerely,
Janet Mitchell

P.S. Thank you for trying to stop Dr. Allgood from cutting the bone wrong. You tried...and I appreciate it!

I reread the letter and felt certain any doctor receiving one like it would respond immediately if there had been a misunderstanding. I marked the letter "personal and confidential" and sent it "certified, return receipt requested," then began counting the days, waiting for a response.

I hadn't felt good about leaving my x-rays with Dr. Ulid, yet at that time, I was too scared for a confrontation because I was frightened that I would upset Dr. Ulid. After all, *he* was the doctor, and *I* was the patient. I told him I would pick up the x-rays midweek. It sounded simple but because of all that he had said and done, my trust in him was gone.

Jane Hall is one of my closest friends. Jane knew all about my appointment with Dr. Ulid. She displayed great patience and love for me as I lived out my pain before her. She did not know me at the time of my surgeries, but she saw my scars. Her compassion and empathy were life preserving. If anyone ever compared me to "Lucille Ball," then Jane was my "Ethel Mertz." Whenever I had an outrageous idea or something wild in mind, Jane was the one I called. So it was quite natural that I asked Jane to be my accomplice to go along to retrieve my x-rays. She and I carefully mapped out a plan of action.

As we headed up the walkway to the medical complex, Jane and I approached the signboard that listed all the doctors and their office numbers. "Guess whose name plaque *isn't* here?" Jane sighed. I stared at the empty space. "Jane," I whispered, "do you think Shannon stole Dr. Ulid's actual name plaque?" I took a second look at the signboard, rubbing my fingers across it. "Oh Jane, this isn't good. Shannon will have to return it."

"Janet, I'd say it is likely that you possess stolen property."

We then walked up to the receptionist who greeted us warmly. I explained I was there to pick up the x-rays I had left with Dr. Ulid. She motioned for us to take a seat and then excused herself. Minutes passed. Returning empty-handed, the receptionist said, "Janet, I can't find your x-rays. As soon as I locate them, I'll call you, and you can pick them up." With this, Jane and I aborted our mission and headed out to buy our usual extra-large Diet Cokes.

---

Weeks later, Marty and I waited nervously for my appointment with Dr. Ulid. It had been a month since Dr. Ulid's original confession. The office was familiar to Marty as well since he had limped there before due to basketball injuries of his own. The physical surroundings had not changed. Yet we felt far less comfortable there than we had been in the past.

Marty tried to break the tension by telling jokes, but nothing he said seemed funny. My throat was dry. I didn't know if I wanted to fight or flee. Leaning close to Marty I sighed. "I don't really want to see Dr. Ulid again. I am so angry with him, I could scream."

"Janet, calm down," Marty said. "I want to hear what he has to say. Maybe he can help make sense of this confusion."

I tightly rolled a magazine in my hands and twisted it, anxiously waiting. *I'm not going to be a victim who can easily be preyed upon again. Someday I'm going to have a chance to tell Dr. Ulid how irate I am. But not today.*

In the examining room, Dr. Ulid greeted us with a brusque, "I bet you two have had a long discussion."

"Yes, sir, we have," Marty answered.

Unlike my last appointment, today I was not alone. I was with my husband who loved me, who wanted to protect me. If it was within Marty's power, Dr. Ulid would never have the opportunity to hurt me again.

Dr. Ulid cleared his throat and looked at Marty as if he wanted to speak with him alone. "I believe that it matters, in retrospect, little as to what the overall situation is. Janet's MRI shows major degenerative arthrosis of her knee joint," he added.

Seeing our confused looks Dr. Ulid continued, "Her knee is simply deteriorating." And then, without giving Marty a chance to respond, Dr. Ulid launched into an explanation of the medical options I faced. I sat motionless, listening to the pros and cons of each painful choice.

"Janet can remain as she is now until she can't bear the pain any longer. Or she can have a total joint replacement with the understanding this would not fix the bow in her leg or replace her ligaments. There are major technical risks and complications when thinking of a total knee replacement."

Speaking methodically and without emotion, Dr. Ulid continued, "Even if successful, the knee replacement will not last her projected lifetime, so she would have to count on two or three replacements in the future. Another option would be to try a fusion, to fuse the knee joint together so it would not give way. *If* this were successful, it would promise a pain-free future."

Marty glanced at me. "I don't believe Janet likes the idea of having her knee joint fused together."

I felt numb. Two men, one who had hurt me and one who loved me, sat there discussing what would be best for me. Was there a "best" in this situation? The best thing I could think of would be to turn back time, for none of this to have ever happened. I wanted to disappear, to go somewhere and hide. For all these years, Dr. Ulid had not wanted what was best for me but what was best for him. I believe he had hidden the truth about my condition to protect his reputation and his financial standing.

My spirit slumped. Why hadn't God protected me?

Marty was cordial while trying to get as much information as he could from Dr. Ulid. It was all I could do to remain calm and quiet. It wasn't easy being an observer, watching this scenario unfold before my eyes.

Marty brought up the subject of my last appointment. Immediately, Dr. Ulid looked away and his semi-friendly demeanor disappeared. The atmosphere chilled, and a sense of a secret meeting emerged.

I asked Dr. Ulid to explain to Marty what he'd shared with me a month before. His threatening glance instantly returned. "Janet, you heard me the first time."

Silence filled the room as an invisible muzzle clamped over my mouth. Breaking the stillness with a crisp, clear voice, Dr. Ulid confirmed, "The bone, the tibia, was cut at a diagonal angle rather than a horizontal one. The cut went through the ligaments."

He then explained that this was why I had needed my past surgeries, and it was the reason my present problems existed. He assured us that I had not injured my knee with my recent fall.

Chills ran down my spine, thinking about what I intended to ask next. I sensed God's presence, and courage came from deep within me allowing me to stare into Dr. Ulid's eyes. Reaching for my pen, I said, "I don't seem to understand what you mean. Was the diagonal cut from side to side or front to back? Will you draw me a picture, please?"

Looking inconvenienced, Dr. Ulid took the pen from my hand and drew two knees on the paper that covered the examining table. He pointed to the front view of one knee. "This is the way an osteotomy should be." Then he drew a line from left to right, back and forth, to emphasize a cut across the tibia a half-inch down from the knee joint. "This is the way your knee was intended to be cut. This is the way I did your left leg. This is the way it should have been cut."

Moving to the second knee, the side view, he started again one half inch down from the knee joint. This time, drawing from the far left side, he ran a line all the way up to the right top corner. In his reporting fashion and with a confident air, Dr. Ulid said, "The mistake Dr. Allgood made was that he cut the bone at the wrong angle and degree. This cut went straight through your ligaments, and because of this cut, you have experienced the instability in your knee and you now have arthritis in all compartments of it."

*No! It's because of your lies that I have arthritis,* I thought.

Before I could even ask, Dr. Ulid answered my question. "Yes, Janet, these mistakes are the cause of the bow in your leg. After the surgery in which we tried to repair things, a varus deformity was noted. That's the bow. I believe that due to the improper cut, the bone gave way and collapsed."

*And this bow makes my leg ugly! I hate it,* I thought.

Dr. Ulid's words seared through my heart, shattering the dam that held back my emotions. I bit my lip, but tears streamed down my face. *I'd like to see you try to walk on a bowed leg for just one day.*

Demonstrating no empathy for the pain he had helped create, Dr. Ulid continued, "Janet, I've told you these things so you can resolve them in your mind as to what happened. But it's water under the bridge. You have to quit crying and decide what to do."

His words released another flood of tears. Nothing could stop them. Marty moved closer to me as if to say, "You're okay. I'm here." He then thanked Dr. Ulid for his time and told him we would go home and talk about my options. We agreed to contact him when I was ready to proceed. Dr. Ulid stood and offered Marty his hand.

I shifted slightly on the table to cover up the drawing. I wanted Dr. Ulid to forget his artwork. I wanted to take it home with me and show it to my parents. Not once did Dr. Ulid examine my knee during the visit. Not once did he mention my "ballerina letter." Not once did he say he was sorry...and for this we were charged a "discounted" fee of fifty dollars?

As soon as Dr. Ulid left the office, Marty and I carefully tore off the picture he'd drawn of my knees. "Shhh...hurry," I whispered. With the drawing secured in Marty's pocket, he muffled the sound as

## Dr. Uild's drawing of Janet's right knee
## 01 September 1992

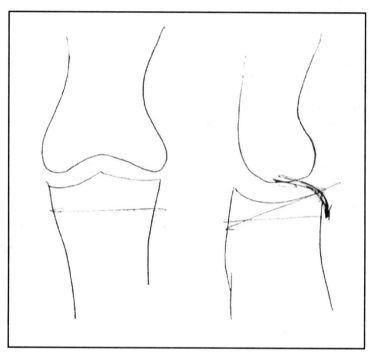

| VIEW ONE: | VIEW TWO: |
|---|---|
| Front view of knee | Side view of knee |

*View One:* The way the operation should have been performed

*View Two:* The way the operation was performed, demonstrating the improper diagonal cut, and the damage to the ligaments

he tore off what was left of the examining sheet and placed it in the covered trash can. He pulled another length of paper down to cover the table. With our hearts pounding, we left the examining room.

Using the hood of our car, I jotted down the only ligament I could remember from Dr. Ulid's description of the drawings. Having nothing else to write on, I wrote phrases and statements on the drawing itself. We were like two children who had investigated a crime and found indisputable evidence.

A mixture of relief and anticipation filled my heart. Marty had heard the famous "water under the bridge" statement for himself. Now he knew for certain that I had heard Dr. Ulid correctly during my first appointment.

"Marty, do you think the mistake really happened? I mean, do you think Dr. Ulid is telling us the truth? Why should we trust him now, when he just admitted to telling me lies for the past fifteen years?" Our conversation held few answers. Yet in my hands, I held the illustrations of Dr. Ulid's story, the nightmare I had lived—the mistakes that changed my life.

It was early evening the following day when Dr. Hughston returned my phone call. The sound of his voice put me at ease. I felt safe talking with him. My mother picked up another receiver and listened in as I wanted her to hear what Dr. Hughston had to say.

After answering Dr. Hughston's questions about the condition of my leg, I went into the story of my visits with Dr. Ulid and his astonishing confessions. "Dr. Hughston, I'm afraid. Dr. Ulid warned me not to tell how I discovered this information. I'm telling you because you are my doctor."

"That's right. I am." Dr. Hughston listened while adding his constant expressions, "Ugh, yeah; go on, sugar."

"Dr. Hughston, I need to know what really happened to me. Dr. Ulid said it was 'water under the bridge,' and I fell apart right there in his office."

"Well, I don't blame you for falling apart. Let's see here. Why don't you start at the beginning? Tell me what's happened since your fall."

Dr. Hughston listened to my story as I gave a detailed account of the visit with Dr. Ulid a day earlier. I told him about the drawing of my knees that Dr. Ulid had drawn freehand. "Did you know that neither my parents nor I knew anything about this?"

"No," Dr. Hughston answered.

"Did *you* know?" I persisted, trying to clarify the issue.

"Great balls of mercy!" Dr. Hughston exclaimed. "I didn't know any of this. Janet, I never received any operative reports from out there. Dr. Allgood said he would send 'em, and then they never showed up."

"Did either of the doctors tell you about the mistakes that were made and that they tried to repair them?"

"No, I can't say they ever did."

"This upsets me. They weren't honest with me, nor with the surgeon who was supposed to fix me."

"Janet, how's your knee holding up today?"

I could barely get the words out of my mouth as I felt Dr. Hughston's deep compassion and concern. My voice cracked as I told him about my recent MRI. "I've got really bad arthritis in all compartments of my knee. Bone chips get caught once in a while, and the MRI shows I have ligaments that are torn and missing." Through my tears, I informed Dr Hughston of the fusion or knee replacements to come.

As he had done in the past, Dr. Hughston was able to help me put things into better perspective. He assured me that, for the moment, I was *status quo*. He added, "Janet, if you're walking now, you're doing okay. I know the MRI doesn't look too good, but ya know, ya don't walk on an MRI."

Dr. Hughston agreed that fusion wasn't a good alternative. He instructed me not to worry about a knee replacement until I could no longer walk. Dr. Hughston had seen me struggle to get out of a wheelchair. He admired my determination to walk. His famous words from the past crossed my mind, "There's no knee that can't get worse by having surgery!" As he promised to get back to me in a day or two, I assured him that I would not have a total knee replacement anytime soon.

Marty and I took a drive to the beach, making a stop by Jane's house. We told her and her husband, Mark, about our appointment with Dr. Ulid and showed them the doctor's artwork. "I see you two were able to get away with a drawing, but what about the x-rays? Did you pick up your x-rays while you were there?" Jane asked.

Realizing we'd forgotten the x-rays, Marty asked Jane to go with me the following week and pick them up. He then told Mark and Jane about the condition of my knee. Marty reminded them that we had met while I was in a wheelchair and assured them that our relationship could and would withstand this storm. Maybe, in a roundabout way, Marty was really trying to assure me.

The four of us sat at the table, staring at the torn piece of paper. This situation wasn't a surprise to God. He'd known about it all along. I wanted to discover why God chose to reveal it to me now. Through Dr. Ulid's two verbal confessions, and now the picture, it was clear there was something he wanted me to do, but I wasn't sure what he had in mind.

As Marty and I stood to leave, Jane slipped her hand into her pocket and pulled out a smooth gray stone, which she placed in my palm. She tucked my fingers tightly around it, wrapping her hand around mine. She nodded. I understood.

Jane and I had been passing "the rock" back and forth to each other for ten years. In 1982, Jane had written on it, "Let God be your strength." She gave it to me at a time when I needed encouragement. I passed the rock back to Jane in the next challenging moment of her life. For all these years, our rock had been passed back and forth between us. We knew that whenever the rock was passed, times were not easy, and we needed to rely solely on God.

I'd grown up believing that God had a special plan for my life. No detail or circumstance was too insignificant for his attention. Genesis 50:20 came to mind, where Joseph so confidently stated, "Even though you planned evil against me, God planned good to come out of it." I've always believed that God could bring good out of evil, but what possible good could he create out of this mess? I wanted to have a heart as gracious as Joseph's. I wondered if Joseph had experienced such a range of emotions along his route to believing.

*Oh God, bless this mess! How can I please you with a heart so full of anger?* I internally wrestled. Back at home, sitting in my favorite rocker, I tried to pray. But no matter how hard I tried to suppress it, my simmering anger surfaced. My teeth clenched until my jaws ached. Every bite hurt to chew. Ironically, food was now more than sustenance; it was a comfort. I refused to look at my legs, because they were a constant reminder of my pain. Vigorously rocking back and forth, my frustration turned into a wailing cry, *God, what am I supposed to do?* My strength was gone. Moving from the rocker, I fell on to the floor and cried myself to sleep.

Life had been tough for the past year or so. Adversity had become a regular visitor, disrupting our lives. Our precious son, Joel, had been born prematurely, and Jenna Marie, our kindergartner, was diagnosed with juvenile diabetes, so the two of them had required thirteen hospitalizations to date. Marty's brother was stationed on the front lines in Iraq; the deaths of my grandparents; layoffs at Marty's work; and now Dr. Ulid's confession—we were overwhelmed.

For thirty-two years, I hadn't known what it really meant to depend on God and his strength. *I* had been a pillar. *I* was resilient. *I* handled everything that life brought my way. *I* was confident. I could do anything, be anything, or solve any crisis. Things were different now. *I* was at the end of me. I could not make my children well. I could not save Marty's company. I could not create peace in Iraq. I could not visit with my grandparents. And I could not change the truth concerning my knees.

My emotions were raw and bleeding. Betrayal ran deep. I wrestled with my despised, vicious enemy—my anger. And I didn't know how to win.

## Chapter Three

# THE STING

DR. ULID'S DRAWING became the talk of my family. Needing advice, I decided to call my cousin Bradley, an attorney in the state of Nebraska. He listened to the story of Dr. Ulid's drawing from a couple of weeks earlier in disbelief. He then asked, "Did Dr. Ulid give you the drawing? Can you fax a copy to me today? I've got to see that." Through our conversation, I began to understand that if Dr. Ulid was correct and the mistake did occur, he and Dr. Allgood would be guilty of fraud and/or concealment, as well as medical negligence.

But what good would it do? What could filing a lawsuit accomplish? I wondered. Then I had thoughts that sent shivers throughout my body. What if my doctors had hurt others? Were they continuing to practice concealment and deceit? If filing a suit could somehow prevent another person from experiencing the pain I'd endured, I'd have to consider it. Didn't I have a responsibility to "take a stand" for God's principles of truth and justice?

Two days later after I had spoken with my cousin, Dr. Hughston called again. "I've been reviewing some records, films, and things of your care here, and I'm getting back to tell ya what I think." He confirmed what I desperately did not want to hear. Calmly and without hesitation he stated, "I've noted in the x-rays from your 9-22-78 surgery that it is shadowed up to or through the joint space."

"What does that mean?" I asked.

"It means the osteotomy was cut about one and a half inches down on one side, then went up to the corner of the joint space on the other side."

"So this proves that Dr. Ulid was right when he said that the bone was cut at a diagonal rather than horizontal?" My body stiffened as we continued our discussion about the cut and its complications.

"You know, I never received any records or operative reports from out there. Not one of your previous doctors sent 'em, even after we asked." Dr. Hughston paused for a moment and then continued, "Janet, you told me after that first surgery you had an arthroscope, and the doctors said you had torn a meniscus. What I believe is that they went back inside the knee to find out how badly they'd damaged the ligament. They had to have known they cut it. Yep, there it is. There's no doubt in my mind that's what happened. Janet, that's what's caused your instability."

Shaking, I read a quote to Dr. Hughston from his own medical chart pertaining to my treatment. "With the second osteotomy, a varus deformity was noted, and it was thought that the varus deformity was putting some excessive pressure in the lateral capsule in order for her to walk straight. This subsequently resulted in a grade-three posterolateral laxity."

"Janet, you're right. You never had a bow in your leg before the first surgery. I didn't realize that. It's the varus deformity that kept stretching out your ligaments. This was caused by your bones being cut up through the joint space. You see, the bones collapsed, and that's why I had to graft bone from your hip. I had to try to correct this damaging deformity."

"Dr. Hughston, they knew they cut my ligaments and caused the varus deformity."

Very softly and with disgust, Dr. Hughston again echoed, "I agree."

There was a long silence because neither of us knew what to say next. Eventually Dr. Hughston spoke up. "Janet, what might you do?"

"I don't know," I said, sobbing. "Dr. Hughston, if they had been honest, I would have found you earlier. I would not have had all of those surgeries. They would have never had the chance to try to fix it. It wasn't until I went in to see Dr. Ulid last month that I knew.

"You have a right to be upset. All this coming up like it has. I'll do what I can to help you. You call me when you need to, and keep on exercising that knee."

Thanking him, I hung up the phone and pondered his words, words that he had never said to me before: "I believe that somewhere down the line your knee's gonna give out. It won't hold any longer. There will be arthritis and pain. When the time comes, we'll have to deal with it."

The reality was I couldn't do a thing to change it. I had no choice but to deal with it. From 1977 until now, I had believed what I'd been told by Dr. Allgood and Dr. Ulid. I believed that my condition was due to "the way God had made me, the way I was formed in my mother's womb." These doctors had used my faith, something they knew was genuine and precious to me, as a way of escape from their mistakes and responsibilities.

Realizing this, I felt my anger simmering. I entered a private war with my own thoughts. *Janet, you've got to stay focused,* I told myself. I could almost hear my grandma say, "Honey, it only takes a half a cup of garbage to pollute a bucket of water."

---

For days we'd been planning our trip to Dr. Ulid's office. With Jane's rock in my pocket, I swung by her home to pick her up. Jane was inspired. She said, "Janet, this time we'll march right by the directory board with our eyes straight ahead. We'll get those x-rays no matter what! Do you hear me, Janet Lynn Mitchell?"

Opening the office door, Jane walked in first. I noticed the faces of the people who sat waiting. Everyone sat quietly, some there for a checkup, others hoping for a miracle. Everything from mothers with children to the elderly sat in that room, relying on and trusting in their doctor. I wanted to scream, "Do you people know your doctor is a liar? You should run away while you can! Get out of here. Find another doctor who is trustworthy."

My name was finally called. Jane and I stood up and walked over to the reception desk. I told the attendant who I was and that I had come to pick up my x-rays. She asked us to take a seat and left to check on our request.

Not long after, the door leading to the examining rooms opened and the attendant called out my name. Jane and I stood and followed her back to a small waiting area. "Why did she bring us back here?" I whispered. "Why couldn't we have waited for my x-rays in the reception area?"

"I'm not sure, but look at this wall," Jane said as she began to count the numerous certificate-of-recognition plaques that hung neatly in rows.

While we studied them, a nurse named Rhonda arrived. "What may I help you with today?"

I told her that I was there to pick up my x-rays. Suddenly the room crackled with tension. "You can't have them. I've been told to guard your x-rays with my life," Rhonda mumbled under her breath.

I was stunned. "Yes, I can," I shot back. "Those x-rays belong to me!"

I felt the blood drain from my face. As Rhonda turned to leave, Jane leaned me gently against the wall. I wasn't sure if she thought that I might faint or that my leg was too tired from standing. "We need to get out of here. Something is really wrong," Jane whispered.

Rhonda returned with my medical file in hand and regretfully stated she couldn't find my x-rays.

"I'm positive I left them in this office," I insisted. "The last time I saw them, they were in Dr. Ulid's hands. Have you looked in the x-ray room or in Dr. Ulid's office?"

Rhonda's right eye twitched. She licked her lips nervously while agreeing to backtrack and check again for the x-rays. Clearly she was trying to comply with her employer's instructions and at the same time appease me. Her eyes darted constantly, as if to make sure no one was listening. Then, appearing confused and distracted, she laid my medical file on one of the benches and excused herself again. I glanced at Jane. She nodded. I grabbed my file and Jane slipped me my jacket to cover it.

Rhonda returned empty handed. I asked her to contact me when my x-rays were found. So without the "mysteriously vanishing x-rays," but with my "hot" medical file in hand, we rushed out of the office toward my car. I wondered if we were breaking any laws. We raced out of the parking lot and down the street. Once we'd traveled far enough from the office to be certain no one had followed us, I pulled over and began to read my file.

```
June 29, 1982: Patient seen and examined
this date, thirty-two-year-old white fe-
male. She had an extremely long history.
She had an extensive other chart here,
which we will pull up. Be that as it may,
dating back to when she was a teenager,
she had three operations under the direc-
tion of Dr. Allgood. This was for tibial
derotation. At that time the osteotomy cut
entered the posterior aspect of the joint
itself. She then ultimately had to have
a derotation. The knee joint continued
unstable. She was ultimately referred by
myself back to Dr. Hughston. Examination
```

> at this time reveals multiple scars. There
> is obvious posterior displacement of the
> tibia on the femur. There is three-com-
> partment crepitation.

Jane snatched the file from me. After all, she was the registered nurse. She thumbed to the back, "These records stop in August of '77, then start again August '78," she said. "I mean one entry is dated June 1977 and just below it is August 1978. Didn't you have several operations during that year?"

"Yes, I did. Keep on looking. Maybe they've been misplaced."

She flipped through the file again. "I don't see them. They're not here and it doesn't look as if they were misplaced. It appears they were removed."

"Keep looking," I cried. "They have to be there."

"Look, I've found your operations during your senior year of high school, but the following year is gone."

"I had four surgeries during that year. I was homeschooled and in a wheelchair part of that year. Oh Jane, the following year was when they tried to fix their mistakes. An entire year of my life can't be missing!"

Jane continued searching for a while and then quietly closed the file. We sat in silence with many questions and few answers. Neither of us had a clue what to do next. We walked through Jane's front door and collapsed on to her couch, not knowing if we should laugh or cry. The last hour had definitely not gone as planned.

Reaching for the phone, I called my lawyer cousin in Nebraska. "How are things going?" Bradley asked.

I began to tell him about my day when he interrupted me. "Janet, I want my partner, Stan, to get on the other line to listen in. He's an experienced medical malpractice attorney who has a heart for the underdog. Now, I want you to begin again and tell us about your day.

I've started the tape recorder so if Stan or I miss something we can listen to the recording."

I'd taken something that I was not sure was mine to take, and now I was about to confess it to a tape recorder. "Bradley, my x-rays are missing," I said and sighed. "The ones Dr. Ulid took from me the day he confessed. Dr. Ulid's nurse, Rhonda, said she didn't know what happened to them."

I heard Jane whispering in the background. "Remember to tell them what Rhonda said. You know, 'You can't have them! I've been told to guard your things with my life.'"

"Janet, is there any form of documentation that would state Dr. Ulid indeed did have these x-rays?" Bradley asked.

"Yeah." I opened the file. "The records state: 'August 4, 1992. She comes in at this time with multiple x-rays from the Hughston Orthopedic Clinic.'"

"What are you reading from? What records are you referring to?" Stan asked.

There wasn't a better time than now to explain to Stan about the medical file I was holding in my hand. "Stan, who do medical files belong to, the doctor or the patient?"

With this question, I disclosed my unorthodox act. I made sure that both Bradley and Stan understood that an entire year of my medical history was nowhere to be found. The relevance of the missing year was becoming clear.

"Bradley, do you understand? The year that is missing is the year I had the fix-it operations. The missing records would have shown my inability to recover from the first operation on the right knee." My heart beat faster as I told him about the thank-you letter I had mailed to Dr. Ulid a month earlier.

"Janet, do you have a copy of that letter?" Bradley asked.

"Sure I do, it's right here in my purse," I said as I began to read it aloud.

A few moments passed before Bradley interrupted me. "Janet, when do you think Dr. Ulid received the letter?"

"The return receipt says the delivery date was August 11, 1992."

"And you haven't received a response from Dr. Ulid?"

"Not yet."

"Well, he's had time. Janet, you need to get that medical file back to the office tomorrow," Bradley insisted. "I'm not sure of California law regarding the ownership of medical records. But I think the sooner they get back the better."

Stan told me to get a piece of blank paper. He then systematically reviewed my medical file with me. He instructed me to add a front page. On the top right-hand corner, I was to write the date. At the top in the center, I wrote, "I have received a copy of this medical record of Dr. Ulid, 1992. These records include…"

Section by section and page by page, I listed the contents. I ended my documentation with "Thank you for making these records available to me. Sincerely, Janet Mitchell."

Bradley and I discussed some ideas about how to return the file. I felt tense but knew Jane and I could come up with a plan. I agreed to call the next day to report on our success.

As Jane and I made copies of my "documentation" and the file, we talked about outrageous ways in which the file could be returned. We devised a legitimate plan and a few alternate ones in case we needed to divert from one plan to another. The laughter provided a welcome though temporary relief.

The next day I picked up Jane just before noon. "Janet, I was thinking maybe, just maybe, we could sneak into Dr. Ulid's office right before they closed for lunch and place the file under the glass window at the receptionist's desk."

*This,* I thought, *will be a challenge.* I couldn't imagine Jane or me sneaking anything anywhere!

"Plan One" went into effect approximately at noon. I slid the file under the glass window; it fell on to the desk, and we fled. Then we headed back to Jane's to call Bradley to tell him about the success of our mission. We all wondered who would find the file and discover my handwritten entry.

During my first conversation with Bradley, he had also suggested that I request my medical records from Dr. Allgood's office. He believed that these records could shed light on what had occurred during my first knee surgery. We wanted to compare these records with Dr. Ulid's and hopefully find the content from the missing year in Dr. Ulid's file. At that time, we thought these records might prove that a mistake had not, in fact, happened. Maybe Dr. Ulid had started "this commotion" because of an agenda of his own. Being punctual lawyers, the subpoena for my records had been mailed immediately. To date, Dr. Allgood had not responded. Technically, he was in violation of court orders.

My curiosity caused me to research. I learned that in the State of California, medical records and x-rays are the property of the health care provider. This surprised me. I paid for them, so why didn't they belong to me? However, the law provides that patients did have a right to access their records and obtain copies. The medical board could be contacted if the records were not made available within a fifteen-day period after a written request.

Days later, I decided it was time to pay Dr. Allgood's office a visit. Maybe they had simply forgotten to mail my records to Bradley. Maybe they'd misplaced the address. Regardless, I was glad my dad agreed to go with me on this adventure. "There's no telling what you might do if you run into Dr. Allgood," Dad said with a chuckle.

We strolled into the office and made our way to the reception counter to talk to Beverly, Dr. Allgood's office manager. Beverly had worked for Dr. Allgood since 1978. She'd seen me pass through these doors countless times, greeting me with her pronounced New York accent. But this time I was ignored. Except for her shade of blonde she looked as I remembered. She still wore her hair teased, perched high on her head, giving her petite body a taller appearance.

After standing at the counter for several minutes, my father cleared his throat, which was my cue to say something before he did. "Beverly, I'm Janet Hepp Mitchell. I'm here to pick up my medical file."

Beverly looked at me blankly. "We don't know a Janet Hepp Mitchell."

"Beverly, it's me, Janet. I had seven surgeries with Dr. Allgood."

"We don't have a medical file on you, or I would have sent it to your lawyers."

"You what?"

"I'm sorry. We've already looked, and there's no file by the name of Janet Hepp Mitchell."

Beverly was the first person to say she was sorry about anything—sorry that they didn't know me, sorry that I never existed to them. I was appalled, yet it almost seemed humorous. I felt the urge to push further.

"Well, if you don't recognize me, maybe you'll recognize my knee," I blurted loud enough for everyone in the room to hear. Then I stepped away from the counter and rolled up my pant leg. In front of the shocked patients waiting for their appointments, I aired the battle scars of my surgeries. The room hushed with all eyes on our little threesome.

"Look," Beverly continued curtly, "we don't have your records or x-rays. You can tell that to your lawyer friends."

"But I saw them here. I held them in my hands at an appointment just eight months ago. X-rays were taken that day. Where are they?"

Beverly briefly scanned the wall of files behind her. "You don't have a medical file here. Legally we only have to keep them for seven years."

"Beverly, I was in this office just a few months ago. Is it your policy to get rid of active records?"

"No," Beverly shrieked. Looking her in the eye, trying to find the person I once knew, I pleaded with her to look again.

"Janet," she snapped, "you're taking up my time. This office doesn't have any records on you. Now, I need to get back to work." Beverly proved again that she was the one in charge. Her word was final. It had always been difficult to get past her, to speak directly to Dr. Allgood.

Now, knowing there was no one above her except for the doctor, I asked, "Is Dr. Allgood here? I'd like to talk with him."

"No. He's not here."

"Can you tell me when he'll be back?"

"He's gone for the day. He won't be back until Monday."

"Please let him know I was here. Tell him I need my records." Practically pushing us out of the office, Beverly said she would tell him.

My dad held the elevator door open for me, and we waited until the door closed. "That woman is crazy to say they don't know me. Dad, how did Dr. Ulid know I wouldn't get a copy of my file from Dr. Allgood? How did he know my file and x-rays would be missing?"

"I don't know, but I bet I've got copies of your medical bills at home. They might jog Beverly's memory."

"You've got copies?" Being the collector he was, I shouldn't have been surprised. My dad saved everything.

"You never know when you might need it," he reminded me as he dropped me off.

Once home, I curled up on my couch and reflected on the day. I found my mind playing ping-pong with my emotions. With every slam of the paddle, anger gave way to worry, which, in turn, slammed back to anger. I tried to think thoughts I believed would be encouraging, thoughts that would please God. Oh, how I struggled to control them. I knew I had to be a gatekeeper and guard my mind. For every negative thought, I needed to input a positive thought or a promise of God. For every doubt or fear I had, I would counter it with God's truth and his Word.

I found a set of index cards held together by wire rings. To the front, I stapled a Bible verse: "Yet, the strength of those who wait with hope in the Lord will be renewed. They will soar on wings like eagles. They will run and won't become weary. They will walk and won't grow tired" (Isaiah 40:31). To the back, I stapled another: "We know that all things work together for the good of those who love God..." (Romans 8:28). This I declared to be my "flip book."

I was now armed for battle, the battle of my mind. Every day I read and added new verses, affirmations, and profound words. My collection included quotations by wise philosophers and fellow sufferers. One of my first entries was by Corrie ten Boom: "Obedience is easy when you know you're being guarded by a God who never makes mistakes."[1] I recited Corrie's words daily. "My God never makes mistakes. My God never makes mistakes..."

Ralph Waldo Emerson brought another profound thought: "What lies behind us and what lies before us are small matters compared to what lies within us."[2] I was grieving over my past and fearful of my future. Now I knew that what lay within me would be my anchor. Daily I read my flip book from cover to cover, reflecting and meditating on these thoughts.

After a few days of digging through boxes of old records, my father phoned me. "Janet, I've found some bills here. I figure I have most of them up until you married. It looks like Allgood and Ulid shared billing statements. Both their names are on the receipts. You had twenty-three office visits during the missing year, not to mention the four surgeries."

I pondered my medical history. Up until Dr. Ulid left the practice with Dr. Allgood in 1979, I had one medical file. I assumed Dr. Ulid made a copy of my chart and took it with him. I wondered if he'd removed the missing year at that time, or whether it had already been deleted from my chart. I didn't know what to think about my x-rays. I found it quite odd that all x-rays of my *right* leg from both doctors were missing or unavailable. Stranger yet, the x-rays of my left leg, the leg that had been "so lucky," were in abundance. Even x-rays taken at the hospital had vanished. It seemed someone had gone to a great deal of trouble to erase my surgical history. If I didn't wear the scars, the proof of my past surgeries would have almost disappeared.

For the first few years of my treatment, Drs. Ulid and Allgood were partners. Rumor had it that sometime during 1979, they got into a tiff, and Dr. Ulid left to open his own practice. Before he left, they shared an office, patients, operating costs, billing statements, and charts. I now believed that they shared a lot more. They shared the hidden secrets and the oath of silence surrounding my missing medical history.

With my "go-ahead," Bradley sent Drs. Allgood and Ulid an Intent to Sue. This was a legal document required prior to filing a lawsuit. It would put the doctors on notice that I was considering a lawsuit against them. I hoped this action would spur them into action to clarify my medical past.

The next day, I received a fax from Nebraska. The first page was a copy of Dr. Allgood's response to my Intent to Sue. Bradley tried to cheer me up by including a cartoon of a pelican holding a frog in its mouth. The frog was definitely in trouble. Its legs were dangling out of the pelican's bill, but its hands were tightly gripped around the bird's neck, squeezing with all its might. The words "Don't ever give up" were printed in bold across the top of the page. I chuckled at the dilemma the frog was in, and yet I had hopes that he, too, would beat the mighty pelican at his game.

I sat down to read Dr. Allgood's response. I was surprised that it wasn't written by an attorney but by Dr. Allgood himself. His letter was ridiculous, his dates were wrong and his "facts" were fictitious.

The letter was a clear demonstration that he was on a deliberate path of deceit:

Dear Mr. Weaver:

I have received your correspondence of October 6, 1992. I am somewhat perplexed at the letter as it has been over fifteen years to my recollection that I treated Janet, and I have not seen her now for the last seven or eight years.

At the time of our treatment, Janet did have derotational osteotomies of the tibias. She was doing well on the left and having some difficulty on the right. At no time were Janet and I ever at "arms" with each other. We continued to work well with this. She was then seen by Dr. Jack Hughston, and I believe some additional surgery was performed on her then, but I do not really have the exact surgical procedures or care at that time.

I do remember seeing Janet at one time either socially or here in the office when she was probably seeing Dr. Blake, but I have no recollection of ever having any malpractice or negligence in her case. I do know that her entire chart at one time was sent back to Dr. Hughston, but I also believe, in discussing with the office managers here, the charts need not be preserved. If the records have been misplaced in storage, it is not because of negligence, it is because of time elapsing.

I, at no time, want to cause any animosity between Janet and myself as she has always been a wonderful girl, and I am sure now a wonderful woman. How the knee is doing may be part of "nature" more than anything that medicine could cause. As far as fraudulently concealing negligent acts from Janet, I take that as a personal affront as much as I do not care one bit whether you are associated with California counsel or not. My only concern is Janet and how she has been doing. To bring something up like this out of the clear blue sky seems to be some type of possible ambulance chasing.

I will be glad to cooperate in this matter in any way I can, but as I have said, after fifteen years, I do not understand your letter.

Sincerely,
Albert G. Allgood, MD

Frustrated and angry over the contents of Dr. Allgood's letter, I agreed with the fact that he and I were never at "arms" with each other. But now things were different. My heart was full of rage!

Marty and I sought counsel from our pastor, elders from our church, and family members. We were challenged, "Sometimes faith requires action." We were reminded how God feels about lukewarm, indifferent believers who don't take a stand for anything. It was unanimous. It was time to move. I needed to find an attorney who was licensed to practice law in the State of California. I had to stand up against what was wrong and take a stand for what was right.

But who could I trust? Who'd believe my story? Who would even want my case with its lengthy history and statute of limitations issues? How could I afford an attorney? I was nervous about seeking counsel where I lived. Drs. Allgood and Ulid were respected in the community. One had even held the position of chief of staff at a local hospital.

Finding legal representation wasn't easy. Most people think personal injury attorneys are in abundance—that they'll represent anyone for a percentage. I quickly learned this wasn't true. Most *medmal* attorneys investigate a case and evaluate it for its financial worth and statute problems. Then they consider if the defendant is a friend or foe. Many times a victim remains "the victim," unrepresented and unable to secure counsel. Many personal injury attorneys represent their clients on a contingency basis. Sometimes they win; sometimes they lose. When they win, they often win big, and it's publicized. When they lose, they lose hundreds of hours of their time, it's chalked up as a loss, and they carry on.

Attorney after attorney turned me away. Although I had an incredible story, not one firm that I spoke with jumped to represent me. Some had an existing "conflict of interest" concerning the doctors.

Others thought the statute of limitations and odds against me were stacked too high, having to prove fraud.

One prospective attorney said it like this: "Janet, I hate to be the one to take the wind out of your sails, but the facts are clear. Ninety percent of all med-mal cases settle. Some settle on the doorsteps of the courthouse, but they settle. Ten percent of the remaining few plaintiffs actually go to trial, and doctors win ninety percent of the time."

"But I believe I'm one of the ten percent who could win," I argued.

Interrupting me, noting my enthusiasm and determination to expose my doctors, he asked, "Do you have proof of these so-called mistakes?"

"Yes," I said. "My left leg is proof. I had the same surgery on it, and it's fine today. I also have surgical records, office notes, and x-rays."

"Records stating the mistakes?"

"No, that is just it. No surgical record states what happened. Presently the x-rays of my left leg exist, but most x-rays of my right leg are mysteriously missing. I think my doctors concealed their mistakes until they thought the statute of limitations had run out."

"Janet, proving concealment and fraud is difficult—almost impossible unless you have it in black and white. Missing evidence could be normal considering the records have existed for fifteen years. Without proof of the mistake, there's no chance."

"But I do have it in black and white. Dr. Ulid drew a picture."

"I'm sorry. I'm sorry. I'm sorry," echoed from each personal injury attorney I approached. One firm, "Day and Day," truly wanted to invest their money and time in my cause. Yet they were already in litigation that involved Dr. Ulid. I wondered if the others thought

I was chasing a dream or perhaps had a story, but not all the facts. Regardless, I felt empowered. I refused to give up my pursuit.

I told Stan in Nebraska about my inability to find local representation. He said he was going to find counsel for me, and in the same state I resided. Then he told me about his sister, Bridget, a confident, well-established attorney in northern California who worked for a firm that specialized in the defense of doctors. *Isn't it just like God to provide me with a "defense attorney" whose entire career was geared to representing doctors in cases like mine?*

God has a history of using the "unexpected" to accomplish his will—Mary the virgin, Sarah the barren, and Bridget the defense attorney. Why not? With my go-ahead, Stan called his sister, and within days, Bridget flew down from Sacramento.

We met at a restaurant. Bridget was an attractive woman in her thirties. Her brunette hair was shoulder-length, permed, and shining with highlights from the sun. Her upbeat, friendly voice had a calming effect on me as we began our attorney/client relationship. Sitting in a large booth, I spread Dr. Ulid's medical records out across the table. I began to point out the discrepancies I had discovered. I then reached into my purse and pulled out Dr. Ulid's drawing.

Bridget held the rumpled piece of paper in her hand and ran her finger along the "mistake." Looking up at me she whispered, "Oh, Janet, I'm so sorry." Shaking her head in disgust and speaking quietly so that others in the restaurant couldn't hear, she whispered, "Do you think Dr. Ulid knows you have this? I can't believe that he drew this for you."

Bridget tried her best to explain to me the legal process of litigation. Even though the firm she represented was located a good four hundred miles away, and even though they specialized in the defense of doctors, they had discussed my case and unanimously agreed to gamble the odds and fight the fifteen-year statute of limitations. They were willing to rise to the occasion and untangle the web of lies surrounding my medical care.

"But how will I pay you? I can't afford—"

"Being a defense firm, normally we don't work on a contingency, but we will. My firm will front the cost of the lawsuit and receive a portion of any settlement or judgment if one is awarded."

"What if one isn't? What if we lose? What then? I could never..."

"Janet, we clearly understand the risk involved in taking your case. We also understand what's happened here."

We spent the next half hour discussing my reasons for pursuing a lawsuit—something I had never imagined I'd do. Over dessert, with my hand slightly trembling, I signed the agreement. I retained Bridget as my lawyer.

Weeks later, Marty and I took our family to the mountains to get away for a few days. Curled up on a couch, I prepared to do my weekly Bible study lesson. My class had been studying how Moses led the Israelites across the Red Sea. My friend Annette had scrawled across my lesson, "Roll up your pant legs. We're going in." True, I was facing what seemed like an impossibility, like the Red Sea, yet we knew that somehow God Almighty would part the waters in my situation. But that didn't mean my feet wouldn't get wet or that I wouldn't have to walk through the mud. Somehow, some way, God would meet the needs of this situation and of my heart.

Gazing out the window of the cabin, I saw nothing but God's creation. I bowed and prayed, committing this time to him and then turned to Exodus four, reading on through chapter seven. I began to answer my Bible study questions. I meditated on the Scripture references and reread my lesson. "God is my source, my sustenance, my strength, and my sufficiency." I pondered the meaning of these words. One by one, I began to apply them to my present circumstances. I grabbed a pencil and began to write:

*God is my source.* I don't have to worry about collecting all the facts. God was there. He saw everything. It was by his hand that my medical records were "made available." I will walk behind him as he conducts my lawsuit. God will provide all the details I will need. He will not allow my doctors to conceal information he wishes to expose.

*God is my sustenance.* He will nourish me and heal me. I will draw close to him, that he may comfort me and wipe my tears.

*God is my sufficiency.* God is just. He knows that my family and I never knew the truth. He knows my doctors lied. God will accomplish that which concerns me. I am not to be weary or afraid.

*God is my strength,* the lifter of my head. He will provide me with the capacity to endure physical pain. He will provide me with strength and endurance as I take a stand and watch for the deliverance he will bring.

With songs of praise, I thanked my God. With great reverence, I knelt on my scarred knees and worshiped him.

*Chapter Four*

# REFLECTIONS

MONTHS PASSED. I tossed and turned and fought sleep. The shock of the mistake and cover-up died down, but my anger intensified. *I said I was going to stand firm, that I wasn't going to let this situation change me. The truth is I've changed. I don't even recognize myself. My heart is cold and untrusting. It's not my legs that are crippling me, but my anger.* My rage resembled an out-of-control fire that leaped into every aspect of my life. Nothing I did could squelch the blaze.

It's hard to hit rock bottom, especially when you have a friend who lives above the clouds. Annette was the most positive person I knew. She found good in almost any bad situation. I, however, could not find nor feel any good whatsoever. It's been said that, "Friendship is a holy tie—made more sacred by adversity."[3] Annette was always there to celebrate and share in my happy times, and because of our mutual trust, she had earned the right to challenge my anger. Annette also understood something I did not—she knew that forgiveness needed to begin with a decision to forgive.

On one of my most down days, Annette paid me a visit. There she was, all five foot three of her, standing in my family room holding a large balloon bouquet in an array of colors. "Today is the day of forgiveness!" she eagerly announced.

Laughing and wondering if she'd accidentally inhaled too much helium, I said, "Is it a Hallmark holiday that I don't know about?"

"Janet, get with it. Today is the day you can forgive the doctors. It's time, you know. I've brought these balloons to—"

I interrupted, knowing exactly where her conversation was headed, "Oh, so you've brought balloons to celebrate? And what might we be celebrating?"

"No, Janet, I brought these balloons to help you forgive."

Now Annette had my attention. How in the world could a silly bouquet of balloons help me with the forgiving process?

Annette gave me a hug and sat beside me. Still holding the balloons, she spoke words that she knew I needed to hear and to act on. "These balloon are for you to *let go*. We'll get a marker and write on them the people and situations you need to forgive—the doctors and all. Then you can take a moment and choose to forgive."

The highlight of Annette's plan was that once forgiveness had taken place, we'd proceed outside where I'd release the balloons to the heavens, setting them free. This would symbolically represent that I'd handed my situation over to God and let go of the pain and anger that held me in bondage. This act would be a symbol marking my decision—the forgiveness that had taken place.

While listening to Annette's idea, my stomach tightened. I was not ready to set balloons free. I was not ready to say that what had happened to me didn't matter. Unsuccessfully hiding my tears, I stood and turned from Annette. With my fist clenched tightly, I shamefully cried, "Don't you understand, Annette? I can't do this!"

My body began to tremble. I felt the tug-of-war of my emotions. Sobbing, I turned back and faced my friend. "I'm sorry, but I'm still too angry."

Annette gave me a moment to catch my breath. Then she walked over and took my hands in hers. "Janet, your forgiveness will not change the past. It will free your future."

Speechless, I sat back down. *What?* How could my act of forgiveness free my future? My friend, who knew me well, had never seen me struggle with these agonizing emotions before. Whatever emotions they were—anger, sadness, or fear—I thought as long as I held on to them, I would stay in control.

It took some work, but I managed to convince Annette that my forgiveness needed to be a personal thing. "I promise when I'm ready, and when it's just 'me and God,' we'll take care of things."

What Annette didn't know was that I was also angry with God. I felt that I had kept my end of the deal. I had loved, served, and honored him, and he had let me down. God was one of the names I needed to write across my balloons, yielding to his plan—ending my fight.

I didn't write my words of hurt, anger, and forgiveness. True, I knew that each balloon was like my heart, and that any moment it might burst. Yet I determined that not one of the balloons would find its way to freedom in the skies that day. I hurried up the stairs, pulling the balloons behind me. I felt like a child trying to hide my unforgiveness; I stuffed the balloons in the back of my closet, covering them with my party clothes.

That night, as I lay in bed, I wondered if Annette had picnicked on her porch, watching the sky for a sign of my healing progress. She understood I was in pain and understood that she needed to allow me time to grieve. I in turn understood that she seemed eager for me to return to the Janet she once knew. *Our friendship will weather this storm,* I assured myself and then rolled over.

Unable to sleep, I leaned over and reached for my "flip book" with one hand and a flashlight with the other. I knew this lack of sleep was detrimental to my disposition, not to mention further complicating my depression. Through the fading beam of my flashlight, I read of David's struggles recorded in the Psalms. He, too, fought depression and was overwhelmed with grief. He, too, cried out to God.

Despite my knee problems, I knew I had much to be thankful for. My children were physically stable. Rusty, Marty's brother, had arrived home safely from the Middle East. My husband's job was tentatively secure. Yet my emotions knew no logic.

The secrets, lies and mistakes, why hadn't we discovered them when they occurred? We would have never allowed my doctors to try to fix their mistakes. *Oh, God, you knew they didn't know how to fix it. Through ten surgeries, I was faithful to you. I fought the fight. I learned how to walk again, and I never blamed you.*

My childhood faith had been shattered. I had always believed that, as God's child, God would protect me—that He was an invisible shield that separated me from anything that could hurt me. In my belief system, God would have miraculously stopped the saw or directed it in the right direction.

But my belief system was *wrong*. God had not promised to be my "insurance policy." He had promised to be with me *through* the trials and unfortunate circumstances in my life. Not understanding this, I wondered where God had been on the morning of February 9, 1977, the day my doctors made their surgical blunder. For the first time in my life, I felt a sense of betrayal and abandonment from God.

My anger turned into deep sadness. Sadness seemed to me a more acceptable feeling to be experiencing, rather than the insanity of anger. Depression festered, sleep was unpredictable, fear of my future surprised me at awkward times, and tears flowed freely as I mulled over and over all that had happened to me.

---

On my first birthday I was diagnosed with a congenital hip problem. I was taken for manipulative surgery and placed in a cast from my waist down, allowing my undeveloped hips to fully develop. I'd seen the home movies several times while growing up. I had vivid memories of those pictures of my shriveled legs just out of their cast. Yet being the spunky child I was, soon after I was up and running.

Growing up, there were no outward signs that I had ever had a congenital hip problem. I did, however, have my own "style" about me. I was somewhat knock-kneed. Never did my family or I think this was odd. We just thought I walked like my dad. I had no limp, no physical limitations. I was physically active. My favorite pastimes were riding my bike, swimming, and roller skating.

It was in high school that my "knee problems" were discovered. While vacationing in Mazatlan, Mexico, my sister and I were in a car accident. The motorcycle taxi in which we were passengers crashed. Thrown from the vehicle, my sister hit her nose. I ended up sprawled on the street, landing like a contortionist, hurting my left leg. I nursed my swollen knee, limiting its use until we arrived back in the States, then immediately made an appointment with an orthopedist.

That was when I met Dr. Albert Allgood, orthopedic surgeon. He was handsome, young, and well tanned, everything a fifteen-year-old girl looked for in a doctor. Dr. Allgood had charisma. Looking back, he probably could have told me almost anything, and I would have believed him. Most important, Dr. Allgood gave me the feeling that he was able to make things all better.

For the next year and a half, I nursed my left knee, guarding it from further injury. Three times a week, I attended physical therapy to strengthen my quadricep muscle. Regardless, my knee continued to lock and give way, requiring surgery to remove the torn cartilage.

During the 1976 spring break of my junior year of high school, I entered the hospital prepared for surgery the following morning. About 8:00 p.m., Dr. Allgood buzzed into my room.

"Hey, kiddo, are you ready for the morning? Why don't you hop up on your bed and let me take a last look at that knee of yours."

Dr. Allgood pulled the curtain around my bed, allowing me as much privacy as a hospital offers. I lay on top of my sheets, wearing a flannel gown. Dr. Allgood slid my gown up over my knees. He took my right leg in his hands and maneuvered it in different directions, seeing if it would catch or lock. He then took my left leg and performed the same exercise.

Looking puzzled, he walked to the end of my bed and grabbed my feet. He held my feet together, pointing my toes to the ceiling. Then, keeping my heels together, he slowly turned my feet outward, keeping a close eye on my knees. Grabbing a pen out of his pocket, he wrote numbers and measurements on the sheets.

Before I knew it, my gown was gathered around my waist and he was examining my hips. I was turned on my right side and flipped to my left. First my legs were in the air and then I was tummy down and looking straight into the bed. He had never examined me like that before. What in the world was he doing?

"Janet, you have a congenital deformity," he announced.

"A what?" I questioned, still face down and talking into the sheets.

"Your knees and feet don't line up. It's a rotation problem."

"It's a problem?" I asked, turning myself over so I could see his face. They'd never bothered me before. Why was it a problem now? "Dr. Allgood, I've been in your office countless times during the past year and a half, and you've never mentioned this before. Has something happened? My parents just left. Should I call them and tell them to come back?" *Should I call them to tell them that I'm deformed?*

What a shock it was to find out as a sixteen year old that I had an existing congenital defect. At first Dr. Allgood appeared surprised, but within minutes, his demeanor changed. Like a miner discovering gold, he left the room and gathered every doctor and resident he could find so he could show off my legs.

With several people now crowded around my bed and the curtain unable to close, I again performed acrobatic tricks. "Janet, I'd like you to take a walk down the hall to the nurses' station and back. We'd like to see your gait—how you walk," Dr. Allgood pressed. "Hold your gown up over your knees while you walk so we can get a good look."

How embarrassing! I shut my eyes for a moment, wishing I could make myself disappear. I suddenly had a mental picture of myself deformed, hobbling into Dr. Allgood's office.

"Janet, we're all waiting," he repeated. "Will you walk?"

It's a girl's dream to be a beautiful model, strutting up and down a ramp with all eyes focused on her. My dream had become a nightmare with all eyes focused on my defective legs. I slid out of the bed and stood beside it. Slowly gathering my gown in my fingers, I heard Dr. Allgood say, "Higher, higher, Janet. You've got to pull it way up."

With blazing cheeks, I began to walk the corridor. Nurses stopped in their tracks to watch the procession of doctors following me as I paraded down the hall. Was my gown high enough—or perhaps too high? I felt tears welling up inside me. *God, you said that I'm perfectly and wonderfully made. Truthfully, right now I feel like the new freak at the circus.*

Dr. Allgood's discovery did not stop my surgery. The following morning, I was rolled down to the operating room. Several hours later, I felt my mother's touch. "Janet, it's all over," she whispered. "Dr. Allgood said your surgery was successful. Your cartilage has been removed. Now your knee won't give way or lock up."

I mouthed the simple word "Good" and then fell back to sleep.

After a few days, I was up, swinging from crutches and learning to maneuver in my Velcro leg brace. I was discharged from the hospital after making a follow-up appointment with Dr. Allgood.

Two weeks later, I returned to Dr. Allgood's office where he and his partner, Dr. Blake, were engrossed, evaluating my congenital problem. For an hour or more, they measured and twisted my legs. The facts were down, numbers and measurements were scrawled out like hopscotch across the paper covering the examining table. Something was wrong.

Dr. Blake cleared his throat. "Janet, we're going to discuss your situation with Dr. Ulid. He's one of our associates who specializes in childhood—or should I say, congenital problems."

"Dr. Ulid is not here today," Dr. Allgood added, "but he's the known expert in his field. Dr. Ulid has seen many a rotation problem."

Within a couple of weeks, my mother and I met the famed Dr. Ulid. He was friendly and immediately tried to get to know me. "Do you know my daughter Stephanie Ulid?" he asked me, knowing we went to the same high school.

Sure, I knew Stephanie. So Stephanie's father was the orthopedic expert.

Within minutes, Dr. Allgood and Dr. Blake appeared at the door of my examining room. Peering inside, Dr. Allgood cheerfully said, "I see you've met our expert."

Dr. Allgood and Dr. Blake stepped inside, standing behind Dr. Ulid as he began his exam. Dr. Ulid had me sit, stand, walk, and lie down. After bending and twisting my legs in all positions, he stepped back and leaned against the wall. A conversation began as each doctor took his turn scrutinizing my legs. X-rays were taken. Then the threesome huddled together outside my examining room to discuss my situation.

Once back inside the cramped examining room, Dr. Ulid began the discussion. "Janet, you have excessive retroversion of your femurs with external rotation of the tibias."

"What? I have what? Where?"

"Putting it in simple terms, your femurs, the long bones that connect to your hips and knees, are turned or twisted. Your tibias, the bones between your knees and ankles, are also rotated, twisted. Yet they're rotated the opposite way, outward."

"What does this mean?" my mother asked.

"Mrs. Hepp, we're going to monitor Janet's condition. We'll have her continue the physical therapy that Dr. Allgood prescribed, but I'm changing the prescription to include both legs. We want to see her again in one month. Anything surgical we would do to help her would probably be done at the tibial level, cutting and derotating the bones."

*Surgery?* "Oh, but Dr. Ulid, I'm not interested in surgery. Really, I think that I look fine and...I don't mind the way I walk, really I don't. And I don't think anyone really notices. Dr. Allgood didn't for almost two years." If this were such a serious problem, how had it been overlooked by my pediatrician for my entire life?

Dr. Ulid shook his head. "It's not the appearance of your legs we're concerned about. It's the way your femurs and tibias are turned. We're concerned about your future."

I suddenly wanted to cry.

"Dr. Ulid, how could this problem affect Janet's future?" my mother pressed.

Dr. Ulid sounded factual as he responded, "Mrs. Hepp, I'm referring to severe crippling arthritis developing in the knee joints. The likelihood of Janet becoming wheelchair-bound is great without surgical intervention. We'll have to keep an eye on this situation and watch for any arthritic changes."

*Wheelchair-bound? Arthritic changes?* In a matter of moments, I went from a happy-go-lucky teenager to one with an unbelievable worry. Throughout the next few weeks, I found it difficult to get my mind off words such as *cripple, wheelchair,* and *future.*

With my doctors' permission, I headed to Badger Pass to go skiing with the youth group from my church. The snow was like cotton under my skis. It was there I convinced myself. If having surgery was what I needed, I'd have it. I'd do whatever I could to prevent crippling arthritis.

Once home and back in school, I found it hard to concentrate. My mind wandered. I'd catch myself daydreaming while my teachers were lecturing. Five days a week, I attended my Regional Occupation Program (ROP) classes at the hospital. By the end of the semester, I would be a certified nursing assistant, accomplishing step one in reaching my goal to be a registered nurse.

With the news of my medical condition, I felt a new sympathy toward the patients I came in contact with. I empathized with the uncertainties of their futures.

As planned, that summer I packed my bags and headed to Forest Home Christian Conference Center, tucked away in the San Bernardino Mountains. I spent several weeks at camp working to develop leadership skills.

Still unable to shake my worries, I sought out a rustic prayer chapel hidden at the end of a trail. In the solitude of the chapel, I walked to the front and knelt below the stained-glass window. *God, I'm so scared. I'm just sixteen, and these worries are too big for me. Please help me, heal me.* Tears streamed from my eyes. Now, for the first time, I truly understood what it meant to have a "trusting cry." I had surrendered myself to God in prayer. I had released the cares of my future to Him.

In the few minutes I spent on my knees, something remarkable occurred within me. I left that chapel at peace. I had a calm assurance that God indeed was in control. He had a plan for my life, and He would work out the details and orchestrate the circumstances.

My summer of 1976 concluded with a four-day backpack adventure, hiking over ten miles of mountain wilderness. My body felt exhausted, but my legs were strong. They provided me with stable footing and served as anchors as I made the uphill climb, journeyed over rugged terrain, and made my descent.

I began my senior year in September, and more doctor appointments were scheduled. In the late 1970s, it wasn't "acceptable" to question one's doctor. Despite the stigma attached, my parents demonstrated wisdom as they insisted I get a second opinion concerning my legs and future surgeries. After hours of networking, they managed to get an appointment with Dr. Kerlan, the team doctor for the Los Angeles Rams, Lakers, and Dodgers.

With x-rays in hand, my mother and I drove to Los Angeles. I soon found myself in a pair of shorts, parading down the halls with all eyes watching me. Several doctors, all men, watched me walk. I felt like Pippi Longstocking trying to compete in a beauty contest, hoping to win first place. Nervously, I wondered if I had altered my gait any. Conscious of every step, I wondered if I should walk with my feet directly in front of me and my knees in, or with my feet pointed outward and my knees straight ahead. Not sure what to do, I did it both ways.

After changing out of my shorts, I joined the task force at a long conference table. Each physician voiced his opinion. I felt that I was in the middle of a brawl as the doctors disagreed on their treatment plans and prescriptions for my health. Some felt that I did need surgery and the sooner the better. Others were not so sure.

The final conclusion of these great minds, and the only thing that they actually agreed upon, was to send me to be evaluated by Dr. Wilbert Gillian, yet another expert in the field. Drs. Allgood and Ulid agreed that I should consult with Dr. Wilbert Gillian. I wondered. Dr. Ulid also made it clear that he and Drs. Allgood and Blake all felt it was necessary for me to undergo derotation of both my tibias. "Dr. Ulid is the expert," Dr. Allgood bellowed. "He's very familiar with children's osteotomies. Really, the mechanics of this surgery should not be too big of a problem."

Dr. Gillian was wonderful—wise, kind, and experienced. Hindsight is perfect vision. Looking back, I wish I had chosen him to perform my surgeries. Dr. Gillian reviewed the x-rays Dr. Allgood had sent, and he took x-rays as well as photos of my legs. As I demonstrated my stride up and down his hall, I broke out in giggles at the sight of the flash from his camera. Now I could honestly say, "In my modeling days, all eyes and cameras stood transfixed on my legs." Never would I mention that I was wearing an old pair of gym shorts, which I now kept in the trunk of my mother's car.

With December came my second appointment with Dr. Gillian. A nurse walked my mom and me back to his office where he sat waiting. Piled on his desk were stacks of notes and x-rays. Suspended from a pole in the corner of the room hung a life-size skeleton. Dr. Gillian took the skeleton's hand, tapping its fingers on my knee. "How are you today?" he asked, pretending the skeleton was talking.

I smiled and whispered back, "I think I'm fine unless you know something I don't."

Dr. Gillian dropped the skeleton's hand. "I'm sorry to have to bear such news, but I believe you do need to have surgery, and on both legs. If these surgeries aren't performed you're certain to be crippled and wheelchair-bound by the time you're thirty. The good news is that once surgical intervention occurs, you'll be fine."

I sat frozen in my seat as I listened to these biting words—the reiteration of Dr. Allgood and Dr. Ulid's words. My mom began to cry, covering her face with her hands. Dr. Gillian quietly excused himself so we could have a few private minutes. Speechless, I watched my mom weep.

I then slipped out of my chair and knelt in front of her. Holding her hands, I prayed. In the middle of our private moment, Dr. Gillian returned. Hearing the door open, my mom and I looked up. "Good for you, Janet. That is exactly what I do when I'm in a tough spot."

I chose to break the seriousness of the moment and tried to be upbeat. "Can Drs. Allgood and Ulid do my surgery?"

"Any good orthopedic surgeon should be able to handle this. It's a simple procedure for a qualified doctor."

"Dr. Gillian, can you please explain the meaning of 'qualified'?" my mom asked.

"Sure, Mrs. Hepp. Any good orthopedic who specializes in children's congenital problems can do this procedure. And the positive side to all of this is that once surgery is done, Janet *will* be problem free. Besides the single horizontal scar just below each knee, she'll walk great, look great, and not have any of the projected problems when she's thirty."

The only remaining question was who would perform the surgeries. My parents thought that Dr. Gillian was the best choice. I, at seventeen, begged them to allow Drs. Ulid and Allgood to perform the surgeries. "But Mom," I pleaded, "Dr. Gillian's hospital is far away. My friends couldn't come to visit me."

My persistence won out. My parents concluded that Drs. Ulid and Allgood were excellent surgeons, and they would perform my surgeries. For it was the doctors themselves who had said, "We'll perform Janet's surgeries together as a team." We understood that with selecting Drs. Allgood and Ulid, we had *two* masterminds with twice the medical experience and knowledge. Wouldn't two surgeons be better than one?

Two surgeons meant two pre-ops, a separate appointment with each doctor to discuss my upcoming surgeries. This gave my parents and me a chance to discuss the surgical procedure and gain understanding of what my post-op treatment would entail.

My first pre-op appointment was right after New Year's in 1977. Dr. Allgood put us at ease by saying, "This surgery will be controlled breaks. It's not like breaking your leg while you're skiing, where the bones might be shattered. We're going to go in and cut the tibias, turn them, then put her legs in full-length casts. We'll use weight-bearing casts so Janet can balance and allow her legs to bear her body weight."

Dr. Allgood used a mixture of history and knowledge as he explained to my father, "You know, George, in World War II they learned that applying pressure against a broken bone helped it to heal better. After six weeks or so in her casts and walking with crutches, Janet will be fine. She'll have straight legs!"

My father sat quietly for a moment. Finally, he said, "Sounds reasonable to me." He then reached into his pocket and pulled out a folded piece of paper that listed all the questions he had thought of to ask Dr. Allgood prior to surgery.

As my dad began to read his list, Dr. Allgood interrupted him. "George, there's no need to worry about a thing." Then, looking my way, he said, "And don't you worry about it, kiddo. I'm going to take care of you."

Dr. Allgood crossed his arms. "You know, I'm the Dr. Kerlan of Orange County," he claimed, using the name of the famous orthopedist. In many ways, his boldness and confidence brought comfort.

Contrary to Dr. Allgood's opinion, Dr. Ulid firmly advised, "Janet's legs should be operated on separately, one leg at a time. The inconveniences of two casts and rehabilitation would be too difficult if both legs were done together." After we agreed with him he said, "Janet's right leg should be first, as it needs to be rotated a little farther than the left. After the surgery, she'll be placed in a full-length cast for approximately six weeks. It will be like having a broken leg.

She'll be able to use crutches to get around and carry on with her life."

With Dr. Allgood's appointment still fresh in my mind, a week later my parents and I met with Dr. Ulid for a pre-op appointment with him. Prepared, we had written down a few questions that my father and I had forgotten to ask Dr. Allgood. Now we could ask the known expert.

Dr. Ulid sounded like a reporter as he listed the complications that could occur during surgery. Possible nerve damage, infection, maybe a difficult time healing, we were told. "We'll be careful not to get too close to the nerve. You'll be given medication for infection. The challenge you're facing isn't the surgery but the rehabilitation."

Dr. Ulid placed his hand on one of my knees. "Janet, there's nothing to worry about. You just pack your bags—a comfortable gown, a toothbrush, and a good book. I expect you'll be in the hospital for six or seven days.

"George, her surgery is scheduled for February ninth. You get Janet situated with her schoolwork and all, and let's do it."

---

My surgery occurred as planned on February 9, 1977. Later that night I awoke. *The pain! Oh, God help me. I hurt!* Pain medication only brought temporary relief, allowing me to sleep. I woke again to the sound of people at my bedside. I watched the doctor use a saw to cut my bloodstained cast open lengthwise, down the center, bringing relief to the massive swelling. "No one ever mentioned I'd need a drainage tube," I said as I saw a small tube leaving my knee, draining blood and fluids.

Two days later I rose from my bed and learned to walk on crutches. Within the week, I was on my way to recovery. I checked out of the hospital and began counting the days. I'd wear my cast four more weeks, and then two weeks later have the same surgery on my left leg. *By summer, I'll be up and running,* I thought.

The big day came and my cast was removed. While still on the examining table, I leaned over and touched my leg. I wasn't prepared to see the deformity, which I thought was caused by the swelling. Tears filled my eyes. I stared at the scars and they stared back. Yet, with my upbeat spirit, I chuckled. "Looks like I made the winning goal and was tackled."

The next two weeks I continued to use crutches since my right leg wasn't strong enough to hold me. Yet this weakness wasn't a concern as Dr. Allgood assured me each day would bring improvements.

Like clockwork, two weeks later Dr. Ulid performed surgery on my left leg along with Dr. Blake while Dr. Allgood was having surgery himself. Waking up from this surgery was different, or maybe I was more prepared. I didn't have the horrible swelling nor did I require a drain.

A day or so later, I was taken to physical therapy. It soon became obvious to all that my right leg was too weak to hold me. Instead of bouncing out of the hospital using crutches, with my left leg in a full-length cast and a weak right leg, I rolled out of the hospital in style—in a wheelchair.

The next several weeks I attended physical therapy instead of going to school. A tutor came to my home. *This is no way to spend my senior year!* I thought. My friends kept me company, and just as I always tried to do, I made lemonade out of lemons.

In therapy, I worked hard trying to strengthen my right leg. At home, I'd repeat the same exercises, thinking the more the better. The day came when my cast was removed. The scarring on my left leg matched the right, yet the leg was stronger and could bear weight. I credited this to the many leg lifts I had done while it was in the cast.

I was once again on crutches, using my left leg to support me and placing as much weight on my right as I could.

Summer came and there was no running. In fact, summer only brought return trips to Drs. Ulid and Allgood. It seemed that the more weight I placed on my right leg, the more bowed it became. More therapy and more healing time were needed. Surgery was performed on both of my legs to remove the hardware that had been used when turning my bones.

In the fall of 1977, I began my freshman year at Point Loma College. By Christmas break, it was obvious that something was terribly wrong with my right knee. On December 19, 1977, I underwent another surgery to have a cartilage removed. When I came out of the anesthesia, Dr Allgood informed me that the cartilage was indeed torn, and he planned to remove it "next time." The next surgery on my right knee was scheduled for January 4, 1978, at which time Dr. Allgood would remove the torn cartilage and also repair the loose ligaments he found, caused by the initial turning of my bone, and further rotate my tibia.

Instead of returning to my girlfriends in the dorm, I wrote them letters. I was once again struggling to recover from major surgery.

I finally made it back to college for the spring quarter in 1978. Still in a full-length cast, I found the hilly campus quite a challenge. I spent four days in excruciating pain. No relief, despite pain medications, left me unable to attend classes.

I called Dr. Allgood's office. Beverly said she would relay my concerns to him. She then reminded me that I had had extensive surgery and I should expect this kind of pain. What I never expected was to have a two-and-a-half-inch pin travel across my leg, go through my muscle, pierce my skin, and appear through a hole it had bored on the other side of my cast.

By August of 1978 my right knee was grossly unstable. Trying to walk was a moment-by-moment disaster. I fell several times a day. Even using crutches, my right knee would collapse, causing me to drop to the ground.

My parents thought that maybe we had reached the end of my doctors' expertise. I thought they were shooting for the stars as they searched for a doctor who might know how to fix my problem. "Honey, we're going to find a way for you to walk again," they'd say. In reality, their dreams were bigger than mine. I did not know where this doctor might be, and I had begun to see my future with crutches or seated in a wheelchair.

Instead of starting my second year of college, I was preparing for a trip. "If there is ever someone who knows about the knee, Dr. Jack Hughston is the man," our neighbor Dr. Martian said after extensive research. With suitcases packed, copies of Dr. Ulid's x-rays, and my dad's big dream, we boarded a red-eye flight headed to Columbus, Georgia—three thousand miles away from home. The roar of the engine matched my dad's determination to find help for me.

We arrived in Atlanta at dawn; the city had not yet awakened. It took most of the day to travel by bus to Columbus. The next morning we met the famous Dr. Jack Hughston at his clinic. He held my leg in position as if it were precious cargo and instructed the x-ray technician to take the picture, knowing his own hands were being exposed to the radiation. He held hope that maybe, just maybe, surgery number eight would fix the problem. Two days later, he performed this surgery.

The pain was excruciating. Every part of my body pleaded to find relief. "Please, someone, help me!" I drifted in and out of consciousness. *My hip, my right hip. Did they do surgery on my hip?* Spasms ran through my body like a knife, cutting whatever was in its path.

*Oh, God, ease my pain, help me! Maybe the price of walking is too great.*

"Janet, open your eyes. I want you to wiggle your toes," a nurse said to me. I could hear, but my body wouldn't respond. My father sat beside my bed, helpless, watching and waiting for any sign of communication from me. The surgery had been more than we bargained for.

I woke up three days later to my parents sitting by my side. My mom reached down to hold my clenched fist. It didn't dawn on me that she had not traveled with us to Georgia. My father had called home and told her that she needed to come.

I was now in a cast from my waist down to my right baby toe to prevent my leg from rotating. Bone had been taken from my hip and grafted to my tibia. I had a drain in both my knee and hip. I wasn't sure I was glad to be awake. My fever caused chills. I was weak from enormous blood loss and was receiving my third unit of blood. I wondered how long it would be before I could attempt to lift my head.

Within a couple of weeks, I was feeling better and up on crutches. I headed home with my parents and spent a month recuperating before I returned to Georgia in November. That time a friend accompanied me and spent a week in the hospital with me. There we watched lots of late-night television. During the day I went to physical therapy, adjusting to the new "Forrest Gump" metal brace I'd need to wear for the next six months. In retrospect, that shocking new contraption was an inconvenience, and yet it was an answer to my prayers.

## Chapter Five

# A Faraway Place

MY CHRISTMAS BREAK from school in 1979 was almost over. Between visiting friends and family, I flew south to see Dr. Hughston for another checkup. Kathy, my twenty-one-year-old sister, volunteered to go with me. Calling it a mini-vacation, we packed light for our two-day trip.

Since I had traveled to Georgia for checkups over the past year and a half, there were several places I wanted Kathy to see. We ventured through downtown Columbus, finding an old-fashioned five-and-dime store. I ordered my first hush puppies in months. I had almost forgotten how good deep-fried cornbread tasted dipped in ketchup.

That afternoon, we took a taxi to the clinic. "I've never seen a waiting room so full," Kathy said with a gasp. "There's at least forty people sitting in here. Are they all waiting to see the great Dr. Hughston?"

A couple of hours later my name was called, and we were taken back to an examining room. Several fellows, doctors in training under Dr. Hughston, entered and examined my knees. Each one evaluated, measured, and moved my knees in every direction possible. X-rays were taken, and then all the fellows gathered around to watch me walk. Up and down the hall I went, grateful I had remembered to bring my gym shorts. I was all smiles as I showed off the progress I had made since my last surgery.

Dr. Hughston arrived, wearing a striped dress shirt, clashing bow tie, and his signature roadrunner belt buckle. It was wonderful to see him again. The fellows stepped back as he greeted me.

Dr. Hughston took hold of my right knee, evaluating its condition. "Sugar, how's this knee holding up?" He asked me to walk down the hall again. I wondered why people weren't cheering, or at least smiling, as I made my way around the corner back to the examining room. My smile faded as Dr. Hughston requested a conference with the fellows, doctors in training. They quietly excused themselves and filed out into the hallway.

Kathy and I tried to listen through the door. What we heard sounded muffled. Then again, we had no idea how to translate the medical terms into plain English. Time seemed to stop.

Finally, Dr. Hughston opened the door and entered the room alone. "Sugar, I'm sorry. But that knee of yours isn't holding. I'm afraid we're gonna have to go back and tighten things down. One of the fellows is calling your parents. When he gets 'em on the line, the nurse will come find ya, and you can talk with 'em, too."

*No! This can't be. I can't do this again. This can't be happening,* I thought as I turned away from Dr. Hughston. My eyes caught my sister's. She reached over and grasped my hand.

Within minutes, I completely understood the grim reality. Once again I needed surgery, and if I delayed, extensive permanent damage would occur. No way was I prepared for this news. We'd traveled to Georgia for a two-day visit. I was to be back at school within the week. But my options were slim. If I wanted to walk in the future, I had no choice.

I was scheduled to be admitted into the hospital the next day. My surgery would be the following morning. I cried out to God, asking for strength to submit willingly to this change of plans. Deep in thought, I didn't hear the nurse when she called my name. "Janet, I've got your parents on the phone."

Kathy and I followed her into a small office. I took a deep breath before placing the receiver to my ear. Somehow, I had to convince my parents that Kathy and I could handle this and that they didn't need to come.

"I'll be in good hands," I assured them. "One of us will call the moment we need you. You're only a plane ride away...Mom, I give you my word. Kathy and I will be sitting by the phone waiting for you to call every evening at eight o'clock Georgia time."

After many long-distance minutes, my parents agreed. Kathy and I would manage things in the South, phoning home with any and all concerns. After saying our goodbyes, I set down the receiver, clutched my shoulders as if I were hugging myself, and wept.

Kathy was at a loss for words as she tried to comfort me. I counted on my fingers my past surgeries, all eight of them. "Will this never end?" I asked.

My question brought tears to Kathy's eyes. Quickly, I changed the subject, knowing we were headed straight for a pity party. "Kathy, you've heard the saying, 'When life gets tough—the tough go shopping.' I think that applies to us. "

It was dark as we took a taxi to Kirvens, a large department store downtown. "The way I see it, all I need is a gown, a robe, slippers, and, of course, a good book and a couple of magazines." Kathy bought pj's, shorts, and whatever else she needed to help keep her busy as she would be staying in the hospital with me, eating in the cafeteria and out of the vending machines, and sleeping on a rollaway bed.

The next morning we checked out of our hotel, caught a taxi, and went straight to the hospital. One step inside, anxiety gripped my entire body. The smell was all too familiar. Kathy staked out a corner in the waiting room while I walked over to the admitting office to check in. As we waited for our room, a young woman in a white uniform caught our eye. She welcomed the patients and seemed to know everyone.

Within minutes, she came over and sat down. We couldn't help noticing her eyes, the color of emeralds that seemed to dance as she spoke. "Hey, my name is Renee. I'm a patient escort. Are you two okay? Is there anything y'all need?" Renee was an example of authentic southern hospitality, even in a hospital. She was friendly and genuine. From our first encounter, I knew that we would be friends. "Janet, the nurses here are great! Don't worry about a thing," she said. "Y'all only have to mash the call button one time, and they'll come a-running. Besides, I'll be checking in on you," Renee stated with certainty. "Someday I'm gonna be a nurse. I graduate from high school this year, and then I'm off to nursing school."

The hours soon passed, and I was admitted to a private room. The nurse brightened the room by opening the blinds while announcing we had arrived just in time for dinner. I could hardly eat. Just being in a hospital was challenging enough, but thinking and preparing myself for the next morning took away every bit of appetite I had.

An hour later, the anesthesiologist dropped by. We reviewed my medical history. When he left, Kathy and I walked the halls and took a tour of the orthopedic surgical floor. Over the nurses' station hung a large clock. "Janet, I didn't realize that it's almost eight. Mom and Dad will be calling any minute. We've got to get back to our room."

As promised, at eight o'clock that night the phone rang. On the line were two parents trying to sound cheerful and optimistic, yet I could hear the undertone of worry and apprehension. "Hi, this is Dad."

"I'm here, too," my mother chimed in.

"We're calling to check in on our domestic travelers."

"Dad, we're fine. Everything is fine. I've even taken Kathy to Kirvens."

After counting sheep, morning finally came, and I was taken to surgery. I spent the next couple of days in "never-never land," experiencing pain so intense only morphine brought periodic relief. Kathy sat by my side, waiting for me to respond to her presence. Dr. Hughston stopped by and talked with Kathy. "I'd say Janet has a fair chance of a full recovery. Yep, I'd say her prognosis is 'fair,'" he reported.

It was while I was "out of it" that Kathy met Stella, the mother of another patient, whose daughter was also off in "never-never land." "You let me know when you have to return to California. I'll look in on Janet and make sure all is well," Stella told Kathy.

A week later my sister headed home since her semester break was almost over. She was enrolled in a nursing program that wouldn't allow time off. I bit my lip as she said her goodbyes and reluctantly left my room.

Within moments, I broke into sobs. *God, why did she have to leave? What if I need someone to tell me I'll be okay? God, I know you promised you'll never leave me, that you will always be right by my side. But God, right now I need you to hold me.* Desperately, I tried to control my emotions. Watching everyone's lives move forward while mine remained on hold seemed almost unbearable. I tried to be brave. But dealing with the surgery, physical pain, and the discouragements of the past years, I felt weary. I missed my friends. I missed my family. I even missed school.

Telling myself, "This pain won't last forever," I did everything I could to make the best of a difficult situation. I remembered the words of Dr. Allgood and Dr. Ulid, "Janet, you've got to make the best of things. You have to accept the fact that this is the way God made you. This is how you were formed in your mother's womb."

I wondered how I'd do it, but somehow I pulled it off. I convinced my parents that they didn't need to come. I knew my surgeries had been costly, and because of my problem, every day of their vacation and sick time from work had been used. Knowing this just added to my stress. I'd just turned twenty. I felt that I should have been able to handle this. I couldn't allow them to come. I simply had to be brave.

I was assigned a room with Terri, a tall sixteen year old with shoulder-length, ash-blonde hair. The male population was her favorite subject. Nothing was ever dull while rooming with her because she livened up any room with her contagious laughter. A free spirit, she definitely lived moment by moment.

I soon met two other girls about my age, Joy and Saundra Lee. Along with Terri, the four of us were constant companions. We became known as "the wheelchair roller derby gals." Joy was blue eyed, seventeen and from Virginia. "I've had three surgeries," she said. "And I've come to Georgia with the dream maybe this will be my last." It took nothing more than those words for us to become bonded instantly.

Joy had been in the hospital for a few weeks. She rarely complained about pain and was always early to bed. Joy's mom, Stella, was staying in the hospital with her. Joy was one of the few patients who had a family member with her, and her mother, whom we named Mrs. Joy, was a petite, middle-aged, spirited Italian lady. Her short, layered brunette hair left wispy ends along her neckline. Mrs. Joy became our patient advocate. Not only was she our legs, getting us whatever we needed, but she tried to make things easier for "her gals," as she called us. She became our cheerleader and went out of her way to make sure we didn't get too discouraged.

Saundra Lee was an eighteen year old from Alabama. I'm sure she was a graduate of a finishing school. She had lipstick to match all of her nail polishes, and her auburn hair was blown dry, curled and frozen in place. Saundra Lee even rolled her wheelchair with style.

Early one evening, Mrs. Joy rounded up the four of us for a little excitement. We called the local pizza parlor and requested delivery of three large pepperoni pizzas. The hospital cafeteria was closed on Sunday evenings, so we chose its dining area to host our private party.

Renee came by to cheer us on as we came wheel-to-wheel in line for the finish. After a few more laughs, Mrs. Joy moved the tables back. The four of us in wheelchairs cheered her on as we rolled around cleaning up the evidence of our party. Our fun was over. It was time to call it a night.

With extra pizza in hand, we all sat in a row, rocking back and forth, waiting for the elevator to go up to our rooms. The doors opened and out stepped a short, red-headed young man holding his left arm out, palm up. After taking a better look, we noticed he was carefully holding three pieces of chocolate candy. "Did you bring that for us?" Terri asked.

"Darlin', I sure did, but y'all have to tell me your names first." Randy Worrell then introduced himself. Being called "darling" was all it took. The four of us teased and flirted shamelessly with him. Definitely flustered and embarrassed, yet enjoying himself, Randy interrupted us. "Now just tell me. What in the world would you four beautiful ladies all be doin' in the hospital?"

This was our chance to have some fun! We quickly invented the mishaps that had caused our conditions. Mrs. Joy helped by adding whatever popped into her mind. Saundra Lee spoke first. "Y'all don't recognize me? I'm a famous fashion model from Alabama," she pompously stated.

Saundra Lee flinched as Mrs. Joy chimed in, "It was a terrible mishap—Saundra Lee was modeling in a New York fashion show and haphazardly fell off the ramp. One minute she was there and the next she had dropped out of sight!"

"I'm an Olympian, a track star. I ran the hundred-yard dash in record time!" Terri blurted.

Trying to decide if I should use the "hit by the train story," I blurted, "I am Janet Lynn, the famous ice skater from California. Didn't you hear about my accident on the ice?" Quickly I glanced at Mrs. Joy, wondering what in the world she might add to my story.

Without cracking a smile, Joy informed Randy that she was a famous skier and injured herself while skiing in the Swiss Alps. "There was a small avalanche," she said. "It went straight through that tiny Alpine village, but everyone survived."

Randy followed each story with, "Really?" It didn't take him long to realize we were all from out of state, which meant we had few visitors. "Ya know," he stammered, "I'm on my way to church. I'm gonna ask the congregation to pray for y'all."

With a little encouragement from Terri, Randy promised he'd come back to visit us the next day. Now we'd done it. This poor guy was on his way to tell his church about the "famous four" he met in the hospital. We laughed as we discussed the possibility of television and newspaper reporters knocking on our doors.

Early the next morning we heard Dr. Hughston in the hallway. Terri quickly maneuvered her bedside tray and closed the pizza box, hiding the evidence of her early-morning breakfast of leftover pizza and prune juice. Grabbing her pizza, she dared to take one more bite before it was too late. Dr. Hughston and his fellows filed into our room.

I asked Dr. Hughston if I could speak with him in private. He motioned for all to leave as he sat down on the side of my bed. "Dr. Hughston, I was walking with a limp when I arrived here, but I was walking," I said. "Now my left leg has lost the strength to support me. I'm not even able to stand. And Dr. Hughston, I think something is really wrong with my right knee. Even in the cast, I can feel it moving all over the place. It kind of feels like it's swimming in a pool with nothing to hold it."

"Shh," said Dr. Hughston when he was deep in thought. "Janet, let's go window your cast right now. We'll take a look and see what that wobble is." Within minutes, I was wheeled to the cast room. One of the fellows cut out a square large enough for Dr. Hughston to examine my knee. Something was wrong. I had never seen Dr. Hughston look so defeated.

He stepped out of the room without saying a word to me. I waited with the nurse, Mrs. Harrington, until he reappeared with nine of his friends. Only a few of his fellows fit inside the cast room. The others stuck their heads inside the doorway or turned their heads so they could hear.

Dr. Hughston didn't look at me as he spoke. He focused toward the ceiling. "Sugar, the ligaments didn't hold. There wasn't much of 'em left to work with. We're gonna have to take you back down and try to repair things."

My heart began to race. A cold sweat began at my neckline and ran down my body. All I could ask was the simple question, "When?"

"We'll go now. You'll be the first on the surgery list. Mrs. Harrington has placed a call to your parents. I want to talk with them, and then I want you to talk with them, too."

I could tell Dr. Hughston found the discovery of the day difficult. The way he looked deep into my eyes told me he was hanging on to hope. "Great balls of mercy! Let's get her ready," Dr. Hughston ordered.

In some ways, it was good that I didn't have much time to think about going under the knife or, in reality, "the saw," again. I'm not sure I would have waited well. Mrs. Harrington, the nurse, brought a hospital gown and helped me change. A gurney was brought to the door.

While temporarily parked by the nurses' station, I was handed the phone, with my parents on the other end. "Really, Mom, by the time you could get here, my surgery would be over. I'm okay. This is just another delay, but in a week or so, I should be up and walking."

While I was in mid-sentence with my parents, a nurse gave me a pre-op shot in my thigh. I hoped the shot would take effect quickly. The sooner I was asleep the better. "Really, Mom, I'll call you tonight," I assured. After hearing how proud my parents were of me and that they loved me very much, I handed the phone back to Mrs. Harrington.

What had I said? I couldn't call my parents that night. I'd never been alert enough to call anyone on the night of surgery. But I had to keep my word. I wanted to reassure my parents, for their daughter was thousands of miles away, and they could do nothing to help my immediate predicament. I had to do this alone. In the past couple of years, I had been through so many surgeries, so much therapy, so much defeat, we all had worn thin. It had become too difficult for me to watch my parents watch me struggle. I had to concentrate on giving my full 100 percent effort to walking again.

Moments before the man in the cap came to escort me downstairs, I asked Mrs. Harrington to please get Terri. Minutes later Terri came riding down in her wheelchair, being pushed by one of the fellows.

Feeling rather important, she asked, "How can I help you, ma'am?"

I groggily reached out my hand. She extended hers to hold mine. We both knew the emotions I was feeling. We had taken this ride many times before.

"Terri, I want you to save some pizza for me. I'll be hungry in a day or two."

"Girl, are you crazy?" Moving her wheelchair closer so none of the hospital staff could hear as they all stood watching us, she whispered, "Janet, you brought me down here for pizza?"

"No," I replied with a half giggle. "Terri, you must promise me that you'll wake me up tonight at eight. I've got to call my parents." She promised. I gave her the phone number because she would have to dial and put the phone to my ear.

The group that had gathered said their temporary goodbyes, and I was off and rolling. Terri and Mrs. Harrington waved and watched as the elevator door closed. I closed my eyes. Queasiness washed over me and tears rolled down the side of my face. I covered my eyes with my fingers while pleading with almighty God that this would be my last trip down this road. I knew it would take a miracle and the skills of an extremely talented surgeon for me to walk again. I wondered how many more surgeries, if any, I would need to have. For a quick moment, I thought, *No more! I can't face another.* But as quickly as that thought came, it was overpowered by *I won't give up. I'll continue until I can walk. I will never be the one who loses hope. Even if the doctors give up, I won't!*

Through closed eyelids, I saw the bright lights of the operating room. "One, two, three," they counted as they moved me on to the operating table. The anesthesiologist started the IV. I flinched as the thick needle entered my vein. My right leg was scrubbed, shaved, and hung up high with a tourniquet tightly squeezing it.

*God, why am I still awake? Please help me to go to sleep.*

"Can't you put me out?" I asked anyone who was listening. I could hear people talking. Dr. Hughston arrived. Hearing his voice brought comfort. I felt my body totally relax, and I trusted my crisis to God.

## Chapter Six

# AN UNBELIEVABLE TIME

"Janet, wake up. You've slept all day." I heard Terri's voice, and yet she seemed far away. I felt her tap my shoulder. "Janet. It's time. You can go back to sleep after you call home." Other voices in the room joined in, calling my name.

I was finally able to open my eyes. Terri stood nearby, leaning on her crutches. Next to her, lined up alongside my bed, were three young men, all looking intently at me.

"Oh, Terri, how am I? How did my operation go?"

"I think fine. They didn't exactly report to me. Maybe Mrs. Joy knows something. I'll tell the nurse you're asking. Do you think you can call home?"

"Yeah, I can," I said in a half-whisper. "Who are your friends?"

"Janet, this is Randy. Remember, we met him last night by the elevator. He brought some friends to visit us." She then introduced me to Steve and Marty.

Barely able to focus, I spoke my first words to my drop-in guests. "I don't always look like this," I said with a sigh while I brushed my fingers through my tangled hair. With my leg stacked high on pillows and wearing a fashionable hospital gown, I pulled up my sheets as high as I could. Modesty wasn't really an option as I met my new southern friends.

"How y'all doin'?" Randy asked, extending his right hand to shake mine. I started to move my hand to shake his. With the pull of the IV tubing, I laid it back down. I wondered who "y'all" was. Was he asking about me, or everyone in the room?

"Okay," I mumbled. Then suddenly I whispered, "Terri, I think I'm going to be sick." As fast as she could, she handed me an emission basin, and I proceeded to fill it—gracefully I might add. I figured this would be a good time for Terri's guests to say goodbye, but instead I heard them conversing.

"Why would they give her such a small bowl to throw up in?"

"I mean, I'd need a big pot."

"Shh, y'all, I don't reckon she's feelin' too good."

"Well, would you, if you had just been cut open?" Offering to help, Randy left to get my nurse, Joanne. When she arrived, Steve and Marty were standing by Terri's bed, whispering to each other while I freshened up. Joanne gave me a shot for pain and one for nausea. I didn't even have to ask.

Before she left, Joanne told the guys, "Five more minutes, then you'll have to leave. These gals need their rest." As soon as she walked out, Terri maneuvered into her wheelchair. One of the guys shut our door, and they all gathered around my bed. I was more alert now and took a better look at my company. I had no idea which one was Steve and who was Marty. I did recognize Randy from the night before. He was definitely the comedian in the bunch.

"Janet," Terri said with a gleam in her eye, "Randy went to his church last night and asked his congregation to pray for us. Then these guys offered to come and visit."

*Oh no,* I thought. *Do they really think I'm an ice skater?*

"Randy's always telling us that he's met some girls and we need to go visiting with him. Randy thinks visiting is his ministry." Steve chuckled.

"You guys are crazy," I said in a weak voice. "You should come back on a day that I feel better." After all, these were my first actual visitors.

"We will, ma'am. It's been a real pleasure to meet y'all," Randy concluded.

Terri offered to roll out to the elevator with them. Better yet, she had a supreme idea. She'd roll with them to the front doors of the hospital and out to the parking lot.

Before Terri left, she helped me place my call. Then the four got up to leave. "Reckon we'll see ya tomorrow," Steve said as the door closed behind them.

"Hi, Mom. Hi, Dad. I heard you both answer at the same time. It's me, and I'm doing fine. I'm a pro at this now."

I felt relieved after speaking to my parents. They had spoken to Dr. Hughston, and even though the diagnosis of my condition was now "guarded," he had given them a "hopeful" surgical outcome. My ligaments were unusable; "like mush" were his actual words. Dr. Hughston had restrung my tendons so they would function as ligaments. Sounded good to me. What sounded even better was the word *hopeful*.

My night was rough. The pain was excruciating. I didn't dare try to move. I sucked on ice chips but didn't eat a thing. Again I was in a cast that began at my waist and ended at my right big toe. I contemplated that if God cared enough to keep track of the hairs on my head, certainly He cared about my physical pain. I mumbled parts of Psalm 121:4, "He neither slumbers nor sleeps." I believe God stayed awake with me through many restless nights, and tonight was no different. I took deep breaths as pain throbbed throughout my body.

About 3:00 a.m. Terri spoke up, "Janet, do you want to hear something funny?"

"Sure."

"Tonight when the guys were here, I took them to meet Joy and Mrs. Joy. Randy introduced his friends to Joy and her mom. What he said was, 'I'd like you to meet Joy and her mom, Mrs. Joy.' I died laughing. Stella never told them that her name wasn't Mrs. Joy."

"So what'd you think of the guys?"

"What guys, Terri?"

"Our visitors this evening, Randy's friends. Don't you think they were cute?"

Before answering her, I remembered that she was a sixteen year old with one interest—boys! I was twenty. I definitely liked guys, but the last thing I needed at this time was a boyfriend. "Yeah, they're all cute," I assured her.

"Well, I liked Steve and Marty."

"Which one was Steve?"

"Steve wore the hospital whites. He's an x-ray technician at the medical center next door."

Trying to be attentive to Terri's interests I continued, "Wasn't Marty the quiet one?"

"Marty was the one with the curly, honey-colored hair. He was wearing blue jeans and a red polo shirt."

In immense pain I whispered, "Okay Terri, you can like Steve and Marty. Why not like them all? Steve, Randy, Marty, and even some of their friends?"

The next few days seemed like forever. Hour after hour Terri met my immediate needs and described Randy's friends to me in great detail. I learned that they all attended the same church. Randy drove for a photo service and worked odd hours. The hospital happened to be directly in the path of his route.

Marty was twenty—a junior in college. As boring as it sounded to Terri, he was majoring in accounting and minoring in computer science. His father had retired from the military and moved his family to Columbus just three years earlier. Marty also worked full time. Steve and Marty played on their church baseball team while Randy went to the baseball games to see just how many people he could meet. All the guys spoke with southern drawls, using words like "reckon," and they were all available.

Each day I felt stronger. Renee came by to visit often, always lifting my spirits and bringing me the latest magazines she found lying around the hospital. For the next few weeks, I was confined to bed and unable to move half of my body. Hospital life carved out its own routine. Randy, Steve, and Marty began to visit us daily. The guys were hilarious and definitely somewhat confused. Randy had gotten our original stories mixed up. Wanting to impress Steve and Marty and make sure they'd want to visit the hospital with him, he'd created his own stories. The guys then came to the hospital thinking that I was a Los Angeles Rams cheerleader! I wondered why they kept asking me about football players!

Each night when my parents called, one of the guys would answer the phone. They talked with my parents as if they had known them for years. These musketeers did have a special mission. They brought friendship and laughter to us at a difficult time in our lives.

---

Days passed and it seemed that I had been continually asked to face challenges I would rather have turned my back on. Nevertheless, I had two choices. I could keep trying, or I could give up the hope of ever walking again.

During one of my emotional discussions with God, explaining to him that I was weary and tired of it all, a nurse came by my room. I tried to figure out if I had seen her before. As if conducting a survey, she asked me what type of candy I liked. I didn't think twice as to why she questioned me. "I love light milk chocolate with chewy caramel centers. Just thinking of them makes me hungry," I replied.

That evening an older couple appeared at my door. Not expecting company other than the musketeers, I wasn't prepared for my guests.

It had been a particularly hard day since I was consumed with "what ifs," wondering if this last surgery was going to do the job. I had planned on spending the evening trying to rally my emotions, giving myself a pep talk. Wiping my tears, I reluctantly invited them in.

"Hey, are you Janet?"

"Yes, I am."

The gentleman walked toward my wheelchair where I was sitting, staring out the window. He reached toward me, offering his hand. "Hey, I'm Joe Posey, and this is my wife, Evelyn. We brought you a box of light-milk-chocolate caramels. I suppose that the caramel is in the middle. I didn't try 'em," he said with a grin. "Say, one of the surgical nurses here told our church about you. She's been with you in your last few surgeries and knew about your situation. She asked us to pray for you while you were here alone in Columbus. Evelyn and I've been prayin', and we thought we'd come by and meet the gal we've been prayin' for."

Wow, was I stunned. A surgical nurse I didn't even remember cared enough to tell her church about me. The Poseys were just the medicine I needed for my troubled heart.

Joe Posey was tall and firmly built. His slate, deep-set eyes had a way of constantly shining, especially when he spoke about his wife, Evelyn, the love of his life. When he first introduced himself to me, he shook my hand. For moments he embraced it, holding it, offering me the touch of another human being. How did he know that I longed for my dad's touch? I noticed Mr. Posey's hands were soft, yet strong. As I got to know Joe, I began to understand that this mixture of softness and strength were characteristics of a godly man.

Evelyn, Joe's blonde, blue-eyed wife, was fun. Her ears were always perked waiting to hear about the activities of the day. In style, she wore oxford shirts with vests and penny-loafer shoes. It was obvious Evelyn adored Joe. That visit was the beginning of a wonderful friendship with my heaven-sent encouragers. The Poseys returned to see me every few days, and Evelyn called daily to check on my spirits and my progress.

On each visit, Evelyn took my laundry and then returned it washed and neatly folded in a bag. If I was lucky, when she had baked cheese sticks for Joe, I would find some for me, tucked way down inside my laundry that she had washed and returned.

Becoming friends with the Poseys helped ease my loneliness when Terri was discharged. I was thrilled for her, but I would truly miss our middle-of-the-night chats. We had shared a season in our lives. I had needed her; she had needed me.

My first day without my roommate seemed endless. The room was too quiet. I wrote letters to my parents, grandparents, and college dorm mates. I rolled down to therapy three times just to pass the morning. When I wheeled myself back to my room for lunch I noticed a teddy bear sitting against my pillow. I maneuvered my way between the two beds, over to my new "stuffed friend." I reached for it with one hand and balanced myself with the other, trying not to tip over in my wheelchair. The cuddly brown bear looked as if he were smiling. I giggled when I noticed the T-shirt the little guy wore. The words "Li'l Marty" were neatly embroidered across its front. Taped to its palm was a note: "Squeeze when lonely. I'll see ya tonight." I started counting the hours until that night.

Going to therapy twice a day was challenging, hard work, and painful, but the nightlife in the hospital was great. That's when the musketeers made their grand entrance. We patients knew to take it easy during the day, even nap, just to be ready for the sun to go down for our night gatherings.

One afternoon Marty and Steve dropped by. Not finding me in my room or at therapy, they searched the hospital for me. Knowing I was a social butterfly, they went looking from room to room, and then found Kenneth, another patient, and me sitting in our wheelchairs at the end of the hall. Steve cleared his throat. "Hey, we hate to interrupt this party, but you have visitors, Miss Janet." Kenneth headed on to therapy, and Marty wheeled me back to my room.

"Where'd you get these flowers?" Marty asked, pointing to the vase by the window.

"Kenneth sent them to me. Aren't they pretty?"

"They're okay," Marty said as he moved them across the room next to the sink. "Ya know, it's been a good two months of incarceration. I think it's about time you got out of this hospital and had a night on the town. You definitely need a change of scenery."

Soon after, the nurse made her rounds. She checked my pulse and blood pressure. It was while I had a thermometer under my tongue that Marty found the courage to ask, "Would it be possible for me to check Janet out of this hospital and take her on a date? I think it'd be good for her to get some fresh air."

The nurse looked at Marty and then at me. With a grin, she said, "I'll see what I can work out for you, Mr. Mitchell. Maybe Janet does need to get out of here for a few hours."

Sitting there listening to the two of them talk, I was glad my mouth wasn't available for comment. Did Marty think this was his big chance to go out with a Los Angeles Rams cheerleader? The nurse slid the thermometer out of my mouth. She jotted down her findings and headed out of the room. Within seconds she reappeared, standing in the doorway.

"Mr. Mitchell, I'll take care of your request," she said with a wink, and that she did.

The next day I received a phone call from Dr. Hughston. "Say, I've been hearing about a young man named Marty. I was just wondering—"

Quickly interrupting, I assured Dr. Hughston, "Marty's a nice guy. We're just good friends."

"All right then. If you want Marty to take you out, have him come to the clinic this afternoon. I want to talk with him. Remember, Janet, your father isn't here. I gave him my word that I'd act in his place when needed." I smiled and thanked Dr. Hughston for his concern. I was eager to let Marty know that it was possible for him to take me out. There was just a little something he had to do.

The next day, Mrs. Joy spent the afternoon helping me get ready for my big night out on the town. She washed my hair while I lay flat on a gurney, hanging my head into the sink. We were novices. The entire floor around us got wet, but my hair was clean. With a limited wardrobe, I had to choose between gym shorts with an elastic band or a pair of maternity pants. To match my blue blouse I chose the shorts that allowed my casts to stick out for all to see.

Marty was excited when he arrived. He acted as if he were taking me to see snow for the first time. Almost every nurse and patient on the floor stood waving as he rolled me on to the elevator. Mrs. Harrington's last words were, "Be back by ten, and don't y'all be late."

I was glad I was just going out on the town with a good friend. I didn't have to worry about impressing him. The crisp air moved over my face as Marty ran, pushing my wheelchair to the car. We laughed as I yelled at the top of my lungs, "I'm out, everyone. I'm free!"

Chatting and watching the scenery through the window, I didn't notice the flashing red light when it appeared in the rearview mirror. Marty pulled over and rolled down his window to speak with the officer. After he handed him his driver's license and car registration the policeman asked, "Son, are you aware your brake light's out?"

Marty got out of his car and followed the officer to the back. He saw the broken brake light. When he had placed my wheelchair in the trunk, he had knocked out the light.

"Sir, we're kinda new at this," Marty told the officer. "It's her first time out of the hospital. I'll have to find a way to strap her chair down so this won't happen again." After instructing Marty to get the light replaced right away, the officer wished us well.

Inside the movie theater, Marty parked my wheelchair in the aisle adjacent to the end seat. Haphazardly, he crawled over me and sat down. I tried to adjust to sitting on a slant while facing downhill. The theater darkened and the movie *Grease* flashed across the screen.

Then it happened, the unthinkable. While squirming in my wheelchair trying to get comfortable, I felt a gush of wetness cover my lap. I heard water streaming off my cast and running on to the floor. Wondering if I'd spilled my drink, I looked around for my cup. Then I realized my catheter bag had somehow sprung a leak.

Immediately I turned toward Marty and whispered, "I have a slight problem."

"You what?" he whispered back.

"Marty, I think I've sprung a leak."

"You did what?" Pushing me out of the theater, Marty asked, "What do you do now?"

Not having a plan of action for this situation, I suggested the only thing that made sense, to give me a few moments of privacy so that I could discover what my problem was. I suggested he push me to the ladies' room. Once inside I sat bewildered, not sure whether to laugh or cry. There I was, out on the town with a new friend of the opposite sex and feeling anything but ladylike.

*Janet, you can handle this,* I told myself. As I pondered what to do, I promised myself I would never breathe a word of this experience to anyone in California. While I was trying to tidy up and fix my catheter so that I would not continue to drip throughout the evening, an elderly woman entered the restroom and came to my rescue. First she blotted my lap with paper towels and then she stuck me under the hand blow-dryer to dry me a little. Within minutes she opened the bathroom doors and gave me a push. I wheeled my way over to my waiting escort. *What is he thinking now? Will he ever take me anywhere again?*

Though the incidents of the night were stressful, Marty and I found them hysterically funny. We laughed so hard we cried. The movie ended later than expected, and we were late. Having missed my curfew, we raced back to the hospital, only to be stopped by the Southern Pacific Railroad. We knew that there was nothing we could do so we counted the cars and joked back and forth.

"Hey, I bet the nurses are thinkin' you went AWOL," Marty chuckled. The train came to a standstill, and we waited for it to slowly change tracks. We were now very late.

Marty took me straight to the nurses' station and said goodbye. All eyes were on me as I sat in soggy clothes, smiling radiantly. Three nurses escorted me to my room, curious to hear about my "date." It wasn't until the door of my room closed that I told them about the disasters of the night. No one made an issue of my tardiness. Instead they offered me a sponge bath, helped me into my gown, and offered their condolences. "Yeah, I hate it when those leak. It's such a mess," one said.

I was tucked in my bed, exhausted, when Mrs. Joy came running down to my room, dressed in robe and slippers. She sat down beside me with a silly expression. "Well, how was it? Was he absolutely wonderful?" she quizzed.

"He's a great guy, Mrs. Joy. We had an unbelievable time!" I then told her the catastrophes of the past five hours.

"Well, did he? Did he kiss you?" she asked with a sparkle in her eyes.

"Did he what? Why would he do that?"

Pulling herself closer to me as if she held a secret, she insisted, "Janet, he adores you. I can see it in the way he looks at you." Mrs. Joy and I spent the next few hours discussing Marty, my disability, and my heart. I tried to explain to her that no guy could be interested in me. I couldn't walk. I had a questionable future. The truth was I had to protect my heart. After much debate, I was out of words. Mrs. Joy tried to out-reason my every excuse. But still, I contended even more strongly that Marty was just a good friend—period!

Mrs. Joy stood to leave. As she approached the door, she turned. In her optimistic, upbeat way she bubbled, "Janet, I think he's a great guy. And by the way, he knows you've never been a Los Angeles Rams cheerleader!"

## Chapter Seven

# A MARVELOUS THING

"REALLY, DAD, I'M FINE," I assured my father over the phone. "Sure, I miss you. No, you don't need to come. I'll be home soon. I'm getting my braces, and then I'll be home." After convincing my parents that I was holding my own in the south, I took a deep breath because truthfully my progress wasn't as rapid as I would have liked.

Every time I shut my eyes, I could see myself walking. The only problem I had was getting my legs to do what my heart and mind envisioned. The next time I saw my parents I wanted to walk into their arms. Like an Olympic runner winning the race, I, too, wanted to cross the finish line and have my parents waiting and watching as I lifted my arms in victory.

In early March I was fitted for braces for both of my legs. It would be several days before they were ready. In preparation, my casts were bi-leveled, cut down the sides so the tops of my casts could be removed and my legs lifted out for therapy. Only while I was in bed or physical therapy could I remove the top parts of my casts. When I was up and in my wheelchair, I had to wear both sides of the casts held together by bandages to prevent unwanted movement.

I've been told that one night when I wasn't quite ready for company, Marty had a heart-to-heart talk with Mrs. Joy. "Janet, he told me that you're a very special girl. He's falling in love with you," Mrs. Joy told me in confidence. Mrs. Joy liked Marty a lot, and with his confession, they became allies. Day by day, Marty and I became closer. Night after night Marty sat by my bedside, talking and laughing with me.

I officially celebrated my fiftieth day in the hospital. Little did I know that only half of my stay was over. Renee brought me an enormous decorated chocolate-chip cookie. Across the top of it was written, "Happy 50th Anniversary." We closed the door of my room, and the two of us sat alone, confident we could eat the entire thing ourselves. Before she left, Renee taped a new sign to my door underneath the V.I.P. sign that Terri had given me. In bold red letters, the sign announced, "Famous Unknown American."

That morning, while on rounds, Dr. Hughston appeared somber. In his gentle way, he talked with me about my future. He was kind, and his words were gentle, but I don't think there was any good way to break the news he had to share with me. Cringing, I sat motionless and listened. "Sugar, we're hoping to get you up walking soon, but I've been thinking. I think your nursing plans had best be put on hold. I'm sure nursing would put too many demands on that right knee."

I was devastated by his words. "But, Dr. Hughston. I could...I could be a nurse in a clinic or something. I could get a job where I wouldn't have to lift patients. I could..."

"Yeah, but sugar, you'd never make it through the clinical training. It's just not a good idea."

"But I want to be a nurse," I cried. I flung back on to my bed and pulled the pillow over my face. I was brokenhearted. It had always been my dream to become a missionary nurse. What would I do with my life now? Sitting with my legs outstretched, knowing they were unable to hold me, my disappointment was monumental. Despite the letdown, I was willing to let go of what I thought I ought to become and concentrate on becoming who God wanted me to be.

I decided not to accept Dr. Hughston's news. Didn't I believe in a God who could part the Red Sea? Didn't God delight in making the impossible possible? Quickly I came up with a plan. I'd wait to see what God did. I'd wait until I could walk. Then I would talk to Dr. Hughston again. Maybe, just maybe, if he saw that I was strong and stable, he might change his mind.

The conflicts and struggles of my situation were great enough; yet now I had a relationship to complicate it further. No matter what I did or how hard I tried not to lose my heart to him, Marty had a way of melting my resistance. I realized that I was falling in love with my good friend. To make matters even more complicated, Marty had quit his job so he could spend more time with me. I needed to set the pace, to slow things down. I made a deal with Mrs. Joy. I would keep my heart open to the possibility of falling in love with Marty if every evening, when Marty visited me, she would make sure that we'd never be alone. We set the plan in motion.

Joy always left our nightly gatherings about nine o'clock. Each night before Mrs. Joy escorted her daughter back to her room, Mrs. Joy would ask me, "Janet, would you like a drink?" She knew I would always answer yes. Then she would ask, "Would you like a straw, too?" If I answered yes, it meant, "Come back A.S.A.P. Do not leave me alone with Marty."

About two weeks later, Earl Howard, Georgia's top manufacturer of orthopedic devices, delivered my leg braces. It wasn't only the fact that they looked like old-fashioned steel polio braces that bothered me. I was appalled at the ugliness of the shoes and shocked that one of them had a five-inch lift attached to the bottom.

Alone in my room when Mr. Howard dropped them off, I wheeled beside him as he moved toward the door, thanked him, and shut the door with an angry push. I then wheeled myself over to the hideous braces and tried to fling them off my bed on to the floor. Acting like a child, I was having the fit of a lifetime. After I had succeeded in tossing the shoes across both beds to the other side of the room, I felt someone's presence and looked up. Wanting to surprise me, Marty had silently opened the door while I was in my tantrum. He stood and watched as I continued in my hysterics.

"Reckon ya don't like the shoes. Are ya finished yet?" Marty challenged.

"Did you see them? Those are the ugliest Buster Brown shoes I've ever seen," I half screamed through my tears. "If I have to wear those awful leg braces, why can't they at least give me pretty shoes?" I gasped to catch my breath and cried, "Marty, is my right leg five inches shorter than the left?"

Marty put his arms around me and let me cry. Finally I'd regained my composure. With a slight giggle I said, "Marty, I told Mr. Howard that his shoes were ugly. I don't think anyone ever told him that before."

Without saying a word, Marty picked up the phone to call Mrs. Joy. "What size shoe do you wear?" he asked. "Reckon y'all could come down to Janet's room and model Janet's new pair of shoes?"

My makeup was smeared, I didn't get to finish my fit, and now my room was going to be filled with happy, smiling people. It just wasn't my day. In moments, Joy and her mom joined us. Randy and Steve walked in right in time to see Mrs. Joy using her high fashion skills, modeling the ugliest shoes in town—walking with a five-inch limp. The decision was unanimous—the shoes were hideous.

Marty lifted me up on to my bed. Without a ruler, Randy, Steve, and Marty used their arms, shoes, or whatever they could find. They all took turns measuring my legs and assured me that they were at least close to the same size. Earlier, Rhonda, my nurse, had paged Dr. Hughston so that I could tell him about the ugly, unpopular footwear with a five-inch lift. Dr. Hughston must have sensed my distress when he called my room. He assured me that the five-inch lift was a mistake and that he would talk to Mr. Howard and see what they could do about the ugly shoes.

Within the hour, Mr. Howard returned to pick up the shoes. Innocently, he walked into a crowd I'm sure he hadn't expected. Everyone in the room paused and listened as I tried to explain to Mr. Howard that his shoes were simply "not my style."

Mr. Howard looked around the room, "Is Marty here?" he timidly asked.

Marty nodded his head. "Yes sir, I'm Marty."

Earl Howard extended his hand to shake Marty's. "Marty, Dr. Hughston suggested that you take Miss Hepp to the mall. Help her find a pair of stable shoes with a solid one-inch heel that we can alter to fit her braces."

With a smile and lots of spunk, I piped up, "Mr. Howard, do you think I could pick out two pairs? A casual pair and a dressy pair?"

I was sure Mr. Howard wasn't about to deny a simple request from a "crippled girl," especially in front of this crowd. "I reckon so; y'all find two pairs. I'll fix 'em up to fit your braces. I'll even leave off the lift this time." With those words Mr. Howard and I became friends.

Learning how to maneuver in the braces was quite a challenge. I felt like a tin man yet with "cool" shoes. My physical therapist and I worked day after day trying to develop quadricep strength so I could lift my legs. "You can do it, Janet, you can!" Anna said, cheering me on. "One day you're gonna surprise us all and walk down these halls."

"One day, I'm going to run," I replied.

Anna wheeled me back to my room after therapy. Marty was hiding behind the door.

"What are you doing here? I thought you couldn't come until tonight."

With a grin, he held up a beautiful bouquet of flowers. "I thought these might brighten your room."

As crazy as it was, I couldn't control my heart. I was falling in love with Marty, a friend who had never seen me walk and who knew there was a possibility I never would. Why did he care for me so much? Didn't he want something more in life than a disabled partner? In spite of my feelings for him, I had to talk with him and convince him that we needed to protect our hearts and remain good friends.

So, later that night while Mrs. Joy tucked Joy in bed for the evening, Marty returned. I knew my time was limited, that within minutes, Mrs. Joy would return with a soda and a straw in hand, so I motioned for Marty to come closer, and I took his hand. "Marty, I need you to listen to me and try to understand. You're a terrific guy. You are a girl's dream." I paused for a moment and then continued. "Marty, you have your entire life ahead of you...You can do or be anything. Right now, I'm not sure what I'll do, or what I'll become."

Marty tried to interrupt me, but I held my index finger to his lips. "I don't want to hold you back. You deserve someone in your life who can do the things you enjoy, someone who can block you when you try to make a basket, someone who can try to catch your hit when it flies over third base." With tears choking my words, I simply said, "Marty, you deserve much more than I can ever offer you."

Looking at me intently, he held my face in both hands and said, "Janet, I know you can't walk now. I know you'll never run again. It's not your legs I've fallen in love with. It's your laugh, your smile. It's what you are inside. You've offered me more than I could ever imagine. I want you in my life. And when you can't participate with me, I want you to be my cheerleader. I've never met a girl like you. Walking or not, I love who you are."

Marty leaned forward and brought his lips to mine. Then without a word, he picked up his jacket and walked out. Seconds later, Mrs. Joy came bubbling into the room. "Where did Marty go?"

"I think he left for the night," I said, breathless.

"I brought you your straw. Guess you don't need it tonight." I wanted to tell Mrs. Joy that she was too late, that my fears had been realized. But I wasn't about to divulge my secret. Maybe tonight Marty would lie awake, analyzing our conversation. Maybe he would discover that I was right. He wasn't obligated to me; he was free to be just my friend. I wasn't sure why Marty had left the way he did, but it had surely made an impact on me. I lay wide awake that night, flat on my back, pondering his words.

Marty continued to visit on a daily basis, yet he gave me time to think about "us." He even showed up at my physical therapy. I hated him seeing me struggle to move my legs as I grasped the parallel bars, yet he stood quietly and watched. After a few steps, the therapist grabbed my wheelchair and placed it underneath me. I collapsed into it with a smile of victory. I had walked two steps farther!

One afternoon I received a package and rushed to open it. I held a handmade dress in pastel pinks and greens. My mother knew I would feel beautiful wearing it to church with Marty on Easter Sunday. Also tucked in the box were some pictures of my family, my favorite perfume, and a pair of earrings. My dad sent a note, letting me know Dr. Hughston was keeping him informed of my "progress," meaning Marty's and my relationship. At the bottom of the box was a large chocolate Easter egg labeled, "For Marty." Apparently Marty had passed the inspections of both Dr. Hughston and my father.

The walls in my room were adorned with cards I'd received from home. My college roommates sent me a row of paper dolls, one doll representing each girl. I strung them where I could sit in my bed and face them. I'd often talk to them, so they knew about Marty and our first kiss.

With each passing day, Marty and I grew closer. He became my best friend, and I loved him. He said he loved everything about me. He even thought my new shoes were beautiful. *Nothing happens by chance to a child of God,* I told myself. At this most difficult time of my life, God had brought Marty and me together. It truly was a marvelous thing!

At the end of April, Marty took me out on pass to his home so his family and I could get acquainted. Agnes, Marty's mother, impressed me by cooking a southern meal of fried chicken, peanut butter cake, and black-eyed peas. Max, Marty's father, was a quiet man, yet he asked me many questions and showed an interest in getting to know me.

During one of my visits to Marty's home, Kim, Marty's twelve-year-old sister, and I got into a bit of trouble. Marty and his eighteen-year-old brother, Rusty, were glued to the television, watching the last of a basketball game. Feeling ignored, Kim suggested we go outside and talk. She pushed my wheelchair to the front yard.

Gazing at the steep grade of the street, I had a mischievous thought. At my urging, Kim pushed my wheelchair up the street. She slowed down as we inched to the top of the hill. Totally ignorant of the speed we would gain, Kim jumped on to my lap, and down we flew. The wheels on the wheelchair rattled violently. Horrified at the thought the wheels could vibrate loose, our hysterical laughter turned into high-pitched screams. "Marty! Rusty! Help us! Save us!"

The street filled with neighbors who heard our cries. They stood by the curb stunned while Kim and I sped past. I doubt they'd ever seen a runaway wheelchair, let alone one with two riders. Rushing to the curbside, Marty and Rusty couldn't believe what they were seeing. They ran toward us and grabbed the wheelchair, braking our speed, and brought us to a peaceful stop at the bottom of the street. Kim and I offered our thanks and promised never again to ride down Ember Drive.

Toward the end of my hospital stay, Louise, the once spunky grandmother, who had filled Saundra Lee's place in our group, now hobbled through the halls with a vacant stare. I knew she longed to be at home, and I fully understood her feelings. A patient can only take so much.

One night Nurse Bailey angrily flew in and interrupted our nightly gathering of lonely patients, sending us all to our rooms. Miss Bailey had taken away the only positive thing we had left—companionship.

That night about midnight, while sitting in my bed chatting with Marty, I gazed out my window. Suddenly, I thought I saw a person stumbling through the parking lot. "Mashing" the call button, I raised my bed as high as it would go to get a better view. I was stunned. I saw a woman hobbling on crutches, staggering through the parking lot, dragging a suitcase.

The next morning a concerned Dr. Hughston entered my room alone without his entourage of fellows. Solemnly he sat on the side of my bed, he asked, "What in the world went on here last night? Do you know where Louise might be?"

"You mean she's missing?

That night the patients gathered in Joy's room for our evening of fun when the phone rang. Mrs. Joy answered. "Hello, Louise. Where in the world are you?"

Louise told her story of how and why she had to get away. She couldn't take being in a hospital any longer. Before sneaking out the basement door, Louise phoned a taxi and begged for help. The cab driver picked her up around the corner from the hospital. He then drove her through Church's Chicken, and on to the airport in Atlanta eighty miles away. She then tipped him a hundred dollars for his mission, and she was now sitting in her favorite chair in Arizona. Louise had made it home, and I was jealous.

The day finally came—I was walking with leg braces and going home. Five months had passed, and my life had been changed forever. I wondered what it would be like to leave behind this southern world that had become a part of me. No one in California had shared these experiences with me. Would I even know where to begin trying to explain all that I had been through? The people I'd met while in the hospital in Georgia had become a part of my life, a part of who I was. Each of them had left his or her mark. I would never be the same old Janet again.

Through his wisdom and his gifted hands, Dr. Jack Hughston gave me back the use of my legs. He took my broken pieces and put them back together. I will be eternally grateful. As Dr. Hughston would say, "Great balls of fire, she's walking, and there's no stopping her now!"

I determined that I would close the door on these past painful years. I wouldn't let myself look back. Instead, I'd proudly walk forward. My future looked promising. I now knew what it was to be in love and to be loved. I was regaining strength in both of my legs. My hope was that with dedication and hard work in therapy, within a year, I would be walking brace free. God had been completely faithful.

Still, I felt torn leaving Marty. There was no denying that he had eased his way into my heart. I was in love! Being on the other side of the country wasn't going to stop it. As Marty had done in the past, he held my face with both of his hands and brought his lips to mine. We embraced for the last time. Despite my tears, I knew I wasn't leaving half of my heart in Georgia. I was taking home a heart that was full of love and gratitude.

The plane took off, ascending high above the clouds. I rested my head against the back of my seat and smiled. I was going home!

*Chapter Eight*

# TAKING A STAND

SIXTEEN YEARS HAD GONE BY since those memorable months in 1980. I'd survived the challenge of ten surgeries, learned to walk, and moved on. Contemplating the new legal challenges ahead, I believed that God would provide the strength I'd need to relive those painful years.

My lawsuit was filed in January 1993: "Complaint for Professional Negligence, Negligent Misrepresentation, Fraud, and Concealment." California has a statute of limitations pertaining to medical malpractice suits. This statute reads as follows:

```
A plaintive must bring action within:
Three years after the date of injury, or
one year after the plaintiff discovers, or
for the use of reasonable diligence should
have discovered the injury, whichever oc-
curs first. In no event shall the time for
commencement of legal action exceed three
years unless tolled for any of the follow-
ing: (1) upon proof of fraud, (2) inten-
tional concealment or (3) the presence of
a foreign body which has no therapeutic or
diagnostic purpose or effect in the person
of the injured person.
```

This meant that Bridget, my lawyer, had to prove fraud and concealment in order for me to win my suit. That was fine with me. It wasn't the mistake that fueled my anger but the fraud and concealment that followed.

My case was placed on "fast track," a system designed by the courts to help eliminate lengthy, drawn-out court proceedings and to get cases to trial in a reasonable time period, usually eighteen months to two years. I figured I could survive almost anything for two years.

I wanted to participate and have full knowledge of my case. Bridget understood and encouraged my involvement. Within weeks, she mailed me medical authorization forms and proof-of-service papers. She instructed me to deliver them to each doctor and hospital that had treated me. These forms required that all medical records pertaining to my heath care be made available within five days. This was another mission for Jane and me. As detectives in training, we hand-delivered these important papers, and again, Dr. Allgood's office ignored the request.

Bridget responded by serving interrogatories to both doctors. These were standard and specialized questions that the doctors were to answer and return by a specific date. These answers would provide the information we needed to begin our investigation.

Weeks later, I received a set of interrogatory questions from the defense. It took me days to draft my answers. It ultimately became a family project with everyone trying to remember dates and important facts. My father again went through boxes of receipts he had long ago filed away.

"I found plane tickets both to and from Georgia," he proudly informed me. "Even found the bus ticket that took us from Atlanta to Columbus years ago."

Marty added up all the expenses, excluding the medical bills paid by my father's insurance company, as they were kept separate. "Janet, I can't believe these extra expenses add up to so much. Your parents paid over $20,000 to cover them, and that was in the late 1970s and early '80s. This doesn't even include their medical deductibles or co-pays." Like a businessman delivering an annual report, Marty continued. "Of course there are over twenty plane fares to Georgia, taxi and bus fares, a couple of exercise bikes, maternity clothes that would fit over your casts, and a few other odds and ends. But what about all of the long-distance phone calls? Didn't they call you every day while you were in the hospital in Georgia? Shouldn't those expenses be added?"

"I don't imagine we'll ever have a full account of the expenses," I replied. "I'm just grateful I had parents who could and were willing to make the sacrifice."

To complete the interrogatory, I recorded every job I ever held, each surgery, and each school I attended. Twenty-seven pages later, I faxed my rough draft to Bridget so she could refine it into legal terms and meet the deadline. My entire life, for the past sixteen years, was now down on paper. I was surprised they didn't ask me for my shoe size.

I faced my medical history head on. Reading every piece of information I could find, I compared the various medical files, with the exception of Dr. Allgood's, and I then made a list, recording each inconsistency. I noted that Dr. Ulid's medical file had entries from both himself and Dr. Allgood, implying that at one point they had shared the same chart. Both doctors noted my walking and "doing fine" when, in fact, I was sitting in a wheelchair, unable to walk, and vital x-rays of my right knee were still missing. Discovery after discovery fueled the flames—igniting my anger. I felt the doctors' betrayal over and over again.

I compared each of my operative reports. On paper, the first surgery on my right knee was successful. My tibia was cut two inches from the knee joint horizontally across the leg. After cutting the bone, my tibia was rotated forty degrees. The report stated, "The foot and the knee were lined up, and the knee was stable."

Flipping the pages, I found the fourth surgical report pertaining to my right leg. It stated that the leg was once more "internally rotated approximately 35–45 degrees, lining up the second toe with the patella." I didn't need a calculator to add the degrees of rotation from these two operations. Something was amiss. My doctors and I both knew it. I had never required that much rotation in the first place.

I thought back to my phone conversation with Dr. Hughston. I pulled out the transcript of his call and read it. He, too, knew that a mistake had been made and even believed that "the doctors had to have known." Within a few days, I was back on track, reviewing files and taking notes. I marveled at the cut-and-paste job that was done to my chart while extracting a whole year from my medical records. I kept wondering, *Who took it out and why? Where did it go? Did it still exist? What did it contain? Would I ever find out?*

Days turned to weeks as I read several hundred pages of hospital records. The nurses' notes provoked memories, accurately portraying my post-op experiences. As I read every word, I felt as if I were reliving each fever, pain shot, and muscle spasm that was recorded. I knew how many pillows had been stacked under my leg and when.

With a cup of hot cocoa, I curled up on the couch and turned to the pages of my last surgery in Georgia, my longest hospital stay. Nurses' names were scrawled adjacent to each entry. Fond memories emerged of their kindness and support. Dates and times were noted of the rendezvous I took with Marty. I searched, to discover if it was actually recorded, the evening when the nurse walked in on our good-night kiss. I found it. It stated, "Patient busy." Other entries were noted: "Patient missing family. Patient in pain. Patient riding halls in wheelchair. Patient in good spirits. Pedal pushes with left foot—good."

I flipped the pages and found the entries of Anna, my physical therapist. These records told a challenging story of a girl who had the determination to walk and a therapist who told her she could. Anna's therapy notes charted everything from wheelchair to leg braces, parallel bars to crutches, defeat to victory.

Days later, I met Jane for lunch. Over chips and salsa, I told her about the doctors' answers to my complaint and their responses to the allegations listed in my lawsuit. "Jane, you'll never guess what the doctors wrote. I can't believe they had the nerve to put it in print."

"Tell me."

I wrestled through my papers. "Dr. Ulid actually had the audacity to write, 'The plaintiff'—that's me—'was negligent, careless, and reckless and so conducted herself as to cause or contribute to the occurrence of her claimed injuries.'"

"Don't you even begin to let yourself believe that," Jane exclaimed.

"I won't, but listen. Then he says, 'In the event that defendant'—that's Dr. Ulid—'is found to have made a misrepresentation of any type, in which supposition is denied and merely stated for the purpose of this affirmative defense, then the reliance upon same by the plaintiff was unjustified.'"

Jane dipped her chip and said, "Janet, that's like saying if Dr. Ulid indeed said what he now says he didn't say, then you're at fault for believing him."

Quickly, I grabbed another page. "Mr. Porter, Dr. Allgood's attorney, scribbled these words on Dr. Allgood's answer to my complaint. 'Plaintiff's congenital deformity has been lessened by numerous surgeries.' That's ridiculous! I could ski, backpack, run, and walk without pain before I met Dr. Allgood."

"He or his lawyer must have stayed up all night thinking of that one," Jane giggled. "Janet, you know the doctors have chosen to continue concealing the fact that you were injured. They completely deny it. So you should expect them to say these types of things. What else could they say?"

"I'm not sure. I wonder if these are standard responses, used in all medical malpractice fraud cases, or I wonder if hidden somewhere in Dr. Ulid's office, these responses are written on note cards entitled, 'Do Not Use Unless...'"

"Unless what? You mess up or have some type of legal emergency?"

Playing with my chip, I used it to stir the bowl of salsa. "Jane, Dr. Allgood states that he hasn't been covered by any medical malpractice insurance policy since 1971."

"You mean, at this moment he doesn't have coverage?"

"Nope—no coverage."

"Can he do this? Isn't there a law that requires doctors to carry insurance?" Jane shook her head no. "That's absurd. You can't drive without auto insurance, but it's okay for doctors to cut someone open, tinker with their insides, sew them back up, and not be insured?"

"I wouldn't take the risk of going uninsured. I have both car insurance and a malpractice insurance policy to cover my nursing career. I'm not about to take a chance of losing my home and everything I've worked for."

"Jane, what if something goes wrong in a surgery, or a doctor accidentally prescribes the wrong medication and the patient can't work to provide for his family any longer? Who helps out? Isn't medical malpractice insurance meant for just these types of things? I know if I were in a car accident, I would readily hand over my car insurance information. This is what it's for—an accident."

"But Janet," Jane interrupted, "patients have abused the system and sued doctors and malpractice carriers when they shouldn't have."

"Yes, but people have also filed fraudulent automobile claims and this hasn't changed the requirement for citizens to be insured.

Car insurance is required so that the people who are responsible or involved in causing harm to another will have the financial aid to offer. It shouldn't be left up to the people of California or one's state to pay for another's error. Doctors should have to take responsibility and obtain insurance, and if they don't, they shouldn't drive or perform surgery."

"Now you're sounding like a politician," Jane said.

"Well, do you agree? I just can't believe that an educated surgeon would take such a risk and not be covered."

"What I do know is that when I worked at the hospital, they provided the nurses with insurance coverage. The doctors weren't employees of the hospital. They were contracted services and required to provide insurance for themselves. Janet, I, too, purchased an additional insurance plan of my own. I then gave a copy of this to the hospital. It is the hospitals that require their medical staff to be covered."

"Don't all hospitals require medical malpractice insurance?" I asked.

"I would think so, but I'm not sure."

"Dr. Allgood states that St. Ann's has required medical malpractice insurance since 1985, but then again, he also states, now in the '90s, he doesn't have it."

"That doesn't add up," Jane said as she took another chip. "Then again, I believe Dr. Allgood makes his own rules, and then only breaks them if it will somehow benefit him. For example, he still hasn't produced your medical chart, even under court order. Bridget had to threaten him just to get him to answer his interrogatories, and he was still two months late."

"I know, but how can he be performing surgery at St. Ann's when he's uninsured? Could Dr. Allgood be such a great surgeon that the hospital allows him to be an exception to their rule?"

"Got me." She shrugged.

We finished our lunches and walked to our cars. "Janet, I wonder if St. Ann's knows that Dr. Allgood is uninsured."

"I don't know, but it's hard for me to feel sorry for him if he's made the decision to go without insurance." Kicking the tire, I mumbled, "I feel that Dr. Allgood is experiencing the consequences of his behavior—you know, 'reaping what you sow.' Unfortunately, I, too, am living a consequence of his behavior, and I am one of those who deserves to benefit from his insurance coverage that doesn't exist. My future medical bills are going to be more than my family can handle."

"Remember, we believe in a God who promises to take care of our every need. There's nothing he can't handle and nothing's ever been too expensive for him. Besides, this lawsuit isn't about money, right?"

"Right," I concluded as Jane gave me a hug goodbye.

Later that evening I called Jane and began to rattle off my thoughts. "I've been thinking. With truth being a confusing issue for Dr. Allgood, I wonder if Dr. Allgood has medical malpractice coverage and doesn't want me to know? Maybe he's been sued before and maxed out his policy by other claims and reached his lifetime allowance. Or could the insurance companies have denied him coverage?"

"Slow down, girlfriend! You sure have been thinking. I think those questions warrant a trip to the courthouse to find out."

Early the next morning, Jane and I went to the Orange County Superior Court. Our goal was to look up the doctors and find out if they had been sued before, and if so, when and why. We planned to write down the names of all plaintiffs and attorneys involved in the suits. Previous detective work had not called us to a courthouse. In unfamiliar territory now, we stood reading the instructions on the wall.

To the right were books listing the defendants named in suits from the 1970s to the present. Supposedly they were alphabetized, but the books were tossed in no particular order on the shelf. The left side held the plaintiffs' books. These were labeled in the same fashion as that of defendants. However, they were stored in a manner that resembled a mountain more than a library. Jane had watched more "Marcus Welby" programs than I, so she directed me to the right where we could discover if my doctors had been sued before.

We began with the defendants' book "A." Dr. Allgood's name appeared not just once but several times. The list ran down the page: "*Goldman v. Allgood*; *Kirby v. Allgood*; *Ruppert v. Allgood*," and so on. Dr. Allgood was no novice to legal actions. Goose bumps covered my arms as Jane counted and whispered, "Janet, since 1977, Allgood has been sued twenty-two times in an Orange County Court. I wonder how many times he's been sued in other counties."

Following the required procedure to review a case file, Jane drew a card out of the box. We listed each file number, along with our names, addresses, and driver's license numbers.

We received three files at a time. One by one, we read the cause of action pertaining to each case. Our joking ceased. Our light-hearted approach became serious. Words such as "medical malpractice," "breach of contract," "tax liens," "medical negligence," "personal injury," and "fraud" jumped off the pages.

"Wow. Dr. Allgood's been sued for all kinds of things—not just medical malpractice," I whispered to Jane.

"Yes, but these suits tell a story of a real character—or lack of."

"Jane, listen to this. Dr. Allgood has been sued for 'diamond fraud.'"

We lowered our heads close to the document and resorted to whispering as we discussed our findings. The room was full of professional-looking people. Yet, we sat in our blue jeans and sweatshirts, taking notes and dog-earring the documents we wanted to copy.

Dr. Ulid's history was just as colorful. We counted a total of twenty-three suits; all but one were for some type of medical negligence. Some included "intentional infliction to cause harm," "conspiracy," "negligent misrepresentation," "fraud," even "wrongful death." One stated that Dr. Ulid covered up the negligence of another doctor. Another read, "Dr. Ulid performed surgery on the wrong site—the wrong location." Several files were stamped with the word *dismissed*. Not knowing exactly what this word meant, I approached the clerk at the counter. "Could you please tell me what the word *dismissed* means as it's stamped on some of these files?"

The young clerk piped up in a less-than-confidential manner. "Means there was a payoff—that's what's stamped when a case is settled out of court."

I leaned over the counter and whispered to the clerk, "You mean all these suits have settled out of court?"

Still speaking as if he wanted the entire room to be apprised of his legal knowledge, he answered, "Well, a judge may have tossed out one or two, or the plaintiff might have dropped a case, but for the most part, I'll say—the doc has made a deal."

"If there are this many suits against a doctor, why would the medical board state that he is in good standing?"

"That's one reason doctors settle cases. When a case settles, the doc's insurance company is to turn in a one-page report to the medical board. It's then the medical board's job to find the victim and get them to sign a release so the board can obtain the records and investigate. But settlements or payoffs come with confidentiality agreements…The way I see it, the doc's virtually paid the cost of his mistakes, and it's a done deal."

"Yeah, but what happens when the same doctor keeps making mistakes and he's never reported?"

"Then people die, ma'am. People die."

The clerk's words sent a chill throughout my body. I walked back to where Jane was busy reading. "We have to get out of here."

One look and Jane knew something was wrong. "Jane, people could have died," I whispered, fighting back my tears. "This cannot keep happening!"

Jane placed her arm around my shoulder, and we walked out to my car. I told her about my conversation with the clerk. "Janet, I'm going to be right here by your side," she said. "You've got to take a stand. You can't be another statistic and settle. Girl, we're in for the long haul on this one." With that, she gave my arm a squeeze.

"But Jane, I can't help but wonder if some of the suits against doctors have been brought about by disappointed parents whose children have experienced a 'poor result' from a surgery. You know, doctors aren't responsible for all poor outcomes. They're not gods."

"Yeah, I think too many people believe that if doctors are not gods, they're at least God's best friends, able to do almost anything and everything. But Janet, you must also remember that your parents once believed that you, too, were a child with a poor result, and now we know better. You had a poor outcome due to a poor surgical procedure."

"I know, but, Jane, it's so hard for me to believe that all this has happened. It's hard for me to believe that so many people have been hurt. I really liked my doctors."

---

Not long after the trip to the courthouse, I placed a call to St. Ann's Hospital and asked to speak to the head of their medical staff. A woman came to the phone. After introducing myself, I asked her what the hospital's policy was regarding their physicians carrying medical malpractice insurance. "Each of our physicians carries malpractice insurance. It's a requirement," she assured me.

"Could you tell me the name of the carrier that insures Dr. Albert Allgood?"

Within minutes the woman came back to the phone. "Dr. Allgood is covered by Physicians and Surgeons Exchange." She then gave me the policy number, when it was renewed, and the expiration date. "The doctors are required to turn in their updated information each year when they renew their policies," she added.

I thanked her for her time and hung up. Either Dr. Allgood was lying to the court and me, or he was lying to the hospital. If he were lying in my lawsuit, I was assured that he would be exposed during trial. But if he had been lying to St. Ann's Hospital, would they ever find out? They might not...at least not until someone was hurt or injured, and then it would be too late.

I grabbed the phone book and tried to find the phone number of Physicians and Surgeons Exchange. With no luck, I called the 800-information line and within seconds I was talking to a representative.

"No. I'm sorry, we do not insure a Dr. Albert Allgood."

"But I have his policy number right here; it's 34914."

"Ma'am, our policy numbers have ten digits. From our records, Dr. Allgood has never held a policy with us."

I thanked the woman for helping me and sat perplexed. Why would Dr. Allgood lie about something as important as this? Then I had a thought. Earlier that year my neighbor, Bob, and I had discussed medical malpractice insurance, as he had sold policies in the past. Bob figured it would cost an orthopedic surgeon like mine approximately $50,000, maybe more, per year to be insured. This meant $50,000 in the doctor's pocket if he went uninsured.

I wrestled with what to do with my newest discoveries. I felt a pressing responsibility to inform St. Ann's of what I knew. Yet I wondered what the consequences might be if I exposed the truth. But didn't Allgood's patients have the right to have a doctor who was covered by a medical malpractice insurance policy?

As I entered St. Ann's, the smell of the hospital brought back a flood of memories. Trying to stay focused, I walked to the receptionist and asked for directions to their legal department. Heading down a hallway, I realized I was being followed by a man wearing an earphone, talking into a walkie-talkie. He stayed ten or so feet behind me, yet he followed my every turn, eventually joining me in the elevator. There, I noticed he was wearing a hospital identification badge. I stood silently as he tried his best to see the documents I held.

I opened the door to the legal department, turned, and motioned to the man, offering to hold the door open for him. Once inside, he stepped back and again stood behind me.

I introduced myself to the receptionist. She wrote down my name and drew a circle around it several times.

"I am in litigation against two surgeons on your staff. Sometime this last year my attorney sent you an Intention to Sue. I chose not to include your facility in my lawsuit of medical negligence, fraud, and concealment. I believe we need to resolve our differences differently. But I also believe that you're a victim of these doctors' lies and deceit."

She asked me to take a seat. I smiled while I imagined where my "shadow" was going to sit. The woman came from behind her desk and took a seat next to mine while the man with the headset stood nearby like a guard.

"A few days ago," I explained, "I spoke to your medical staff department and was informed that Dr. Albert Allgood was covered by Physicians and Surgeons Exchange. After calling the insurance company, I have reason to believe that Dr. Allgood has not only lied and altered my medical records, but perhaps he has submitted fraudulent proof of medical malpractice insurance to you. I ask that you verify his coverage. I feel this present 'misunderstanding' has put people at risk."

Clearly alarmed by the issues I brought to light, the woman made a few notes and then looked up. "I'll check on this matter and clarify any confusion." Without hesitating, she added, "Our findings in this matter will be confidential."

We stood and shook hands. With appreciation and a promise that I'd receive the red carpet treatment the next time I was a patient at St. Ann's, the receptionist said goodbye, and "the man" escorted me to the hospital doors. I wasn't sure what I'd accomplished. But I had been obedient to what I felt God had asked me to do, no matter how uncomfortable or outrageous the situation had been.

*Chapter Nine*

# FACING THE PAST

MONTHS CREPT BY. Each day I had the opportunity to hurry up and wait. I stayed abreast of the developments in my suit and often wondered if I was an attorney's dream or an attorney's nightmare.

Due to Allgood's citing "scheduling conflicts," Dr. Ulid would be the first to be deposed. There was no question as to whether I'd attend his deposition—I was going. Finding the courage to face him was another story. Fear struck the moment I heard the date because I remembered Dr. Ulid's stern warning not to tell who had divulged the secrets surrounding my medical care.

Since Marty had a last-minute conflict at work, my father agreed to attend Dr. Ulid's deposition with me. "I'll go to keep you in line," my father joked. "On second thought, I think we'll need to keep each other in line."

I knew my dad wanted to be with me when I sat and listened to the medical details of my past. I also knew that it would be difficult for any father to face the man he had trusted with his daughter's medical care and who had deceived him.

We met Bridget in the parking lot and walked together into the office of Keen, Murdock and Wiley, Attorneys at Law—Dr. Ulid's attorneys. Politely greeted by a young, sharp-looking woman, we were escorted through a maze of offices. Tasteful artwork lined the walls. The receptionist, who was poised like a fashion model, led us to large conference room, smiled, and motioned for us to enter.

A man inside the room looked up. "Good morning. I'm Michael Keen," he said as he shuffled the papers he was studying. "Take a seat. Can I offer you something? Coffee? Tea? Soda?"

Already on edge and not needing caffeine, I opted for a glass of water. Sitting between Bridget and my father, I looked around the room. Surely this firm had won many lawsuits. My hand brushed over the smooth leather covering my chair. I watched as Bridget and Mr. Keen got acquainted and made last-minute preparations. Studying Mr. Keen, I noticed he had a much smaller stature than the doctor he represented. His brown hair was perfectly combed, parted to the side. In a jet-black suit and wearing a starched white shirt and solid red tie, he looked dressed for the Supreme Court.

Keen came from a powerful, prestigious, well-established firm where he was a partner. Dr. Ulid's medical malpractice insurance company had selected Keen to defend him. This insurance company was both powerful and wealthy, and it had chosen to play hardball. It would direct Mr. Keen in how to conduct the defense.

I was told that Dr. Ulid was obligated to cooperate fully in the investigation of his case. If he failed to do so, he would jeopardize his insurance coverage and protection. I wondered how Dr. Ulid's insurance company compensated Mr. Keen. The longer my suit stayed in the court system, the more Mr. Keen had to gain. I was pretty sure he was paid by the hour. Win or lose, Mr. Keen would be compensated. What did he have to lose? Still, what I saw of him, I liked, but I wasn't sure he liked or believed me.

Soon we were joined by a man whom I knew had to be Alvin Porter, attorney at law. Porter was large in stature. His dark charcoal suit was stretched across his middle, his buttons strained and threatened. His wiry, silvery hair reflected his age and experience.

"I'm here, so let's get started," he bellowed. Bridget introduced herself, handing Mr. Porter her business card. Porter responded, "Oh, you're the attorney. I thought you were a sister or something."

Mr. Keen managed to gain control of the conversation before Bridget began a women's liberation march. Mr. Porter took a seat across the table from Bridget, and Mr. Keen left the room to retrieve his client. I reached into my pocket and rubbed the smooth rock Jane had given me, reminding myself that my strength comes from God; I didn't have to manufacture it or pretend it into being. I took a deep breath, realizing that at any moment I would be sitting across the table from Dr. Ulid.

The doctor entered the room, towering over his attorney. Head bowed, he didn't look up or lift his eyes to meet mine. He stared straight ahead as he took a seat one away from Alvin Porter. Mr. Keen sat at the head of the table, adjacent to his client. Seconds later, Dr. Ulid removed the paper clip from the stack of papers before him and began moving it between his fingers.

"Dr. Ulid, my name is Bridget Halvorson, and I represent Janet Mitchell in a case arising out of care and treatment she received from you and others dating back to 1977. You understand, Dr. Ulid, that you are under oath, and this is just as if you were testifying in court?"

"I do."

"After your deposition is over, it will be typed and put in booklet form, and you will have a chance to read and review it and make any necessary corrections. If you do make changes in your testimony, I would then be able to inform a jury or judge that you changed your testimony, which may affect your credibility. Do you understand?"

"I do."

"Dr. Ulid, what year did you go into private practice?"

"1964."

"Are you board certified?"

"I am."

"Do you recall when Janet Hepp Mitchell first came into your office on Fourteenth Street?"

"No, ma'am."

Question after question was answered with either "I do," "I don't," or some other short, snappy, to-the-point answer. It was obvious to all that Dr. Ulid was annoyed about being put in this situation, and he wasn't going to let his guard down.

"Dr. Ulid, other than this lawsuit, have you ever been sued before?"

"Yes."

"Were those medical malpractice situations?"

Dr. Ulid finally looked up and reported with a slight grin, "With thirty years in private practice of orthopedics, the answer is yes."

Mr. Keen interjected, "It is not a statistical inevitability."

Bridget continued. "Do you recall approximately how many times?"

I squirmed in my chair and bit my lower lip to keep from blurting out, "I can tell you. Twenty-three times."

"There have been very few in my career," Dr. Ulid said without flinching.

"From 1975 until 1978, I believe that you and Dr. Allgood were associates. Did you and Dr. Allgood part on good terms?"

"Did we part as friends? I don't know. You must define what you mean by good terms, because…"

"Was there any professional disagreement between you and Dr. Allgood that caused you to move your office from Fourteenth Street to La Mesa Drive?"

"Of course there was," Dr. Ulid replied in a huff.

"What was the professional disagreement?"

"Who took what and where."

The room was silent. Bridget reviewed her notes and changed her line of questioning. "Dr. Ulid, is the chart that you have with you today your complete chart on Janet Mitchell?"

"I do not believe it is."

"Do you offer any explanation as to why there are portions of the chart missing?"

"No, ma'am, I do not. I think it is a miracle that this chart is still even in existence."

*Miracle? I know it's a miracle,* I thought.

"May I see your chart, Dr. Ulid? I would like to have the entire chart marked as Plaintiff's Exhibit 3."

"Excuse me," Mr. Keen abruptly interrupted. "Let me tell you… I'll be straightforward about this. We went through the record, and we noticed there seemed to be no entries about any care for Janet Hepp Mitchell between August 1977 and August 1978, which makes us wonder whether something was missing…" Mr. Keen then tried to explain away the missing year by stating this could have occurred when the doctors went their separate ways.

Bridget continued fishing for any information regarding its contents. "Dr. Ulid, at some point there may have been two charts, one left with Dr. Allgood and one that you took with you when you moved your office. Is this correct?"

"That sounds reasonable," answered Dr. Ulid. "I just don't know for sure."

"The records that you have provided for us jump from August of 1977 to August 1978. You have no idea what happened during that period of time?" Bridget quizzed.

"I know Dr. Allgood took some staples out."

"Do you recall seeing Janet at all between June of 1977 and August 1978?"

"No, I do not."

I could hardly contain the eruption that was about to explode within me. In my mind I blasted, *What? You performed surgery on me. You know you did!* I turned my head in disbelief and caught my dad's eye. I could tell he was thinking the same thing I was. Either Dr. Ulid had become very forgetful, or he was outright lying.

"Do you think it was kind of odd that Janet was seeing both you and Dr. Allgood at the same time, having an appointment with you and kind of going back and forth?"

"Do I think it odd if a patient has a problem and she knows another physician, that she would get another opinion in an area where she lives? No, I don't find that odd at all. Patients do it all the time, and they do it in Sacramento just like they do it here," Dr. Ulid pointed out sarcastically.

"Have you talked with Dr. Allgood about whether he has a chart on Janet Mitchell?"

"I have not."

"Have you had the opportunity to review the operative record from the 1977 surgery?"

"I have."

"In reviewing the record, does it bring back any memory of something unusual happening during that surgery?"

"It does not."

"Okay, after the surgery on Janet's right leg, you performed surgery on her left leg. This would be the osteotomy dated April 6, 1977."

"I believe that is correct."

"Now, from reviewing all the records, do you recall what kind of result Janet had from the surgery you performed on her left leg, April 6, 1977?"

"I believe the result was very good."

Dr. Ulid sat motionless except for his fingers, which were still playing with the paper clip.

Bridget continued. "Dr. Ulid, Janet came into your office in April of 1992. Would you mind reading your handwritten note found in her medical chart pertaining to this date?"

Like a machine, he read, "Night of riot, walking, left knee slipped. Right back, and landed on right knee. Moderate swelling. Packed in ice. Seen by neighbor—internist..."

"Now, in the typed history, in the third paragraph, you say, '...This was for tibial derotation. At that time the osteotomy cut entered the posterior aspect of the joint itself.' Dr. Ulid, do recall why you included this information?"

"Because at that point in time, like we have discussed here for the last two hours, it was my recollection that the cut may have been off a little bit. I was probably talking a little bit out of school. I have a tendency to do that. Looking back, I don't think what I told Janet Hepp Mitchell at that appointment was true."

"Okay."

"I think I had a misassumption as to what the real situation was," Dr. Ulid added.

"But, Dr. Ulid, you had some vague recollection in June of 1992 that the osteotomy, the cut that Dr. Allgood performed on the right leg, was high, and you had a vague recollection that she had had problems with that knee?"

"I had a—no, I had a vague recollection, which I believe at this point in time to be incorrect. I think I made a mistake. I'm not the only one in this room that's ever done that, but I believe I made a mistake. And I think with review of all these records and these operative notes there is no indication a mistake, which I thought might have happened, did, in fact, happen. Putting everything together sitting in this room today, I think that was wrong."

"Dr. Ulid, again I ask, do you have a recollection of telling Janet in June of 1992 that you thought the osteotomy cut entered the posterior aspect of the joint?"

"I may have made that statement to her with regard to the fact that if that could have happened, it could have injured her ligaments."

"Back to my question, Dr. Ulid," Bridget said sternly.

With a slight glare directed toward Bridget, Dr. Ulid ranted, "The answer is that my clinical thought at that point in time was incorrect. I was wrong. I may have stated that wrong assumption to the patient. If I did, I am in error, and that has been laid to rest."

"Dr. Ulid, I am trying to ask—"

"The questions have been asked and answered," snapped Mr. Keen.

Bridget brought her glass to her lips and paused. She took a drink, swallowed, then cleared her throat, providing a cooling time for tempers that were about to fly. Within a minute or two Bridget began again, trying to find the answer she was looking for. "I'm trying to find out, Dr. Ulid, if you remember telling Janet that the cut went through the posterior aspect of her knee."

With a huff of anger, Dr. Ulid fumed, "If I wrote that in the chart, I probably did tell her that."

"Thank you. Now, on August fourth, a couple of months later, you again saw Janet. Did you continue to think, as of that date, that the cut had entered the posterior aspect of the joint?"

"Yes, what I thought at that time is described in the second paragraph of my typed note." For the record, Dr. Ulid read out loud, "I believe that it matters really in retrospect little as to what the overall situation is..." Looking up at Bridget he explained, "I believe, as I stated way earlier in this deposition, I had come to an incorrect conclusion. I advised the patient of my incorrect conclusion. And in retrospect, what I thought was going on and what I thought had happened didn't—I was wrong."

With a look of surprise, Bridget confronted Dr. Ulid. "You advised Janet of your incorrect conclusion on August fourth of 1992?"

"No, I'm sorry. I did not."

"Was there some reason that you did not tell Janet you had made a mistake when you explained to her that the osteotomy cut had entered the joint space of her knee?"

"I didn't feel at that point in time it made any real difference as to what—how we got to where we were. We were now trying to deal with the problem and how it would impact her life."

"Oh, I see…" Bridget said while trying to make sense of Dr. Ulid's logic.

"Mrs. Halvorson," Mr. Keen interrupted, "can we go off the record for a moment? I need to know how much longer you'll be. I do have some questions that I'd like to ask, and I assume that Mr. Porter does as well. It's already well into the afternoon, and Dr. Ulid is to be in surgery within the hour."

"Mr. Keen, I'm not nearly finished with my examination. I know I have taken most of the morning. But I flew down from Sacramento, planning on spending the day and flying home tonight. You did not inform me, nor the court, that there was a conflict concerning time."

Dr. Ulid spoke up. "Ms. Halvorson, I'm scheduled to perform surgery in an hour or so. I'm sure my patient has already been taken to pre-op."

Bridget guarded her words and looked sternly at Dr. Ulid. "Well, I guess you or your attorney will need to call the hospital and tell them you will not be available."

"For surgery?"

"Not until I deem this deposition over."

Frustrated, the doctor and Mr. Keen walked out of the room to call the hospital. Mr. Porter followed them, I think out of his own curiosity. Bridget stood up, running her fingers through her hair. "They're tough," my dad said with a sigh. "But I believe they've met their match. You're doing a terrific job, Bridget. Don't let them bully you around."

"Janet, are you doing okay?" Bridget asked. "I mean, this is the first time you've seen Dr. Ulid since all this happened."

"I'm fine. It's my dad I'm worried about."

"Don't you worry about me. I'm sitting here pretending I'm at a movie, and an action-filled one at that!"

When we were certain the halls were clear, my father and I wandered down, finding our way to the restrooms. We were not up to an informal meeting with the doctor outside the rest rooms. It felt good to stretch our legs. I could tell that I was tense by the way that my shoulders had begun to ache. I now wondered for my own sake how much longer this deposition would take and what excitement it might bring.

About fifteen minutes later, Dr. Ulid, his attorney, and Mr. Porter filed back into the conference room. They took their seats across the table and waited for Bridget to resume the deposition.

We were back on the record in *Mitchell v. Allgood and Ulid*. Starting right where she had left off, Bridget began, "Dr. Ulid, did you ever tell Janet that you were mistaken or wrong when you explained that the osteotomy cut went into the joint space of her knee?"

"No."

"Did you know that she was upset by what you had told her?"

"Upset? I don't think so."

"Did you know that she called your office for a referral to a psychologist?"

"Uh? The girls frequently don't tell me those things. She may have, but I wouldn't know a psychologist's name if you asked me right now."

Bridget continued, "Now on September 1, 1992, Janet came in, accompanied by her husband, and at that time you again discussed at length the situation and Janet's options for what she could do about her problem."

"Correct."

"But before that, had you received a letter from Janet thanking you for telling her what had happened?"

"It was delivered," Dr. Ulid mumbled.

"This handwritten letter is Exhibit 4, from Janet to you. It says at the bottom of the page, 'When I asked you in your office why no one had ever told me that Dr. Allgood cut my bone in the wrong direction, you stated: "Janet, we never thought it would come to this."' Did you say that, Dr. Ulid?"

"I don't have an independent recollection. If I did say that, I think I was wrong."

"Did you tell Janet you had tried to stop Dr. Allgood from cutting the bone wrong?"

"If you have a hammer in your hand, and you're hitting something, could you tell someone to stop? Don't be silly."

"Did you tell Janet that Dr. Allgood had destroyed her medical records?"

"Certainly not!"

"Do you know where Dr. Allgood's records might be found?"

"I do not."

"Did you instruct Janet at her appointment with you in 1992 to go and see Dr. Allgood and tell him that she had found out what had happened in her February '77 surgery?"

"I suggested that she go back and discuss the situation with Dr. Allgood. What she elected to do was of her own vein."

"Dr. Ulid, did you tell Janet that you didn't want her to tell anyone that you were the one who had told her that Dr. Allgood cut her bone wrong?"

"Of course not! I don't think I told her that," he fumed.

"Do you remember Janet crying at any of those appointments in 1992 when you told her what had happened?"

Slowly articulating each word, Dr. Ulid replied, "A lot of patients cry."

"But do you remember her crying?" Bridget shot back.

"Not specifically."

"What was the reason you didn't respond to her letter of August 8, 1992?"

Red-faced, Dr Ulid glared in my direction. My father adjusted his posture, pressed his back against his chair, and looked back at him. I could tell that my dad also wanted an answer to this question.

"I don't believe that letter requires a response," Dr. Ulid grunted.

Bridget ignored his rudeness and moved on. "So, then, on September 1, 1992, Janet and her husband came in. You again had a long discussion. At that time, did you again tell Janet that you thought the osteotomy cut had gone into the joint space?"

"I don't believe so."

"Did you draw a picture for Janet of what you thought had occurred?"

"I don't believe so."

Bridget then pulled the drawing out of a manila envelope and placed it directly in front of Dr. Ulid. The paper clip that Dr. Ulid had toyed with throughout the entire deposition shot across the table, falling to the floor. Everyone in the room focused on the piece of paper. Obviously, this diagram was a shock to Dr. Ulid as well as to Mr.

Keen and Mr. Porter. My dad showed a slight grin, and I took a deep breath. Now Dr. Ulid knew that Marty and I had taken his artwork.

No one said a word. Dr. Ulid sat there looking like a child who had been caught cheating on a test. He looked dumbfounded and confused.

Bridget carried on. "I would like to show you a diagram that Janet says was made by you at the September 1, 1992, meeting. You don't remember making this diagram, Dr. Ulid?"

Dr. Ulid looked to his attorney for direction. Mr. Keen raised his shoulders as if to say, "I can't defend you when I'm unaware." Dr. Ulid then stumbled through his words, "Now that I see it—yes, I did—you stung me—and now I have a red mark!"

"No, you don't!" Keen firmly interjected.

Mr. Porter appeared to enjoy watching this scenario unfold, as this wasn't his immediate problem but that of his colleague. I was certain that the very moment Bridget produced the drawing, Mr. Keen's eyes were opened to the character of his client.

"We have marked your drawing as Exhibit 4. Dr. Ulid, do you now recall drawing this?"

"Independent recollection of drawing it, no, I do not have," he said while his index finger covered his lips. "But it is probably my drawing. It is the kind of drawing I would make because that's the way my hand works. But that is not my writing."

"So as you look at Exhibit 4 and you look at the diagram, can you tell me what these lines are meant to show?" Bridget asked.

With exasperation Dr. Ulid replied, "It's meant to show the views of the knee, and if the cut exited high, did the cut sever the ligament. And that's long since been put to rest."

"Dr. Ulid, wouldn't you agree that it would be a mistake if the osteotomy went into the joint space?"

Looking defeated, he sighed. "Yes, I would agree that it would be a mistake."

Bridget ended her examination, and for the next hour or so Mr. Keen pumped question after question to Dr. Ulid, trying to paint a picture of a gentle, caring man. His medical questions were highly technical in nature, certain to confuse any jury.

Mr. Porter, on the other hand, asked just a few questions. He treated this deposition as though it, in the scheme of things, really didn't matter. Mr. Porter tried his best to get testimony stating that my original condition was the worst case Dr. Ulid had ever seen. At one point the doctors' attorneys were at odds. I was certain that Mr. Keen's words, "Don't get testy on us, Porter," would become part of my household vocabulary.

There were just a few days between Dr. Ulid's and Dr. Hughston's depositions. It wasn't long before I was on a plane headed for Georgia. I was glad that Mr. Porter would not be attending Dr. Hughston's testimonial. Because Mr. Porter wasn't an immediate threat, I turned my thoughts toward Mr. Keen, who truly was a kind man. His confidence in the law shined. I could see it in how he verbally responded and conducted himself, yet I couldn't understand how Keen could represent Dr. Ulid with all the known facts. What did Mr. Keen think about his client who could cause such an upheaval in someone's life and then claim that what he said and drew didn't really happen?

I thought back to the months before I filed the lawsuit. I had gone to see Dr. Hughston. Before I turned lives upside down, I needed to talk with him in person. I wanted to look him in the eye and ask, "Is it true? Were mistakes really made in the first surgery on my right knee? And if so, why didn't I know about it?"

Dr. Hughston and I had a long talk. He assured me that mistakes had been made. And the same doctors who had made the mistakes had also made poor attempts at trying to correct them, only creating more damage. "Here it is," he said as he showed me my x-ray dated 9-22-78. "This shows the mistake—without a doubt." With his pencil he traced the osteotomy cut and showed me how uneven it was. Starting at one point in the front of my leg, the cut ended much higher in the back at the joint line. "Janet, it's like a table leg. If you're gonna cut it and turn the leg some, you have to make a level cut, or it won't fit together anymore. They didn't. They cut your leg on an angle, cut through your ligaments, and then set it in a cast. Oh, mercy me," he had added with a sigh.

My in-laws met me at the airport and took me to their home. The next morning my mother-in-law drove me to the deposition. With a hug and a prayer, she promised to pick me up when I called.

I met Bridget outside Hughston's Medical Research building, which sat between the clinic and his hospital. We chatted for a few minutes and then found Dr. Hughston by the elevator. "Hey, Janet, it's good to see ya. I'm glad to see you're using the elevator. You have no business walking up stairs, ya know."

I introduced Dr. Hughston to Bridget. Knowing that the clock was running, Bridget promptly asked Dr. Hughston a few questions regarding medical terms and human anatomy. Dr. Hughston enjoyed sharing his knowledge with her.

Within the hour, Keen, Bridget, Dr. Hughston, and I took our seats in a conference room, around a long mahogany table. The court reporter was set up and ready. The video technician completed his setup and steadied his camera on Dr. Hughston. Due to Dr. Hughston's age and health, his deposition was to be videotaped. Lights, camera, action—the proceeding began. Dr. Hughston was sworn in and given instructions regarding the deposition and videotaping. Bridget cleared her throat, introduced herself, and launched into her questioning.

"Dr. Hughston, this case began with a condition known as external tibial torsion, which Janet had. Can you explain for the record what that condition is?"

"Sure, that's where the tibia, which is the bone between the knee joint and the ankle, is rotated externally, rotated outward."

"And in 1977, was there an accepted method of correcting that condition?"

"Yeah. You could correct it by doing osteotomies—cutting and turning the tibia, that is."

"Okay. Perhaps we can start with a brief explanation of terms. Dr. Hughston, can you please explain the term *derotation*?"

"It means that you're rotating or turning something in the opposite direction."

"Could you explain what the posterior capsule is?"

"Well, that's the ligaments on the back side of the knee joint."

"Thank you, Dr. Hughston. And what is posterolateral instability?"

"That's part of the posterior capsule that you're speaking of. That's where the ligaments on the back and outside of the knee joint are loose, so that they don't hold the joint in position."

"If one has that condition, can that cause his or her knee to go out, to give way?"

"Buckle, yes," Dr. Hughston said.

"Dr. Hughston, can you please explain how a derotational osteotomy was performed in 1977?"

"Well, the bone was cut and turned."

"Okay, did you have an understanding that Janet Hepp Mitchell had a condition that we've described as external tibial torsion for which she had osteotomies before she came to you?"

"Yes, ma'am," Dr. Hughston said, nodding.

Lifting a couple of papers off the top of a small stack sitting in front of her, Bridget continued. "I have marked as Exhibit F-1 this two-page letter from Dr. Allgood dated September 6, 1978. Do you have a copy, Dr. Hughston?"

"Yes, ma'am."

"When you received this letter from Dr. Allgood, did you also receive any medical records?"

"Not that I know of."

"Did you know Dr. Allgood prior to Janet's referral?"

"I think I've met him, but as far as know him, no."

"You do know that Dr. Cameron Blake is associated with him?"

"Yes, ma'am."

"And prior to 1978, Dr. Blake was a fellow here at the Hughston Clinic, right?"

"Yes."

"And you yourself operated on Dr. Blake at one point, didn't you?"

"Yeah."

"Now, in Dr. Allgood's referral letter it states in the third paragraph, 'Following our examination here by myself, Dr. Cameron Blake, Dr. Ryan Ulid, and other consultants, we feel what has happened is that the posterior lateral capsule of the knee has been involved in the osteotomy, causing some of the initial laxity.' Dr. Hughston, upon your examination of Janet, did you see anything which would support Dr. Allgood's statements that 'the posterior lateral capsule was involved in the osteotomy'?"

"Yes, I can interpret it. The examination of the right knee revealed evidence of posterolateral laxity."

"And would you agree then, with Dr. Allgood, that the osteotomy involved the posterior lateral capsule, based on that finding?"

"Objection!" Mr. Keen protested. "Leading and suggestive!"

Calmly Bridget turned to Mr. Keen and countered, "Why? Dr. Hughston is an expert."

"So what?" Keen said in a disgusted tone of voice.

"You can lead an expert."

Mr. Keen sat there, shaking his head, while the witness looked to Bridget for the go-ahead. Bridget nodded.

"Yes," Dr. Hughston answered matter-of-factly. "Janet had posterolateral ligamentous instability, yes."

"Okay, going back to Dr. Allgood's referral letter. Dr. Hughston, do you have an understanding of what Dr. Allgood meant when he said the posterior lateral capsule of the knee was 'involved' in the osteotomy?"

"Yes, ma'am."

"Do you have an understanding of what Dr. Allgood meant when he used the word *involved*?"

"I know what 'involved' is," Dr. Hughston replied with a grin.

"Objection!" Mr. Keen hollered. "This question calls for speculation."

Dr. Hughston looked perturbed. "Where's the letter?" he asked as he shuffled through the papers before him.

Without making a sound, Bridget slid Dr. Hughston another copy of the referral letter.

"Yeah," Dr. Hughston mumbled as he used his index finger to find the word *involved* written in the letter. After pausing and rereading portions of the letter to himself, he spoke. "*Involved* means it was cut. I would interpret the word to mean it was injured or cut, or something of that sort, in the osteotomy."

Everyone sat silently as Bridget continued. "Dr. Hughston, if the posterior lateral capsule of the knee was involved in the osteotomy, would you be able to see a cut or tear in that capsule on x-ray?"

"Let me object to the question as being uncertain and vague," Mr. Keen snapped. "Your question assumes that involving the posterior lateral capsule is evidence of a surgical misadventure."

Dr. Hughston looked to Bridget for direction. "No, you wouldn't see it in an x-ray," he articulated clearly.

Bridget paused and smiled slightly. "Thank you." She nodded.

"Dr. Hughston, is it a normal result of a derotational osteotomy to have capsular instability?"

"No, it's not."

"Would you say, Dr. Hughston, that if the posterior capsule is torn or cut in a derotational osteotomy, that's a mistake?"

"Objection," shouted Mr. Keen. "Inadequate foundation for the question, inadequate, hypothetical."

This time, not waiting for direction from Bridget or permission to speak, Dr. Hughston looked into the camera and spoke his mind. "You know, it's just as Dr. Allgood stated in his letter—the posterior capsule, the ligaments have been involved in the osteotomy!"

This was a moment that I am sure Mr. Keen was dreading. Yet it was the moment I'd been waiting for. Bridget paused, looked Dr. Hughston directly in the eye, and in a hushed voice rephrased and repeated her question. "Would you call it a mistake?"

"Yes, ma'am," Dr. Hughston confirmed.

Mr. Keen leaned forward as if he might take to his feet. "Let me just move to strike the answer," he vented.

"Denied," Bridget stated under her breath.

"You're not ruling," Keen shot back in frustration.

For a quick moment, I think the attorneys had forgotten that they were on "candid camera" and that their performance might be shown to a jury of twelve. The next few hours Bridget continued to question Dr. Hughston about my past surgeries and his findings. Medical terms were used that sounded like a foreign language. I hoped that

Bridget understood because I could hardly follow the discussion. Exhibit after exhibit was numbered and added to the stack. X-rays were numbered and discussed in detail.

My ears perked up when I heard Bridget say, "Dr. Hughston, do you recall ever discussing with Janet and her parents that the posterior lateral capsule was involved in the first osteotomy performed by Dr. Allgood?"

My heart began to race. I knew that he had never told us. I knew that to prove fraud and concealment we had to prove that I didn't know—that we were never told. But what kind of a doctor would he appear to be if he indeed said no?

"I don't know...I don't know how I discussed it with them. You'd assume that everybody...I mean, Dr. Allgood had written when it had occurred in his letter to me. So other than discussing it with them and with Janet, that we were going to try to correct it, I don't know that I had any other statements I deserved to make at the time."

"Okay, so you can't recall specifically talking about the capsule being involved, or a mistake being made?"

"No, ma'am."

With my stomach turning flip-flops like an acrobat, I thought I finally figured it out. If Dr. Hughston had indeed told me of the mistakes—or if he told everyone who was ever referred to him of his suspicion of medical blunders—word would get out. Doctors would quit referring patients to him, and patients would not walk.

"Do you remember, dating way back, that you told Janet she could not go into nursing because of her condition?"

"I've got a bunch of letters telling her not to do a lot of things."

"Did Janet ever discuss with you what she states Dr. Ulid told her in 1992 concerning a mistake being made in her original surgery?"

"Yes, ma'am."

"Do you recall what she said in that regard?"

"She told me that Dr. Ulid broke down and said they did something wrong at the time of the operation."

"Okay."

"And that got her excited. Then she said she took her husband back to see Dr. Ulid, and he said it again."

"Okay. And do you recall telling her that you agreed with Dr. Ulid, that you thought a mistake had been made?"

"Well, obviously, a mistake had been made. As Dr. Allgood said, 'They involved the ligaments on the lateral side of the knee joint at the time of the osteotomy.' The ligaments had to be torn or severed at some time. Otherwise, we wouldn't have had the scar tissue and the instability."

"Dr. Hughston, you kept in touch with these doctors who referred Janet over the years, did you not?"

"Yes, ma'am, I dropped them a brief letter now and then."

"Were you aware that, off and on, Janet continued to seek treatment from those physicians over the years?"

"Yes. She told me in telephone conversations."

"Did you know that Janet had the same surgery, a tibial derotation osteotomy, on her left leg?"

"Yes, ma'am."

"And there were no problems with the left leg?"

"Yes, ma'am."

After asking several more questions Bridget concluded. "Dr. Hughston, I'm finished. I want to thank you for your time. I'm going to let Mr. Keen go ahead with the questions he has. I might have a couple of follow-up questions when he is through."

After introducing himself, Mr. Keen dove right into quizzing Dr. Hughston. "What is your age, sir?"

"Mine?"

"Yes."

"Seventy-six."

"Are you still actively practicing here at the clinic?"

"Clinically I am. However, I am not doing operative work anymore."

"How much time have you spent in the last forty-eight hours reviewing Janet's medical records?"

"I have no idea, sir!" Dr. Hughston responded in disgust.

"Did you know that Dr. Ulid was Janet's surgeon at the left osteotomy?"

"Just hearsay. I never received any medical records from out there."

"Did you know that Dr. Ulid was only the assistant during the surgeries that were performed on Janet's right leg?"

"Recently, I think that Janet has told me that."

"I take it you have no idea the extent to which he participated in her surgery."

"No, sir, I do not."

"Dr. Hughston, I'd like to direct your attention to your operative report of 9-22-78, which has been marked as Exhibit 1."

"All right, sir."

"Dr. Hughston, did you actually dictate this operative report?"

"No. It says it was dictated by Dr. Matherson. Yes, I remember him."

"And in 1978, who was Dr. Matherson?" Mr. Keen quizzed.

"Dr. Matherson was a fellow here at that time."

"Does this operative report of 9-22-78 appear to be accurate as far as you can see?"

"Yes, sir."

"Did you form an opinion as to what was causing Janet's continuous instability and her need to have three surgeries performed by you?"

"Well, I knew what was causing it. It's partially due to the fibula collateral ligament, a ligament in the posterolateral capsule. This ligament is never discussed in any operative report because it's not there. I've never been able to pull it back to graft or make another one." Sounding defeated and tired, Dr. Hughston sighed. "There's simply no way to restore it."

"As of your last examination of Janet in November of 1992, did you draw a conclusion as to whether she had been exercising as you had recommended?"

"I think so. She's been real good about it...People hit a point where they go and give it up for two or three days or so, and then something reminds them they'd better get back to doing it. I think she's been very diligent about it over the years."

Mr. Keen had heard all that he wanted and he concluded his questioning of Dr. Hughston.

Bridget jumped back in with a few final questions that she had thought of and questions that I had jotted down and wanted her to ask. "Dr. Hughston, I'd like to show you another x-ray. If you could, would you please put this up on the viewing screen?"

Dr. Hughston stretched his stiff legs as he got up and placed the x-ray in position. For the next several minutes, a discussion took place outlining the shadows of the osteotomy cuts. The shadows were covered with scar tissue, and the shaded areas represented arthritis.

"Dr. Hughston, is there an x-ray that would clearly show the first osteotomy cut on Janet's right leg?"

"Well, we had one."

"You don't have the x-ray?" stuttered Bridget.

"No, it's not here."

"Can we go off the record for just a second?" Bridget asked urgently.

The cameraman stopped the tape. I closed my mouth that had dropped open with hearing the word no. And as politely as Bridget could, she questioned Dr. Hughston about our crucial piece of evidence that was now missing.

Moments later we were back on the record and the videotape was rolling. "Dr. Hughston," Bridget asked, "when Janet saw you this past November, you showed her an x-ray dated 9-22-78. This x-ray, you stated, clearly showed the osteotomy cut and the mistake. You informed Janet that 'not all of the x-rays showed the cut because of the angle at which the x-rays were taken.' Dr. Hughston, where is this x-ray?"

Head bowed, he didn't look up. "The x-ray is missing," he admitted. "I pulled it to make copies for you all, and somehow it's been misplaced. I didn't mean to..."

I felt my body start to shake when I heard Dr. Hughston's words. Yet it was obvious that this fact upset Dr. Hughston. I didn't know what to think. Dr. Ulid's x-rays had mysteriously disappeared and Dr. Allgood's x-rays had vanished. And now the one and only known x-ray clearly showing the cut had been misplaced.

## Chapter Ten

# CASTLES OUT OF RUBBLE

STAN'S SECRETARY CALLED ME from my cousin's law firm in Nebraska. A Mr. Kent Wallace, an attorney from California, had returned Stan's call of weeks ago. Mr. Wallace was presently representing a client against Dr. Allgood. Within minutes I was part of a three-way call, listening silently with the phone pressed tightly against my ear. Stan recapped the highlights of my case, and then Mr. Wallace broke in with his thoughts.

"Before I discourage you, Stan, I want to say, if you have evidence to demonstrate the doctors actually knew Janet's injuries were caused by malpractice, and if the doctors knew they had really screwed up and went out of their way to not tell her about it and made sure she could not and would not find out about it, and if she the patient asked them point blank, 'Doctor X, why is my leg like this? What happened?' And the doctors answered, 'Oh, honey, it's just a congenital defect. Don't worry about it. God did it to you.' Stan, if you have something like that, then I think that you can get around the intentional concealment section while proving fraud. It's at least worth a try."

"Well, I believe we can prove fraud," Stan said.

"Personally I think you'll have an uphill battle to get around the statute. The courts are very tight in linking fraud."

"Doesn't that make your Friday before Labor Day?" Kent asked. "But in any event, I suggest you examine the fraud aspects of your case because the statutes are clear. The defense is entitled to a bifurcated trial. To first 'try' the case and resolve the statute issue—barring time. If there's a verdict, they then go after the medical negligence and damages. In every case, and let me underline those words several times, in every case, where there is any possibility of the question of statutes, lawyers invariably want that bifurcated trial for two reasons. One, they are very likely to win, and two, it generates defense fees and they can get the carrier for it."

"Okay, tell me, Kent. What about malpractice insurance?" Stan asked. "Have you found that Allgood has coverage?"

"Not for my case," Mr. Wallace replied with a grumble. "Allgood was bare in the ' and he's bare now. He didn't have coverage then and he doesn't have it now. His attorney in my case is suing him for attorney fees because he hasn't been paid to the tune of thirty-two grand. Needless to say, his attorney is not amused," Mr. Wallace added with a chuckle.

"Good grief!" Stan exclaimed.

"Allgood isn't a newcomer to litigation. He has prolific lawsuits against him, so the likelihood of any malpractice insurance carrier in California giving him prior acts endorsement is none. I know because I do a great deal of work for the various medical malpractice insurance carriers, both for and against them. I can't believe they would write Allgood under these conditions."

"Kent, I'm curious. How come you're going after him if he doesn't have any coverage?"

"I'm stuck with it. We filed and I didn't learn about this until his deposition. And, boy, was I surprised. Yet I do have another party. It's an extremely well-insured hospital that goofed at least as much as Allgood did. I'm involved in a case where the family demanded they provide an infectious-disease consultant and the hospital dropped the ball. So you see, I have a deep-pocketed hospital that has already offered $700,000. So, I am not in such bad shape. Stan, what about you? You know Allgood's bare, so why in the world are you going after him? The guy simply does not have funds."

"Well, first of all, we didn't include the hospital in this suit. Janet believes the hospital was in the dark on this one, that they were as deceived as she was. Regardless, someone's got to stop Dr. Allgood."

"Oh," Mr. Wallace murmured, sounding somewhat surprised. "Tell me, Stan, did Allgood have an assistant in your case?"

"Yes, a Dr. Ryan Ulid. He was the expert. He knew Allgood was cutting the bone wrong. He tried to stop him."

"Okay. California law states that the surgeon is the captain of the ship. He is the general contractor. He is liable for all the acts of his subs. However, I can tell you this, knowing Dr. Allgood and having seen him in deposition, he wouldn't hesitate to blame the other doctor. I assure you, when you take Allgood's deposition, you'll find him absolutely charming. He's very nice looking, an athletic guy, well tanned, suave, well spoken, extremely articulate, and well dressed. Juries will love him. I've got to tell you, he isn't your classic enemy that is going to look like a worm or wimp. He is anything but that."

"Can't wait to meet this character," Stan said with a chuckle and a sigh. "I'll make sure I tell my sister this news. She's taking Allgood's deposition in a couple of weeks."

"So does this cheer you up?" Mr. Wallace teased. "Seriously though, is there anything else you'd like to know?"

Stan and Mr. Wallace went on for another ten to fifteen minutes. I sat quietly, taking notes and listening to the strategies, the plans they each had to help them win.

A few days later, Bridget called. "Stan reported an earful," she said. "Now I want to hear your take on the Stan and Kent phone hour."

"Truthfully," I replied, "I think they've both missed their callings. I think together they should host their own talk radio show. I was thoroughly entertained listening to them."

Bridget laughed. "Stan told me that you didn't say a word, but he thought he could hear your pencil writing, fiercely—taking notes."

After Bridget and I reviewed the contents of Kent's call, Bridget spoke up. "Janet, there's another item we need to talk about."

"What's that?"

"This past week I received a letter from Dr. Allgood's office manager, Beverly Lacasto."

"You did?"

"Oh yeah," Bridget moaned. "Beverly was quite dramatic as she described the moment you and your father stormed into Dr. Allgood's office demanding your records. Beverly would like 'to keep the peace' in her office and has blatantly said you're a threat to that peace."

"I'm what? We went one time, to ask for my records. The most excitement that occurred was I rolled up my pant leg!"

"I know this is ridiculous," Bridget said while trying not to laugh. "But as your attorney, I must inform you that if you and your father choose to go back to Dr. Allgood's office, she said she'll file a restraining order against you."

"A restraining order? For what?"

"Who knows what she might come up with and tell the police? I know you've done nothing wrong, but to protect yourselves, just stay away. I'm sorry I asked you to hand deliver the request for records in the first place."

"I think it's kind of funny. My father and I are the least likely individuals to have a restraining order filed against them. I can't wait to see his reaction to this news!"

"Don't give it another thought. Just file it away. We have more important things to be losing sleep over than this."

"Hey, Bridget. Did Beverly mention my missing medical records in her letter to you?"

"Well, she stated that 'your records have not yet been located.' Janet, I doubt anyone in Allgood's office will ever produce them."

Bridget then spent the next forty-five minutes prepping me for Dr. Allgood's deposition that was scheduled the following week. "Dr. Allgood will probably be surprised to see you. Most plaintiffs don't appear at the depositions, even though they have every right to be there. Sometimes they do request to be there and their counsel decides it's in the best interest of the case that they not attend. But in your case, I think it's great you want to be there," Bridget added. "I think it will make it tough for Dr. Allgood to expound on his stories and lies with you sitting there looking at him. I think it might make him realize that you mean business and are acting as   in your case. Janet, all joking aside, I want to make sure you're really ready to face him."

As Bridget had just a few days to finalize the questions she'd ask at Dr. Allgood's deposition, she asked me for my input. I read off a list of thoughts I'd been jotting down since our first meeting. It seemed almost every thought prompted another question, but school had just let out and my children needed Mom's taxi services. We agreed to talk again later in the week to compare notes and strategies, and then planned to meet an hour or so before Dr. Allgood's deposition.

Dr. Allgood's deposition was scheduled to take place in Porter's office, which he shared with his partner, Richard Arnold. Their office was local. I'd probably driven by it several times, yet I had never noticed it tucked away across the street from a park. Bridget, Marty, and I gathered our notes and legal pads from the car and filed through the front door, only to be greeted by Mr. Porter himself.

"Come on in," he bellowed. "I've been waiting for weeks to host this meeting with the famous Janet Hepp Mitchell."

Not at all prepared for this type of greeting, I smiled slightly and allowed my attorney to return the formal greeting. After shaking our hands as if he were a member of a welcoming committee, Porter led us across the room and into another. There—hunched over a long conference table and wearing a crisp navy suit, sorting his paper-work—was Mr. Michael Keen.

I had no idea what it would be like to face Dr. Allgood, the man who had once been my hero and now my adversary. In my dreams, I'd told Dr. Allgood how his mistakes and lies had affected my life and others.' Yet within the next moment he would not be in my dreams but my presence. I took a deep breath. Marty squeezed my hand, reminding me that he was sitting by my side.

Dr. Allgood was the last to join our meeting. He moseyed in a good fifteen minutes late, implying he had control of the situation, since we could not proceed without him. He seemed to be taken off guard when he entered the room and saw Marty and me sitting at the table. I noticed a slight hesitance in his movements and a fleeting look of uncertainty as his eyes met mine. Then his eyes shifted toward Marty and offered a slight glare as he took his seat beside his attorney, Alvin Porter. There we were—Porter, Allgood, Keen, Bridget, Marty, me and the court reporter. Bridget winked at me, sat straight up in her chair, and called the deposition to order.

The court reporter began, "Dr. Allgood, will you raise your right hand? Do you solemnly swear that the testimony you may give in the case now pending before this court shall be the truth, the whole truth, and nothing but the truth?"

Without flinching a muscle, smooth-talking Dr. Allgood noncha-lantly stated, "Of course I do."

I watched Bridget gain momentum as she began to question the doctor. I wondered how she felt, being a young, aspiring female attorney from out of town, surrounded by highly experienced and powerful men. Marty and I sat motionless, occasionally jotting down thoughts that came to mind.

"Dr. Allgood, prior to this case, have you ever been a defendant in a medical malpractice case?

"One time, yes," Dr. Allgood said with a nod.

*One time?* I reflected. *Ask him about* Ruppert v. Allgood *or* Goldman v. Allgood. *I've got a list.*

I could hardly contain the urge to blurt out the truth. On my legal pad, I angrily scribbled a note to myself so I'd remember to ask Bridget about this answer—"One lawsuit!" I was sitting there watching a man who had moments earlier taken an oath to speak the truth, and he took a simple question, one that could easily be proven one way or another, and he lied. Why would he choose to lie about this?

"And can you tell me the nature of that case?" Bridget asked.

"It was a traumatic knee injury. The patient's family wanted him to go to another hospital to recover after our initial treatment. From the treatment at the latter hospital, the patient's knee subsequently got infected, so I was named in the lawsuit. It was later settled by me. I paid a minor sum."

"And in the last, say, fifteen years, is this the only lawsuit that's ever been filed against you for medical malpractice?"

"Other than this one, yes," Dr. Allgood said.

Bridget jotted down a note to herself, then looked up and caught my eye. Her quick glance assured me that she was well aware Dr. Allgood had not told the "whole truth." She then took the questioning in another direction and inquired about my medical records. I had to sit tight and remember the goal of a deposition was just to obtain information. It would be in the courtroom, in front of a jury, that Bridget could disprove Allgood's claim of one lawsuit.

"I have no records and no x-rays," Dr. Allgood replied matter-of-factly.

"You have no files relating to Janet Hepp Mitchell at all?"

"None."

"Did you have your office staff look?"

"I think they did that on their own after Janet came in the office, and then my staff told me they couldn't find them."

"And your staff reported to you that they found nothing?" Bridget firmly asked.

"Yes."

"I see. Janet's records seem to have mysteriously disappeared." Bridget huffed.

Mr. Keen interrupted Bridget before she could ask her next question. "Mrs. Halvorson, you're talking about a period that began fifteen years ago. That's not so unusual."

*But it's unusual for a doctor to lie! I saw my records, held them just a year ago when I was in Allgood's office for a checkup. I didn't see Allgood, as he was on vacation, but I saw Dr. Blake. And I held my chart in my hand. It was at least five inches thick.*

Dr. Allgood became almost belligerent as he faced Bridget and shot back, "Are you accusing me of something?" Sitting staunch in his chair he barked, "Well, if you don't mean it, don't say it, because that's calling on my integrity."

I tried to maintain a blank look as I listened to Dr. Allgood's response. Bridget tried to calm the situation by speaking softly. Yet with an awkward stare in my direction, Dr. Allgood continued to murmur, "I don't think I ever hid any of your charts. I have no reason to hide them."

Ignoring Dr. Allgood's mumbling, Bridget continued. "From August of '77 to August of '78 all of Janet's medical records seem to be missing or removed from Ulid's chart. Have you ever seen them?" Bridget pressed.

"I'm sure I've seen them, because we did major surgeries on her knee and there would be follow-up. Where those charts are now, I don't know. They sure weren't burned or thrown away."

"Dr. Allgood, have you located any of Janet's x-rays in your office or in storage?"

"No."

"Have you ever seen this patient to examine her or treat her since 1978?"

"No, not since August of '78."

"Dr. Allgood, did you ever read Dr. Hughston's letter dated January 10, 1987? This letter was written by Dr. Hughston to you, Dr. Allgood, regarding Janet's progress."

"No, I didn't see that," Dr. Allgood stammered.

"I would like to admit this into evidence as Exhibit G. Dr. Allgood, did you ever tell Janet that you made a mistake in her February '77 surgery?"

"No. No, I don't think so."

"Did she ever request that you no longer be her doctor?"

"Not that I can recall."

"Dr. Allgood, in your interrogatories you stated you do not have medical malpractice insurance. Why is that?"

"Since 1972 until the present, I haven't carried it. I always felt that the relationship with the patient in explaining things to them and handling them is a lot better than having a shotgun coverage of malpractice. Besides, I would never attempt to do something I didn't feel I could handle. I would never treat patients where I felt that they would sue me. And mainly this has worked, so I've just kept that philosophy. I treat the patient rather than the medical/legal system."

Bridget, Porter, and Keen all sat silent, trying to make sense of what he had said. Bridget boldly continued, trying to get the doctor to provide any additional information regarding his insurance. "Dr. Allgood, did you ever disclose—"

"Not in twenty years—" Allgood abruptly interrupted.

Bridget nodded and then continued, "Dr. Allgood, do you know if St. Ann's presently requires their physicians to carry malpractice insurance?"

"Yes, I think they do, to perform surgery."

"Do you know when St. Ann's first required their physicians to carry malpractice insurance?"

"I believe it was in 1985."

"And did they require continuous coverage?"

"Yes."

"So you obtained coverage and in early 1986 it lapsed right away?" Bridget.

"I wasn't aware it had lapsed. I thought we were keeping it, but it must have lapsed. I wasn't familiar with this until you brought this up, and then we found out."

*Wait a minute. Didn't Dr. Allgood just say since 1972 until the present he hasn't had medical malpractice insurance? And that he'd rather treat the patient than the medical/legal system? How in the world can he now say he wasn't "familiar" that his coverage lapsed?*

"Dr. Allgood, who is the 'we' you are referring to?"

"Beverly Lacasto my office manager, and myself."

Bridget brought up the subject of how I found Dr. Hughston. Marty knew this was a sensitive subject for me. He lowered his arm under the table and patted my leg.

Dr. Allgood stated that he recommended I see the world-renowned Dr. Hughston. He chose Dr. Hughston because "Janet was moving to Georgia and this would kind of take care of two birds with one stone."

I was never moving south. My parents found Dr. Hughston and then asked Dr. Allgood to write a referral. It was a hardship on my family to get me to Georgia, and I didn't know a soul there. This blatant lie brought tears to my eyes, reminding me of such a painful time.

While I was wiping my face with a tissue, hoping my mascara had not bled and given me two black eyes, Bridget sorted through her stack of papers. "Here it is," she said. "We will label this Exhibit M. It's a referral letter that you, Dr. Allgood, wrote to Dr. Hughston in 1978. Because you have no records pertaining to Mrs. Mitchell, I will let you read this copy." As Dr. Allgood reached for the paper, Bridget requested he read it aloud so that the court reporter could transcribe it—for the record.

```
September 6, 1978
Jack Hughston M.D.
RE: Janet Hepp Mitchell

Dear Jack:
This is an initial referral letter on a
young lady you will be seeing September
18. Consultation is for a deformity of her
right knee that has been brought about
by derotational osteotomies that has re-
sulted in a varus deformity with poste-
rior lateral laxity. When first seen this
patient was walking down the street (i.e.
like Charlie  or with her patellae fac-
ing one another). She underwent bilateral
```

derotation osteotomies of the tibia with excellent results on the left leg but with resultant difficulties on the right. The rotational laxity was noted following the initial derotation on the right knee and correction was subsequently attempted at a second surgery. The second surgery consisted of additional derotation osteotomy of the tibia as we had only corrected half of the 70 degrees that she was externally rotated and soft tissue tightening up of the posterior lateral corner of the knee. She was   for 4 to 6 weeks and upon coming out of this was tested to be fairly stable and with no complication in healing of the osteotomy. In the interim from her surgery, which was 1-4-78, the patient has continued ambulation and schooling with increasing posterior lateral laxity of the knee that had resulted in your consultation.

Following our examination here by myself, Dr. Cameron Blake and Dr. Ryan Ulid and other consultants, we felt that what has happened is the posterior lateral capsule of the knee has been involved in the osteotomy causing some of the initial laxity. With a second osteotomy, a varus deformity noted with the patient lying supine and the knees together, the varus deformity is causing her to put excessive pressure on this lateral capsule in order for her to walk straight and this has subsequently resulted in this Grade IV posterolateral laxity. It is felt by myself and Dr. Blake that your input into this and subsequent treatment if desired by the family would be most appreciated by us.

We are including with Janet the x-rays we have taken that hopefully will be of some help. If you desire any of the specifics of her follow-up in our office, we will be glad to send these charts to you.

Thank you very much, Jack, and, also to Nick, if he takes a look at this knee. Our plan of treatment for this would be, in a two-stage operation, correct the varus deformity at each osteotomy site, allow this to heal and then do a posterior lateral capsule repair and reconstruction for the posterolateral laxity.

Thank you very much again. This is a very nice family and very trusting of our profession.

Sincerely,
Albert G. Allgood, M.D.


Head bowed as if he were still reading the paper lying on the table, Dr. Allgood concluded, "This is a very poor letter that I dictated."

Mr. Porter jumped in before Allgood could complete his thoughts, "Bridget, let me say on the record that I have a neurosurgeon coming here to review some x-rays for another case. I have to name him as an expert no later than Thursday, and I can only get him today. I thought we'd finish by 4:00 or 4:30, but we haven't. I'd like to take a little recess here."

While waiting for Bridget's response, I wrote Marty a note: "The difference between Porter and Keen is that to Keen, Bridget is Mrs. Halvorson and to Porter, Bridget is just Bridget—a school girl."

"Mr. Porter," Bridget asked, "you don't have anyone here who can fill in for this deposition?"

"No. Richard had a two o'clock elsewhere."

Not sure if this was a ploy to distract from the questioning, but realizing she had to let Mr. Porter know right away that she also knew how to play the game, Bridget spoke up, "I flew here from Sacramento, and I obviously wasn't notified of this change in schedule. I don't want to make two trips, and I don't want to take an hour break. I want to finish today. I think the best solution would be for you to try to find someone to sit in."

Mr. Porter turned toward Mr. Keen saying, "Richard Arnold isn't here. There's nobody else to sit in unless you want to represent two clients."

Tapping his pencil Mr. Keen looked up. "I don't think that's appropriate."

"Well, Bridget, I don't know what to do. That case is set for trial—this one isn't."

"Yes, it is," Bridget confirmed. "This case is set for February fourteenth, less than four months from now."

We took a short recess so Mr. Porter could solve his problem. We all stretched our legs while Bridget used this time to refocus and review her questions pertaining to Allgood's referral letter. Marty and I stayed in the conference room because we did not want to find ourselves face to face with Dr. Allgood. Soon we were back in our seats and Bridget returned to questioning Dr. Allgood.

"Now again, Dr. Allgood, I'm referring to Exhibit , your referral letter. In this letter you write, 'Janet has a deformity of her right knee that has been brought about by derotational osteotomies.' Are you saying the osteotomies caused the deformity of her right knee?"

"Well, I'm saying that she didn't have it before we did her knee. What we're trying to say is that—let me see that—which sentence is this...?"

Bridget moved on through the letter. Things were going as smoothly as one could have hoped, until she hit the word *involved*. "Dr. Allgood, could you please explain what you meant when you wrote, 'We feel what has happened is that the posterior lateral capsule of the knee has been involved in the osteotomy causing some of the initial laxity.'"

"I can't see how you can pick out one word. It's a bad choice of words," Dr. Allgood admitted.

Bridget tried several approaches, but no matter how she asked the question, Dr. Allgood failed to explain what he meant by the word *involved*. I wrote a note and slid it close to Marty. "I bet only a judge can get the meaning of involved out of Allgood."

Throughout the deposition, I felt myself churning inside. I kept my eyes focused on Dr. Allgood, thinking that might make it more difficult for him to lie. I was wrong. At one point he asked why I had to "stare" at him. What he didn't seem to realize was that all eyes were directed at him—Porter's, Keen's, Marty's, Bridget's and mine. At times, even the court reporter paused to look up at him. We all sat there in amazement as Dr. Allgood insisted that even if my posterior capsule had been cut, "these ligaments would have healed themselves" and I would not have needed to have them repaired. "For example," he explained pretentiously, "if you're playing football and you plant your foot and tear your entire posterior capsule, that will heal today even non-surgically."

"Dr. Allgood," Bridget said, "before you performed the derotational osteotomy on Janet, had you performed this procedure before?"

"No," he said without emotion.

*He'd never done it before? Oh, God, help me. I was a guinea pig,* I realized.

"Did you discuss with Dr. Ulid whether he had ever done any derotational osteotomies?"

Perking up, Dr. Allgood replied with certainty, "Oh, I'm sure he had, yes. I discussed this with him and relied on him to do this case right."

"Objection," Mr. Keen cut in. "I'm going to move to strike the answer as speculation."

Dr. Allgood continued to put as much blame on Dr. Ulid as he could. He babbled freely, providing answers without being asked. He concluded his monologue by adding, "Dr. Ulid was probably the best children's   in Orange County and one of the best in the West, if not the country. I'm sure he knew what he was talking about when we discussed Janet's case."

"Now you mentioned earlier that it was your understanding that you and Dr. Ulid were doing Janet's surgery as a team. What did you mean by—?"

"I definitely would not have done this without Dr. Ulid because he recommended the surgery. Dr. Ulid was going to show me how to do it, but he felt that I should still continue managing the patient," Dr. Allgood said while nodding his head. "But, I would have never done it without Dr. Ulid because he was good at this."

Bridget moved on to her next question as if Dr. Allgood's answer hadn't fazed her at all. Holding up another paper from her stack, she said, "I'd like to mark this document dated 2-8-77 as Exhibit Q." She read a section from it. "'I authorize and direct A. Allgood, R. Ulid, C. Blake, M.D.s to perform the following operation…' Do you recall why all of your names were listed on this surgery consent form?"

"Yes, and there is another one there, too," Dr. Allgood noted.

"A house staff? Physician?" Bridget questioned.

"She could have had the resident perform the surgery. That's the house staff. The patient could come in and even though my name, Dr. Allgood, would be here and Dr. Ulid's here, a resident could have done the surgery. That's what can happen in a teaching hospital!" he said boastfully.

*Wow, someone other than a patient's doctor can perform a surgery and the patient will never know? Is this legal?*

Bridget decided that it was time. She thumbed through the remaining documents in the stack before her and produced the drawing that Dr. Ulid had sketched for Marty and me months ago. For the first time, Dr. Allgood saw the artwork of his former partner.

"I'd like to introduce Dr. Ulid's sketch of what was supposed to happen and what did happen in Janet's first surgery as Exhibit P."

Looking directly at Dr. Allgood, Bridget added, "This is a diagram that Dr. Ulid said he indeed did draw."

Immediately Dr. Allgood's face turned red. He looked at the drawing intently. He ran his finger across the two views of my knee, half stood and spurted, "This is a bunch of—" The room fell silent. No one spoke or made a sound. Slowly dropping back into his chair, Dr. Allgood took his pencil to the drawing.

"Don't draw on this," Bridget snapped, ready to grab the pencil from his hand.

Mr. Porter spoke and tried to calm his client. "Albert, just stop talking and wait for a question." He then looked at all of us sitting there watching, as if it were a scene in a movie. With a shrug of his shoulders, he offered a simple explanation. "My client reacted. That's all."

Placing his head in his hands, Dr. Allgood said, exasperated, "Dr. Ulid drew wrong."

After sitting quietly for what seemed like an entire day, the deposition concluded only after Mr. Porter and Mr. Keen got their chance to question Dr. Allgood. By the end, everyone was worn out and my nerves were on edge. Marty, Bridget, and I were eager to be alone so we could talk. We hadn't gotten to the car before Marty sighed. "Alvin Porter, attorney at law, what a character."

"Porter reminds me of someone from a gangster movie," I blurted.

"And how many gangster movies have you seen, Janet Lynn?" Marty questioned.

"I don't know. But I'm sure Mr. Porter could get the part if he auditioned."

"Janet," Bridget joined in, "I'm not at all surprised that Dr. Allgood retained Porter to defend him. They're two peas in a pod. They both think you were moving to the South."

"At what cost, Bridget? Do you have any idea what his hourly rate might be?" Marty asked.

"I'm almost positive they worked some kind of deal. Remember, Dr. Allgood says he doesn't have malpractice insurance, so he's responsible to provide for his own defense," Bridget said.

"Wow, that's got to cost him," Marty exclaimed.

"Who knows?" I chimed in. "Maybe Dr. Allgood bartered one service for another. Maybe Mr. Porter has a trigger thumb that needs to be fixed."

"Oh, Janet," Marty said, "I think you're tired. After we drop Bridget off at the airport, I'm taking you home and fixing you a warm bath."

Fighting traffic, the three of us discussed the day. "Janet, you described him and Mr. Wallace described him," Bridget said. "But Dr. Allgood is someone one has to meet for himself. He is amazing!"

"I agree," Marty said while clutching the steering wheel. "I found it tough sitting there listening to the man who hurt my wife and isn't a bit remorseful. It's a good thing for both of us that I believe that vengeance belongs to God."

"Facing him today wasn't as hard as I thought," I announced. "See, I've faced the pain of my past head-on—and I'm okay."

That night, while I enjoyed a warm bath, Marty went out and picked up my favorite Chinese food. The phone rang just after I took my last bite.

"Janet, this is Carl Kirby, an ex-patient of Dr. Allgood's, returning your call. I'm sorry to hear you, too, were injured by him. This guy gets around."

"I guess so. Carl, thanks for calling. Tell me, how are you? How's your leg?"

"I'm okay, but my leg's another story. It'll never recover from its moment with Allgood."

"Are you in pain?"

"Always."

"I'm so sorry. But Carl, have you been able to, you know, move on with your life?"

"Just returned to work after a couple of years on disability. I'm still in physical therapy. My life has been altered because of Dr. Allgood. Can't help it. My anger burns to this day."

"What are you doing about your anger, may I ask?"

"It should have fueled me to fight this thing, the injustice. Instead, only the folks I care about see it. I'm not proud of this but..."

Carl's tone of voice, mixed with his stuttering words, made me realize that this was a painful topic. I quickly spoke up, "I'm in physical therapy too. I like the people, but some days it sure is hard to face the therapy doors."

"Janet, I listened to your phone message. Our cases do sound somewhat alike, yet there's years between them. Dr. Allgood must find it acceptable to treat his patients this way. I can't figure how the guy lives with himself. So tell me, Janet, how many of us are out there?"

"In his deposition, just today, Dr. Allgood said that other than mine, he's only had one med-mal case against him. But I know there are plenty of us. I spoke with a nurse who was working at the hospital back in the late '70s, early '80s. She, too, had surgery with Dr. All-good, experienced a medical disaster, yet never sued. The difference was she was educated and smart enough to figure out the mistake, and had access to her medical chart. She noticed that her records had been changed. But she wasn't brave enough to say or do anything about it. She figured it would cost her her job. She did ask me to forgive her and then cried, 'Janet, if I had only had the courage to report him, maybe this would not have happened to you.'"

"Wow, I never thought I'd be short of words, but I don't know what to say."

"Carl, I'm creating a list of tangible ways patients can help prevent medical disasters. I'm seeking different ways patients can keep one step ahead by monitoring and managing their own health care. Do you have any suggestions, any earth-shaking advice you'd like to contribute?"

"You're amazing! You're actually trying to make a castle out of a pile of rubble." Carl chuckled. "Yes, as a matter of fact, I do. In my case I sensed that something was wrong, but I waited until it was too late before I got that second opinion. I'd say, if your heart's telling you something—listen! It's truly better to be safe than sorry."

"I agree 100 percent."

"Another thing I'd add is this. I knew what Dr. Allgood told me regarding my medical care didn't add up. Out of respect, or stupidity, I didn't question or challenge him. I never dreamed a medical error would happen to me. Up until it happened, I'd never have believed that my doctor would lie to me. I kept thinking Dr. Allgood was all good and I must be misunderstanding something. I'll tell anyone who will listen, doctors can make mistakes. There's no such thing as a perfect doctor, after all—they're human beings. Surgical mistakes are made daily, just as often as you and I make mistakes. Many doctors are honest, above board, informing patients of their new medical challenges—the mistakes. Yet a handful lie, or remain quiet, and I didn't realize this."

"I'm curious, Carl, if you believed Dr. Allgood injured you, and you felt you could prove that he fraudulently concealed his errors from you, why did you settle? Why didn't you go all the way to trial?"

"Allgood wore me down. Out of the blue, he was threatening to sue me. If you haven't learned yet, you soon will. I believe that Allgood's way of fighting a suit is stalling. He'll do anything he can to stall. He even threatened to declare bankruptcy."

"We've seen some of his stalling tactics," I said.

"Janet, tell your attorneys this for me. 'Carl says, don't agree to anything that allows Allgood to stall.' Now that I look back, I'm sorry I settled. Someone needs to find the strength and courage or plain nerve to call him on his threats to go bankrupt. Someone should insist on a jury trial and expose this quack. Someone needs to get this to the medical board. I'm sorry I didn't go all the way. I'm sorry I didn't do enough to try to prevent Allgood from hurting others. I'm so sorry..." Carl faltered, his voice choking with emotion.

Tears welled up in my eyes as I heard his words. I tried to steady my voice. "Carl, I'm not going to settle. I'm in this until a jury reaches a verdict and the medical board hears my complaint. I'm in this for you and others who have been hurt in the past and those who are the unknowing victims of the future."

"And I'm behind you," Carl said. "Let me know if there's anything I can do to help. And if you ever feel like giving up, give me a call. I'll remind you that in many cases a financial settlement is basically a way of pretending that nothing ever happened. The only problem is, no matter how hard I try, I'm not good at pretending."

My phone call from Carl ended an emotionally filled day. I lay in bed, snuggled up close to Marty. "Thanks for being with me today. You know, just when I think my anger is under control, one of the doctors lies again. It's like they open a wound that has only begun to heal."

"I guess I have a big job ahead of me," Marty whispered as he brushed my hair away from my eyes. "I guess I'll just have to hug you till you heal."

And with this Marty held me in his arms and kissed me good night.

## Chapter Eleven

# A STARTLING REALITY

JUST DAYS AFTER Dr. Allgood's deposition, Bridget was on the phone. "Janet, I've been thinking. It's time we hire a private investigator to check out the doctors. We need to find out about their history and assets. We need to stay ahead of the game and not be taken by surprise. Don't you have a cousin who once worked for the FBI? I wonder if he could recommend a detective in your area. I know several private investigators, but they're all in Sacramento."

I gave Bridget my cousin's phone number. "I'll call him now," she said. "I'll let you know if he thinks he can find us someone."

At the end of a tough week came a day I had dreaded for months. Per Dr. Hughston's instructions, I'd made an appointment to be seen by Dr. Donald Richmond. In Dr. Hughston's opinion, Dr. Richmond was the "best in the West" in orthopedics. Armed with a copy of a four-page letter from Dr. Hughston explaining my medical history and the doctor's blunders, my father and I set out.

As my dad fought the morning rush hour traffic heading into LA, conversation was mostly nonexistent. It all seemed so familiar. I couldn't help but think back to all the trips my father and I had made seeking medical help so I could walk, and I'm sure those same thoughts returned to him as well.

The office buzzed with people. It reminded me of Hughston's clinic, yet it was only a fourth of the size. Wheelchairs, crutches and canes, neck braces and slings—there were patients with all of them. I sat and filled out the medical history and patient information sheets. I then flipped to a form I'd never seen before titled: "Physician-Patient

Arbitration Agreement." Under it were paragraphs of legal words, words I'd need an interpreter to decipher. At the bottom of the page, directly above the dotted line hoping for my signature, was printed in brilliant red: "Notice: By signing this contract you are agreeing to have any issue of medical malpractice decided by neutral arbitration and you are giving up your right to a jury or court trial." I wondered what would happen if a patient refused to sign the agreement. Would the doctor refuse to see the patient? I wanted to add a sentence or two beside the dotted line. "I might agree to neutral arbitration per any issue of medical malpractice, as long as it doesn't include concealment or fraud." I reluctantly signed my name, angry that I was asked to give up my rights just to be seen by this doctor.

When my name was called, my father and I followed the nurse to a small examining room. There I handed the nurse Dr. Hughston's referral letter.

"I believe Dr. Richmond received a copy of this letter with the x-rays Dr. Hughston sent. I'm sure he's read it, reviewed your x-rays, and understands your history. You can keep your copy," the nurse instructed.

I handed the letter to my father. He folded it and slid it into his pocket. I was then led down the hall to a restroom where I slipped into my one and only pair of shorts. Then I found my way back to the examining room.

Three doctors entered the room and studied my x-rays, which hung along the wall. Not one of these men was Dr. Richmond. They were all young doctors in a fellowship under him. Each fellow took his turn at examining my right knee. They compared it to my left. Then they looked at it while I stood and they measured it every way possible.

Fifteen minutes later, Dr. Richmond appeared at the door and introduced himself. Upon his entrance, the fellows stepped back and lined the far wall. Right away, I could tell that Dr. Richmond did not have Dr. Hughston's social charm. He reminded me of a scientist, tall, thin, and wearing a white lab coat with his name embroidered across the pocket. He walked toward the table where I sat with my legs dangling. Picking up my right leg, he held it out and fully examined my leg. When he was finished, he stepped over to the x-rays.

Looking over toward the fellows, Dr. Richmond quietly said, "Please state your given diagnosis and treatment plan." One by one the young doctors walked over to the x-rays and pointed out problems they had observed. When the training consult concluded, the fellows excused themselves. Dr. Richmond leaned against the wall, folded his arms, and began to talk.

"Surgery is a certainty in your future. At this time, you should go as long as possible before we try to perform a total knee replacement. When you're going to walk further than the length of a few houses, you need to use a wheelchair. Otherwise, I suggest you use a cane. You never know when that knee will give out." He continued, "Janet, you have tricompartmental degenerative arthritis with subchondral sclerosis."

*Subchon...what?* I thought.

"There is obvious rotational malalignment, wearing of the femoral condyle, and the joint line is tilted. This, along with your ligament instability and the bony abnormalities, makes your future surgeries anything but routine."

Without any sign of emotion and still in a monotone, Dr. Richmond shocked me with me a dose of reality. "Janet, with each surgery one has on a knee, it increases the chance for complications in a future surgery by 10 percent. With your history, the condition of your knee and the nerve damage present, your chances for complications are great. You could end up losing your leg—becoming an amputee."

*What? Lose my leg?* Astounded, my father and I sat looking at the doctor, trying not to look at each other. I wondered if Dr. Hughston had sent me to see Dr. Richmond because his heart would not allow him to tell me such devastating news.

"Janet, I recommend you go as long as you can, live with the pain, and deal with the instability. When the time comes when you can't take the pain one more day, that will be the day to take the risk and deal with the outcome."

"What about getting a second opinion?" my father asked.

"The way I understand it, she's had a second opinion and a third. Dr. Hughston knows the condition. Even Dr. Ulid recommended a total knee replacement. Remember, this won't be a routine procedure; you'll need an expert. Even then, no promises can be made."

Dr. Richmond picked up my medical chart and headed for the door. "Janet, I'm sorry I've met you on this end of things. I'd sure like to have been doctor number one." With his hand on the doorknob ready to walk out, he looked toward the floor. "Give me a call when it's time," he said quietly as he walked out and closed the door behind him.

I wanted to be alone. I wanted to scream so loudly that boulders would topple down the sides of mountains. Instead, I swallowed my anger about my past and my fears of my future and tried to give my dad a pep talk. "You know, Dad, I'm in pain, but no way am I in the kind of pain he's talking about. I think he might be overreacting a bit."

My dad wiped a tear from his eye. "I don't think you need to be doing all the walking you do. When you go shopping, you should use a wheelchair. Let's preserve what you do have."

I had fought the idea of using a chair. I didn't find it...fashionable, nor did I want people to see me walk one day, use a wheelchair the next, and wonder if I were a hypochondriac. I limped back into the bathroom where I changed out of my shorts, again covering my legs with a pair of long pants. I then met my father in the waiting room where he held a handful of papers.

"They gave me a couple of prescriptions. One's an arthritis medication, and one's for pain." My father showed me another form. "This one is for a fitted leg brace. Dr. Richmond said they need to cast you in order to make the brace, so take shorts when you go. These others are for a new pair of crutches, a cane, and a wheelchair."

That did it. I broke down. "Let's get out of here, Dad. I've heard too much." With tears streaming down my cheeks, I went and paid for the appointment.

The ride home was even quieter than the ride there. Each sound I heard seemed ten times louder than usual. My dad, on the other hand, seemed to tune things out. For five straight minutes, the blinker clicked away, my father not even realizing it was on. Eventually he pulled up in my driveway.

"Thanks for going with me," I said as I crawled out of the car.

"Honey, I wish we hadn't gone," he replied.

Once inside I threw myself on to my bed. "God, help me!" I screamed into my pillow. "I hurt so bad. God, if you're not ready to take away my anger, and if you're not going to heal my leg or change my situation, please, please—numb the pain for a day or two."

Without moving from my bed, I thought about what I had just prayed. "God," I added, "and if you're not going to numb the pain I'm feeling just now, you're going to have to somehow resuscitate my heart." I tried to catch my breath and calm down. "God," I said once more, "you're going to have to help me. I'm not getting off my bed until you do. I would help myself if I could, but I can't."

Two weeks went by, and I used the time to regain my focus. I did everything I could to get myself prepared for my deposition. From taking vitamins, exercising, getting plenty of sleep to reading through my flip book, I did it all.

Finally, the long-awaited day came, so I drove to meet Bridget at the hotel where she was staying. We planned to spend the entire day preparing for my deposition the following day.

Once inside her room, I noted stacks of my medical records, all sorted across the dressers. Scattered across one of the beds were legal pads scribbled with notes and an open briefcase filled with court documents. We settled down at the small round table next to the window. I could see Orange County stretching for miles below. Bridget looked at me with a "go-get-'em" smile and then said, "Let's do it!"

"Janet," Bridget began as she held her pen in the air, using it as a pointer reading down an invisible checklist, "you must remember that a deposition is a tool used by lawyers to gather what we call 'discovery.' It's where one side questions the other side or a witness in a case. It helps us get answers to our questions. As you know a depo is conducted under oath, and everything that is said is recorded by a court reporter. Depositions are used in trial as testimony sometimes to help remind a forgetful witness or sometimes to impeach a witness. Your deposition will be used to provide information.

"First of all, during your depo, I want you to be courteous and polite. I know it might seem funny for me to be telling you this since you are courteous and polite, yet they may ask some questions that upset you. They may also try to get you riled. Do not, whatever you do, let them rattle you. Show respect."

"What if I do get upset? What if I start to cry? Ever since my appointment with Dr. Richmond, I cry if someone looks at me."

"I don't want you to cry. This shows weakness, like you're in victim mode. Especially try not to cry in front of the jury. We want to present you as a person who has been injured and has tried to make the best of things."

"Well, I have."

"I know you have. Now let's just communicate that to the other side and then to the jury. Janet, you have the truth on your side. You're not trying to remember and keep track of lies. You just tell your story—answer their questions. If you can't remember something, say, 'I'm sorry sir, I don't recall.' You don't have to offer dates and times that you can't remember. They can always be added into a depo before you sign its declaration."

I wrote fiercely as Bridget spoke, jotting down key words to remember. Bridget didn't let my hand rest. She continued, "Never guess or speculate. Only answer the question asked. Do not offer information that is not asked, as this can only lead to more questions. Make them work and figure out what questions need to be asked."

We continued for hours, taking breaks when needed. Bridget reviewed her notes while I watched a video informing me about depositions. Exhausted from such intense concentration, we grabbed our purses and went out for dinner.

"Bridget, I'm ready, I'm really ready. Not only do I want to get this deposition over, but I can feel the adrenaline. I can't wait. For the first time, they'll hear my story and from me!"

"Janet, you're right. You're ready, and I think the other side has some surprises waiting for them."

Over dinner, we talked about the Nebraska connections that had originally brought us together. "I did see my brother Stan this past month," Bridget chuckled. "I asked him if he'd chased any ambulances lately."

After dinner, I walked with Bridget back up to her room so I could gather my things. Bridget noticed the blinking light on her phone. "Hey, wait a minute," she said. "Let's find out who left a message. It might be for you."

I paused as Bridget listened. I watched as her facial expression turned from happiness to disappointment to disgust. She set the receiver down and placed her hand on her hip. "Janet, they've managed to delay again." With a huff, Bridget continued, "Both the attorneys knew when I was flying down here. They both know this depo should go forward. If one is sick, then a replacement should be sent in his place."

I felt such a letdown as I heard Bridget's words. Instantly, I remembered Carl Kirby's words, "Allgood's way of fighting a suit is stalling. He'll do anything he can to stall—even go bankrupt." But I remembered it was God who ultimately held the schedule pertaining to my case, and he knew all about this delay.

I looked at Bridget. She stood silently leaning against the wall. I watched her as she contemplated the situation. Passionately she spoke. "Janet, listen to me. We're not going to let them get us down. You will be deposed, even if I need to get the judge involved to make it happen. I'll make some calls as soon as I get back to the office and then let you know what's up."

I looked down at my notepad on top of the stack of papers I held tightly in my arms. Bridget's instructions stared back at me. "Bridget, my notes say, 'They may try to get me rattled. Do not, whatever I do, let them rattle me. At all times be courteous and polite.'" I looked up at Bridget with a slight grin. "I think you'll need to add the word *firm* to your list. 'At all times be courteous, polite, and firm,'" I chuckled, trying to hide my frustration regarding the delay. I said goodbye and headed home.

I felt disappointed, but at this point, I was more concerned about Bridget than about myself. Had Bridget known what she was really in for when she agreed to take my case? Was she up for the battle that Drs. Allgood and Ulid were prepared to fight? Just how many more trips down to Orange County was she willing to make?

I arrived home into the arms of Marty. He remained calm as I demonstrated a grand performance of my emotions. "I am so angry," I cried. "Those doctors have ruined my leg. They have altered my life, and they act like this lawsuit is a game—a sport in which only the best player will win!"

Marty continued to hold me, saying nothing. I ranted on for another five minutes. My fists were clenched, and my body was stiff. Between sobbing and gulping air, I hollered, "And the doctors aren't even sorry. Don't they know that 'sorry works'? If they had just been sorry and told me the truth—I would never have sued!"

After crying for a few more minutes, I quieted. I looked up at Marty with my tear-stained face. Still holding me securely in his arms, he spoke. "Are ya done yet?"

Marty understood my anger, yet he was concerned for me. He could see the stress that the litigation and circumstances were creating for me. He was aware of my trouble sleeping and frequent crying. He observed that I had begun to pull away from social activities.

"It's just easier for me to stay home. Remember the reaction I got when the Smiths found out? 'Christians don't do this kind of thing,' they said. I wanted to tell them all about the fraud—but I didn't have the strength. The way I see it, the problem with some Christians is that they don't take a stand—for anything."

"Honey," Marty said as he tried to calm me, "I understand. We're doing what we feel God has asked us to do—nothing more, nothing less. This doesn't mean that what lies ahead of us will be fun or easy, and it doesn't mean that others will accept and understand. In fact, I can say for certain that it is going to be downright difficult. Janet, you've got to promise me something. I need to know that when the 'hard' gets too hard, you'll let me know."

Early one morning my phone rang again. "Janet, I'm glad I've gotten hold of you," Bridget said. "I've talked to your cousin, our FBI man. You're to meet with Forest Wilson, a private investigator, next week. I'm not sure that's his real name, but that's the name he goes by. Call your cousin after we hang up, and he'll give you the details of where to meet and when."

A week later Marty drove me to Lake Elsinore, which was about forty minutes from our home. We met my cousin for lunch and then drove together to an out-of-the-way motel to meet with Mr. Forest Wilson.

"No one would ever see us meeting out here," I said.

"The room's just rented for the night," my cousin replied. He knocked, and a man wearing jeans and a red T-shirt answered.

"You must be Janet and Marty," the man speculated. "Come on in," he welcomed. "And Janet, my friends call me Forest."

We entered the room with our arms loaded with information.

"Looks like you've come prepared," Forest said.

"I've made you copies of some of my medical records, letters to and from the doctors and my attorneys, and additional information that I've found pertaining to my doctors. You know, like other suits and all."

We then spent a couple of hours informing Forest of all we knew pertaining to Drs. Ulid and Allgood. My cousin added his thoughts of what he felt the investigation should include and Forest took notes.

"Janet," Forest concluded, "I've already done some research, and I'm fairly certain that the doctors' lawyers are checking you out. I'm sure they've begun a full background check on you and certain they want to find dirt and make it shine in public. Get my drift? They want to discredit you—make you unbelievable in front of a jury."

Wow, this was a whole new world. I was used to finding the good in people, not working to destroy others. I stood up, needing to stretch my leg that had cramped from sitting too long. I walked a few steps and rested against the wall.

"Janet, one last thing before you head out. I know that you have nothing to hide. But the other side doesn't know this yet. I want you to be aware of your surroundings—who might be watching you and when and where."

"What?" I shrieked. "Who is watching me—where?"

"I think that it's only fair you know," Forest said. "I believe you're being followed."

## Chapter Twelve

# A GATHERING STORM

ONE HUNDRED AND TWENTY-THREE days after my "postponed" deposition, my father escorted me to Mr. Keen's office. For weeks I had reviewed Bridget's instructions: *Never say "never;" say, "I don't believe so" instead. Always say "yes, sir" and "no, sir," not "yeah."*

"This is it, Janet, your time has come!" Bridget said as we met in the parking lot.

"I'm ready as I'll ever be," I replied with a smile. "Let's do it."

Once inside, I was faced with the news that Mr. Keen, the defense lawyer whom I at least liked and respected, was hung up in trial and unable to conduct my deposition. Instead, a newly hired associate, a young, energetic female lawyer, would be taking his place.

"Ms. Mitchell," she said, "my name is Leeza Raddock. I represent Dr. Ulid in this litigation that you've brought about. Please take a seat, and we'll begin in a few minutes."

Ms. Raddock rubbed me the wrong way. I felt her scrutinizing glances as she looked over her new opposition—me. She wore a tight-fitting navy skirt and matching jacket set off by matching high-heeled shoes. Her hair was ash blonde, tightly pulled back and knotted in a bun. I watched her brashly give orders to her secretaries while she made last-minute preparations for the morning.

Not a minute late, Ms. Raddock joined us at the table and began the deposition. She recited her opening instructions, and I tried to relax, noting that Mr. Porter had not shown up yet. "Ms. Mitchell," Ms. Raddock said crisply, "do you understand that you have just taken an oath, and everything you say today will be said under penalty of perjury as if you were in a court of law?"

"Yes, I do," I answered.

"As you can see, the court reporter is taking down everything that is said. You will have the opportunity to review the transcription and make any changes to it. But I have to caution you, if you do so, those substantive changes may be commented on, and you may be called to explain them." With a slight smirk she added, "This may embarrass you, affect your credibility, or prove harmful to your case. Ms. Mitchell, is there any reason you feel your deposition cannot go forward at this time?"

Despite feeling almost every emotion I possessed causing my stomach to churn, I surprised myself and answered with confidence, "No, there isn't."

I sat back in my chair and took a deep breath. Seconds later the door to the conference room swung open. Fashionably late, Mr. Porter stepped inside and grunted. "I'm here." He took a seat across the table from me while I unconsciously stared him down. He smiled and then gave me a wink.

"For the record," Ms. Raddock recited, "I might add that while I was giving the admonition, Mr. Porter entered the room. He represents Dr. Allgood in this litigation." Looking at me as if she was informing me of something I might not know, she added, "He, too, will be asking Ms. Mitchell questions this morning."

I had expected to be questioned by both Mr. Porter and Mr. Keen. I had also expected the deposition to begin by asking me basic questions such as where I lived, if I was married, and how I first met the doctors. Instead, Ms. Raddock's first questions surprised me.

"Ms. Mitchell, how many letters have you sent to Dr. Ulid?" she asked.

"From what I can remember, it would be two."

Ms. Raddock reached for the stack of documents before her. Holding the ballerina card I had mailed Dr. Ulid days after he confessed, Ms. Raddock grilled me. "It's my understanding in regard to this August 8, 1992, thank-you letter that you were at least happy with the treatment Dr. Ulid himself provided to you. Is that right?"

"For my left leg, not for my right leg," I answered.

"And what in particular was it that Dr. Ulid had done in regard to your right leg that you were dissatisfied with?"

"Just a minute," Bridget said. "I think this calls for speculation, and it lacks foundation. It's vague and ambiguous." Pausing a moment, she looked over to me and quietly said, "Janet, you can answer."

A tad rattled, I licked my dry lips, faced Ms. Raddock, and began a monologue. "Ms. Raddock, Dr. Ulid was not honest with me. He took it upon himself to determine and to make decisions for my medical care that were not his to make." I paused and looked over at my father. "These decisions were for my parents and me to make. It was our right to make them." I turned my head back toward Ms. Raddock. I fought my emotions. My voiced cracked as I continued. "If Dr. Ulid hadn't lied, and if he had told me about the mistakes when they occurred, I would have found Dr. Hughston earlier. Dr. Ulid would have never had the opportunity to try to fix the errors."

Ms. Raddock shuffled through what would become her exhibits. "Ms. Mitchell, I have another letter here, dated September 8, 1992. Is this your handwriting?"

"Yes, it is."

A moment of panic hit me. This was the note Stan and Bradley had me write and slip into the front of my medical records before Jane and I snuck the file back into Dr. Ulid's office. *Had they found out we took the file? Was I in trouble?* I remembered Bridget's instructions: "Answer only the question at hand."

"Ms. Mitchell, who is this note directed to?"

"To the people at Dr. Ulid's office," I replied after I took a sip of water.

"We'll mark this as Defendant's Exhibit B," Ms. Raddock instructed. "Ms. Mitchell, I'm wondering, why did you send this particular document to Dr. Ulid's office?"

"Because I wanted him to know that I knew what was in my file."

"Ms. Mitchell, think back. Have you sent any letters to other physicians concerning this particular litigation, other than those your attorney may have referred you to?"

"Yes, to Dr. Hughston and...I believe that's all."

Ms. Raddock scribbled a note on her yellow pad. When she finished, she looked up. "To your best recollection what did that letter say?"

"My purpose was to thank Dr. Hughston for taking the time to talk with me on the phone the day before. I also explained the photos that I had enclosed with my letter."

"The photos? What were they of?"

"Pictures of me as a child. I wanted to prove to Dr. Hughston that as a child, I never had a bow in my leg."

We then spent the next few minutes reviewing my conversations with Dr. Hughston.

"Ms. Mitchell, how long did this telephone conversation last approximately?"

"I'm not sure. Fifteen minutes, maybe. If you need to know exactly, Dr. Hughston's phone bill might reflect it."

"On this first conversation, did Dr. Hughston call you, or did you call him?"

"He called me."

"During any conversation with Dr. Hughston, did he review your x-rays before he criticized the way the cut was made?"

"Dr. Hughston told me the cut was made at a diagonal angle, not a horizontal. The cut went to the joint space and cut the ligaments by the fibula head. I referred to these errors as 'mistakes.' Dr. Hughston agreed to my terminology."

"Okay, let me break this down a little bit," Ms. Raddock said. "First of all, during this conversation did Dr. Hughston say that a diagonal cut was an improper cut?"

"Yes, he did. And Ms. Raddock, I just remembered more details of my phone conversation with Dr. Hughston. I asked him why I had to have bone taken from my hip and grafted to my leg. Dr. Hughston told me that this was done to straighten my bow. He said, 'Because the diagonal cut had been made, there wasn't much strength in your bone at the top, and that part of the bone had collapsed, and that's what caused your bow.'"

"Let me ask you again," Ms. Raddock said, sounding frustrated. "I don't think I understood you." Slowly she articulated her words, "Ms. Mitchell, did Dr. Hughston say the diagonal cut was an improper cut?"

Quickly responding to this question, Bridget broke in. "Janet has just testified to this. I believe she's answered the question."

I looked at Bridget and waited for some type of instruction. "Janet, you may answer the question again," she said with a nod.

Clearly upset, Ms. Raddock cut in before I could answer. Firmly she said, "Ms. Mitchell, what I'm trying to figure out is, are these the words that Dr. Hughston used or an interpretation of Dr. Hughston's words?"

"Those are his words," I said. "I never knew the term *fibula head* even existed."

In a huff, Ms. Raddock continued, "Did Dr. Hughston specifically name the ligaments that were cut during surgery?"

"Yes. He said the posterior lateral ligaments were cut during my surgery."

"Did he say during which surgery those ligaments were cut?"

"Yes, he said during the first surgery on my right leg."

"And did Dr. Hughston tell you what he was referring to when he made that statement? In other words, was he looking at medical records, or was he looking at an x-ray when he made that statement?"

"He was looking at several things. He was looking at my x-ray, at his medical records, and the copy of Dr. Ulid's medical records that I had sent him. He also had my referral letter from Dr. Allgood."

"And what x-rays was he looking at?"

"The x-ray that he was looking at was the x-ray that shows and proves the angle of the cut. The x-ray dated."

Ms. Raddock paused while she and Mr. Porter scribbled the date of the x-ray across their legal pads. I took another sip of water and assured myself that I was doing okay.

"Ms. Mitchell, can you tell me about the third note you sent to Dr. Hughston, what was the substance of that one?"

"I wrote that letter after Dr. Hughston's deposition. In it I asked Dr. Hughston what had happened to the x-ray that clearly showed the cut."

"Did you ever call Dr. Hughston after his deposition was taken in reference to his deposition?"

"Yes."

"And what was said during that conversation?"

"Dr. Hughston said, 'I want to explain to you why I didn't testify about the x-ray at my deposition.' Then he went on to break the news, explaining to me—'this x-ray is missing.' He said that he 'started to testify about the x-ray during his deposition, but Mr. Keen wouldn't let him because it wasn't there, so it was not evidence.'"

"Did Dr. Hughston mention to you the date of the x-ray that he was referring to?"

"Yes. The 9-22-78 x-ray."

"Ms. Mitchell, to the best of your knowledge, has that x-ray ever been located since Dr. Hughston's depo?"

"No, ma'am."

"Ms. Mitchell, have you had any other phone conversations with Dr. Hughston that you haven't told us about?"

"Yes. A conversation this past July."

"Go ahead. Tell us about it," Ms. Raddock said, appearing somewhat annoyed.

"Dr. Hughston called me to find out how I was doing. He wanted to hear about my appointment with Dr. Donald Richmond, the orthopedic specialist in California he had referred me to. After I told Dr. Hughston about my appointment, he told me he wanted me to keep walking, not to use a wheelchair or my crutches full time, at least at this point. He said once I stop using my leg, I won't be able to use it at all. He also asked how the lawsuit was coming along. With emotion I responded, 'Dr. Hughston, I'm hurting a lot of people, and if you tell me today that the mistakes didn't happen and the lies did not occur, I'll drop my lawsuit.' Stumbling for words, Dr. Hughston replied, 'Janet, I can't tell you this because it happened. They cut the ligaments, the arcuate complex'—whatever they want to call it—'they did it,' he said..."

Once Ms. Raddock gained the information she was seeking regarding my conversations with Dr. Hughston, she then flipped to a clean sheet of paper. "Ms. Mitchell, what is your date of birth?"

A slew of simple questions followed. After forty-five minutes of answering factual, non-emotional questions, Ms. Raddock brought me back to my childhood and reviewed my entire medical history up until my first surgery with Drs. Allgood and Ulid. I cringed as

I spoke. I watched my father wipe tears from the corner of his eye while listening to the past he knew all too well.

"But before you went to Dr. Allgood for the first visit, had anyone ever teased you about the way you walked?" Ms. Raddock asked, sounding curious.

"No."

"Ms. Mitchell, do you recall when it was that Dr. Allgood first noted the rotation problems with your legs?"

"Yes, it was the night before he performed surgery on my left knee—the surgery to remove the torn cartilage."

"Who was present during that particular examination, other than you and Dr. Allgood?"

"Dr. Allgood did bring in some other doctors. I know one of them was Dr. Gate."

Apparently surprised by my answer, Ms. Raddock asked two questions at once, not waiting for me to answer one before she rattled off another. "And how do you remember Dr. Gate's name? Did you continue to see him at some future point?"

Realigning my posture, I smiled and answered, "Dr. Gate was a resident at the hospital and present at my surgery when the mistakes were made. And yes, I have seen him."

"Do you know where his office is today?"

"In Beverly Hills."

"And to the best of your understanding, is he also an orthopedic surgeon?"

"Yes, he is."

Ms. Raddock asked me questions as if she was unaware of Dr. Gate and his role in my medical care. Just a month earlier, I had had an appointment with Dr. Gate. I had asked him what he remembered about my surgery and my aftercare. I had shown him Dr. Ulid's drawing. Dr. Gate, too, drew me a picture of his recollection of the mistake. He told me about Dr. Allgood and Dr. Ulid and the fights that had taken place between them during the actual surgery. Even though I wanted to brag about my visit with Dr. Gate, I stayed silent, remembering Bridget's instructions, which were not to offer information that wasn't asked.

"Before your first rotation surgery, did Dr. Allgood tell you that Dr. Ulid had specifically done this exact type of surgery?"

"Excuse me, I understood both doctors had performed surgeries like mine."

"But you don't know whether it was the exact same surgery or just an osteotomy?"

I wondered how many times I would have to answer the same question, yet worded in a slightly different way. "I don't know if I would have known to ask that at the time," I said with a sigh. "When the doctors said, 'We've performed this procedure before,' I believed they had done it before."

"Ms. Mitchell, you said the doctors were acting as a team. Did Dr. Allgood or Ulid specifically describe what role each doctor would be performing during the surgery?"

"I knew they would be working together. But I had no idea what each of their roles would be. I didn't know to ask—I had no reason to. My doctors were going to perform surgery on me. That's all I knew."

"After your first surgery on your right leg, did Dr. Allgood and Dr. Ulid go into your room and say, 'Surgery went okay,' or 'Surgery went bad,' any statement to that effect?"

"The doctors told my parents, 'The surgery went well.' My leg was lined up."

"After this surgery, when you were out of your cast, was there something you noticed that caused you concern?"

We spent the next two hours discussing my first two surgeries and then took an hour-and-a-half break for lunch. Refreshed, we again took our seats, and Ms. Raddock addressed each additional surgery and the facts surrounding them. Obviously tired, but somewhat curious, Ms. Raddock probed, "Ms. Mitchell, do you recall if your mother or father ever asked Dr. Allgood or Dr. Ulid why your unexpected result was not mentioned as a possibility before surgery?"

"Yes, they did ask that question. I even remember asking it myself. We were told by Dr. Allgood and Dr. Ulid that the unexpected poor result from my surgery was due to the way that God made me, the way God created me in my mother's womb—you know, with my rotation problem. I understood this to mean that because of my congenital hip problem at birth, this was a result of the surgery they hadn't expected."

"Did you ever ask them whether anything had gone wrong in the first surgery?"

"I asked them what had happened, and they answered. I believed their answer."

"What specifically did you ask them?"

I tried not to show my frustration at her constant nitpicking and answered, "I said I asked my doctors, 'How did this happen to me? Why do I need to have more surgery?' I told them I didn't understand. I asked them why my leg would not support me." I tried to stop the tears but failed. My father quietly handed me a tissue. "Ms. Raddock," I said exasperatedly, "I asked Dr. Allgood and Dr. Ulid a lot of questions. For me to have had to leave school and have more surgery, I asked questions!"

"And when you said, 'Why do I need more surgery' what was their response?"

Bridget abruptly spoke up, "It's been asked and answered." She then gave me a consenting nod and gave the go-ahead. "Janet, you can answer it again."

"Ms. Raddock, I asked Dr. Allgood and Dr. Ulid both, 'What happened to me?' I...I did not go to my doctor and say, 'Did you mess up in my surgery?' I trusted my doctors. They looked upset about it. I was upset about my condition. Yet I still had no reason not to believe their words."

"Regardless of what they told you, Ms. Mitchell, did you in your own mind ever feel that the doctors had done something wrong during your first surgery to your right leg?"

"No, Ms. Raddock, I didn't."

The room was quiet. I watched Ms. Raddock while she processed her thoughts and reviewed her notes. My dad reached over, refilling my glass with water. It appeared that my missing records were a mystery to Ms. Raddock, too, yet she actually had the nerve to bring up the subject.

Hesitantly she quizzed, "Ms. Mitchell, do you have any ideas where your medical records from 1974 to 1981 are today?"

"Yes," I answered while Ms. Raddock's eyes lit up with interest.

"You do? Where?"

"Where Dr. Ulid told me they were."

"Where did he say they were?"

I glanced at Bridget, seeking support. I then looked to Mr. Porter and back at Ms. Raddock. Boldly I answered, "Dr. Ulid said that Dr. Allgood had gotten rid of them. Dr. Ulid assured me that they would not be found."

Obviously stunned, Ms. Raddock replied, "So Dr. Ulid told you that Dr. Allgood intentionally got rid of his records?"

"Yes, ma'am. He said the records would show the mistakes."

My answer led us into another two hours of questioning, pertaining to Dr. Ulid's admission of the mistake, up to the appointment when he drew the diagram.

After a break, we all returned to our seats at the conference table. Mr. Alvin Porter began his questioning, and I felt my stomach draw up in knots. I was prepared to hold my own and not allow this man to trick, confuse, or downright bamboozle me. Mr. Porter's demeanor was nothing like Ms. Raddock's. Rather than being shrewd, he behaved very casually, as if we were buddies.

Addressing me by my first name rather than "Ms. Mitchell," he said, "Janet, going back to the appointment when Dr. Ulid drew the picture, the diagram of what was and what should have been, did Dr. Ulid indicate it was Dr. Allgood who ran the saw and made the cut?"

"Yes, he did, sir."

"And did Dr. Ulid actually tell you, 'I tried to stop Allgood, but I couldn't'?"

"Yes, sir."

"Was Dr. Ulid actually crying at your appointment in 1992 when he said, 'I tried to stop Dr. Allgood, but I couldn't'?"

"He had tears in his eyes."

"In other words, your thank-you letter to him, written on this ballerina card, dated August 8, 1992, is accurate?"

"Yes, sir."

"Janet, in your pre-op discussions with the doctors, weren't you told by one or both of them that it was Ulid who had done this type of surgery before?"

"No—excuse me. I was told that both doctors had done this kind of surgery before."

"Dr. Allgood didn't say, 'Dr. Ulid is going to assist me because he's done it before,' did he?"

"No," I replied. "I never understood that Dr. Ulid was going to assist. I thought my doctors were going to do it together and that they both had performed the surgery before."

"At any point in time until your appointment with Dr. Ulid in 1992, did you ever become suspicious that perhaps something had gone wrong in the 1977 and 1978 surgeries that Dr. Allgood and Dr. Ulid performed?"

"No, sir."

"And did you ever discuss with your parents or husband—or speculate with them—that maybe something had happened during those surgeries to cause the remaining problems in your right leg?"

"No."

My examination by Mr. Porter lasted just a few more minutes, and suddenly he stopped. It was painless. He looked at me, then toward Ms. Raddock, and smiled. "Leeza, I think that's all. Thanks," he said while he flipped the pages, rearranging his notes.

Ms. Raddock reviewed her notes again. She asked the court reporter to read back the last few questions that Mr. Porter had asked me, thus leading to another hour and a half of questioning. When it appeared that Ms. Raddock had asked her last question, she flipped the pages of her notepad over with the first page showing. It caught her eye. Hours ago she had written the name "Matherson," followed by a question mark across the top of the page.

"Ms. Mitchell," she said with a sigh, "who is Dr. Matherson?"

"He's an orthopedist I met while I was in Georgia. He was one of Dr. Hughston's fellows. He was present at my first surgery that Dr. Hughston performed."

"Your recent interrogatories state that you saw Dr. Matherson this past July and August. Is that correct?"

"Yes."

"And why is it that you went to see him?"

"I wanted to talk with him about my knee. I also wanted to find out what he knew about my medical history."

"And what did Dr. Matherson tell you he noticed during your surgery in Georgia?"

"He told me that when Dr. Hughston was performing surgery, Dr. Hughston told the doctors who were observing I had had ligament damage in a previous surgery."

"What else did he tell you?"

"I asked him, 'When a doctor cuts and performs an osteotomy, does he intend to cut ligaments? And if so, do these ligaments heal?' He answered my question."

"What else did he say?"

"He said in the osteotomies that Dr. Hughston trained him to do, ligaments were not cut. He went on to say, 'Any good sports orthopedic surgeon should know that ligaments are not to be cut.'"

"Have you asked Dr. Matherson to be a witness on your behalf in this case?"

I looked to Bridget. "Isn't that attorney-client—?"

Interrupting me, Bridget slowly repeated the question while I listened. "Janet. Have you asked him?"

"No," I replied.

It was now after 6:00 p.m. Everyone in the room was exhausted. Ms. Raddock asked a few more questions that, in turn, led to the grand finale saying, "Ms. Mitchell, I'm not asking whether you knew there was a mistake, but whether you suspected there might have been one." Not wavering, I folded my arms, allowing my body language to speak for itself. I paused, wondering how many different ways this same question had been asked and answered.

"No, Ms. Raddock," I repeated. "Before Dr. Ulid informed me, I never knew a mistake had been made. I never suspected that my doctors did anything wrong."

Bridget's eyes caught mine. She grinned and then gave me the look of "Well done, it's over for now." I'm sure I returned a look of "Can we get out of here?" I took Bridget home with me where piping hot lasagna, French bread, and a tossed green salad were waiting for us. After dinner, the work began again. Marty and my parents were going to be deposed in the morning and wanted some last-minute advice. Bridget answered their questions.

The next day my parents made it through their depositions. I tried to stay calm while I sat and listened to the way Ms. Raddock tried to manipulate them into admitting or acknowledging that they had suspected a surgical error all along.

"Did you think, from your observation of Janet's postoperative condition, that something had gone wrong during any of her surgeries? Did you ever discuss with your husband the possibility that perhaps something had gone wrong during the surgeries to her right leg that might have caused the bow? Were you concerned at all that your daughter was in a wheelchair for a period of time? Did you ever wonder whether something had gone wrong at any point in time regarding any of Janet's surgeries?"

Throughout their depositions, the only surprising information the defense may have learned was that my mother had listened in on the phone calls I'd had with Dr. Hughston. And that my father had found invoices dating all the way back to the late 1970s documenting my treatment with both Dr. Allgood and Dr. Ulid. Besides hearing the facts surrounding my case, the only additional information they offered was that they both were in "utter shock" when I shared with them the contents of Dr. Ulid's confessions, and that this lawsuit was supported by an entire family who had been betrayed.

Marty's deposition brought back sweet memories. Ms. Raddock was curious regarding the circumstances in which Marty and I met and fell in love. As she asked her questions, Marty factually answered her while I traveled in my thoughts back to our wedding day—the day I shed my leg braces and was married in my home church...

My mother had planned ahead for this day by placing large ferns and small trees at the front of the sanctuary. Behind a fern sat a stool, just in case I needed to sit down. Randy and Steve stood as grooms-men and grinned as they watched Marty enter from the side and stand at the front. Close friends who had stood by my side for the past few years now prepared the way for the bride.

My father and I began our descent down the center aisle. He held my arm as if I were precious cargo. Slowly but surely, we made our way to the front. I turned, not to Marty but toward my dad—the man who had made this day possible. I gently kissed him on the cheek and whispered, "We made it!"

Soon Ms. Raddock's voice broke through my daydreaming. I regained my focus on the deposition at hand.

"Mr. Mitchell, you say that Janet fell at LAX. Did your wife just slip, or did she fall to the ground?"

"She slipped on something and dropped to the ground. As usual, she had my arm, but I was unable to catch her."

"After this fall I understand that she was seen again by Dr. Ulid. At some point did you go with your wife to an appointment with him?"

"Yes, I did."

For the next hour, Marty was questioned about my appointment with Dr. Ulid the day he drew the diagram depicting the mistakes. I'm sure that Ms. Raddock asked Marty every question she could think of pertaining to the time we had spent in Dr. Ulid's office.

"Mr. Mitchell, did you happen to read any or all of either Dr. Allgood's or Dr. Ulid's deposition?"

"I read both depositions and attended Dr. Allgood's deposition."

Ms. Raddock raised her eyebrows and looked up. "You attended it?"

"Yes," Marty replied.

Ms. Raddock jotted herself a note and then continued. "And why did you read part of Dr. Ulid's deposition?"

"My wife asked me to."

"And was there anything in Dr. Ulid's deposition that surprised you or that you disagreed with?"

This was the moment for which Marty had been hoping. He had longed for the opportunity to state his opinion and speak his mind, yet he never dreamt that he would have the opportunity to state it on the record. "Ms. Raddock, I was surprised that Dr. Ulid said he was mistaken—that he now, at his deposition, recalled the incident wrong and that he was mistaken about what had actually happened."

"Why did that surprise you, Mr. Mitchell?"

Sitting up and folding his hands before him as they rested on the table, Marty began his monologue. "Ms. Raddock, it just seems odd to me that a person would err in this way. To recall a mistake like Dr. Ulid did and to tell the injured person that this mistake had been made—and then remember later the mistake really didn't happen is odd. I think that most people would tend to err saying that they hadn't made mistakes if there were any questions in their minds. But when I went to Janet's appointment, Dr. Ulid was very matter-of-fact about what had happened. He described the mistakes while drawing pictures for us, clear examples of what had occurred. There seemed to be no doubt in my mind as to what he was saying. There was no guesswork. Dr. Ulid even described how Dr. Allgood operated more quickly than he preferred. It was apparent that Dr. Ulid was directing the surgery in some manner since he told us that he was trying to tell Dr. Allgood to slow down—he was going too fast."

"So," Ms. Raddock said with a sigh, "Dr. Ulid said, 'This is exactly what happened,' as opposed to, 'We think this might have occurred'?"

"Yes, Ms. Raddock. Dr. Ulid was very sure of what he was saying. There did not appear to be any speculation on his part."

Quickly, Ms. Raddock changed the subject away from Dr. Ulid's confession to my past appointments with Dr. Hughston. From there she questioned Marty about my past compliance in using my crutches and my attendance at physical therapy. The deposition ended with questions about Marty's employment and his insurance benefits. What portion had his medical insurance paid, and how much had Marty paid out of pocket for my care?

Relieved that all of our depositions were behind us, Marty and I drove Bridget to the airport while my parents picked up our children. An hour later, my parents, Marty and I, and our children sat in a restaurant ready to celebrate. We shared our stories of tense and funny moments that had occurred during our depositions. We all went home thankful that this day was over, and so very thankful for being part of such a loving and supportive family.

## Chapter Thirteen

# JUSTICE FAILS

A COUPLE OF DAYS AFTER MY DEPOSITION there was a knock at my door. My children raced to greet our visitor. "I got here first," Jason shouted while they waited for me to get to the door.

"Hi, are you Mrs. Mitchell?" the young man asked.

I nodded. Like a salesman, he began his speech. "Mrs. Mitchell, I'm here to…"

I knew why he was here. My wheelchair had arrived. I thought I had prepared myself for this moment, yet blinking back tears, fighting sudden nausea, and riding a wave of anger that hit me like a storm, I was caught off guard. I stood speechless in the doorway as he instructed me on the use of the chair.

"I selected this special chair just for you. I hope you enjoy it," the young man said as he fitted me to the chair, made the needed adjustments, smiled, and waved goodbye.

What I saw sitting before me was a reminder of my past, something I wanted to run from, yet couldn't if I tried. Breaking the tension of the moment, Jason jumped into the chair and took off. "Look, Mom, I can teach you how to do a wheelie!" Within the next few minutes, my kids took my new mode of transportation out on the street and offered rides to the neighborhood children.

Understanding my distress regarding the wheelchair, Marty ingeniously planned a family trip to Disneyland—an "intervention" in disguise. Marty assigned himself as "pusher." And for the sake of my family, I pretended I was enjoying myself at the "happiest place on earth." However, I'm sure it was obvious that I wasn't feeling at home cruising in my new wheels.

The reality was that no matter how hard I tried to prevent it, the stress of my medical condition and the lawsuit, mixed with my intense anger, was wearing on me. I didn't remember the last time I'd slept through the night, not getting up to wander through the house. With little energy or desire to socialize, I'd almost shut out the rest of the world. *No one is ever going to have the opportunity to hurt me again,* I told myself over and over. But I was wrong. As long as I was involved in a lawsuit, I would be open to be hurt. As long as I lived in a world full of humans, I would be vulnerable and exposed to being hurt.

A month later Bridget called and told me about a letter she'd received from Mr. Porter. "Janet," she said, "I'm going to break the letter apart. I'll read you one paragraph at a time, then share my opinion before reading the next. Porter has a mouthful to say, and I want you to understand how ridiculous this letter is. Even so, we do have to respond."

Bridget read:

Dear Ms. Halvorson:

It was clear before Dr. Allgood's deposition, and it is even clearer now, that Dr. Allgood has not seen your client as a patient since 1978, when he referred her to Dr. Hughston and was aware that her family was moving to Georgia. This lawsuit was filed fourteen and one half years after Dr. Allgood last saw her as a patient, so it would be difficult to argue that the statute of limitations had not run in Dr.

```
Allgood's favor a very long time ago. This
is not the case with Dr. Ulid, however.
```

"Bridget, he's lying or has been lied to."

Bridget reassured me, "I know your family never had a thought about moving to the south. We have proof of most of the dates that you saw Dr. Allgood, but it doesn't really matter. Mr. Porter is trying to say that you had to have an ongoing relationship, or you don't have a right to sue. This is just not true when fraud and concealment are issues." Continuing on, Bridget read:

```
Dr. Allgood is no longer performing surgery
and has only a limited office practice. This
litigation is therefore extremely taxing
for him, both financially and emotionally,
since he obviously has no insurance cover-
age. I therefore strongly recommend that
you take a close look at the possibility
of a malicious prosecution action taken by
Dr. Allgood against you if you keep him
in this lawsuit and he ultimately attains
favorable termination. And he has asked me
to convey his covenant that the ultimate
outcome of this lawsuit, if you keep him
in it, will be judgment for Dr. Allgood and
a malicious prosecution action against you
and your client or a thoroughly uncollect-
ible judgment against Dr. Allgood. On this
last point he suggests that you run a TRW
credit check on him if you have any doubts
about his financial picture.
```

"Okay, Janet, calm down. I can hear your heart beating from here," Bridget joked, trying to lighten the moment. "We both know that St. Ann's was informed of the facts surrounding Dr. Allgood's medical malpractice insurance. I believe he can't perform surgery anymore due to St. Ann's finding out about his lack of malpractice insurance. Look at it this way. Allgood doesn't have a chance of hurting one more patient during surgery, and I believe it's because of you."

Bridget took a deep breath. My stomach nervously tightened into knots as she read on, adding her own interpretation. "Mr. Porter wants me to inform you that if you keep Dr. Allgood involved in this litigation, he will win, and then he will in turn sue both and you and me for malicious prosecution. Now, Janet, before you get upset, let's think about this. Per Dr. Allgood's history of past litigations, it was just a matter of time before this threat hit us. We've expected it. Remember we're in this together. We will deal with this if and when it occurs." Pausing for a moment to clear her throat, Bridget then continued reading Mr. Porter's letter:

> I will concede that you may have had a probable cause, as the term applies to malicious prosecution litigation for including Dr. Allgood in the litigation until Dr. Ulid gave his deposition and recanted his claim that Dr. Allgood "cut into the joint." It is clear from all of the x-rays that Dr. Allgood did no such thing, and it is also clear that Dr. Allgood was relying heavily on Dr. Ulid during that initial surgery, since Dr. Allgood had no derotation experience and Dr. Ulid was a recognized expert in pediatric orthopedics.

"So, Mr. Porter is saying that my parents allowed me to have surgery performed by a doctor who had no experience and was relying on his assistant to show him what to do? How absurd. What parent would ever willingly and knowingly allow a doctor to do this?"

"Yep, you've got it. That's what he writes. And notice how he mentions that Dr. Ulid recanted his story, therefore, acknowledging the fact that Dr. Ulid did indeed confess to you in the first place. Janet, let me read the last two paragraphs. You've got to hear Mr. Porter's conclusion":

> Now that Dr. Ulid has retracted his thoroughly unjustified statement to your clients and invalidated his thoroughly inaccurate diagram, I suspect you have no medical support for a claim of malpractice against Dr. Allgood. That being the case, I recommend and request that you sign the enclosed Request for Dismissal of Dr. Allgood (only) and return it to me for filing, in which case Dr. Allgood will waive all claims against you and your client and will testify at trial as a medical witness if properly called and paid professional compensation.
>
> Please give me a response to this request within the next few days so that I know whether to invest the time and Dr. Allgood's money in a Motion for Summary Judgment on the statute issue.
>
> Sincerely,
> Alvin V. Porter

"Janet, I wish you could see this letter," Bridget said with a laugh. "In fact, I do have a copy in the mail to you. But let me tell you now, Mr. Porter used thick, black ink to sign his signature, and his name is over an inch tall and close to four inches long."

"Bridget, there are only twelve letters in his name. This man has confidence!"

"You're right. And it's absolutely ludicrous for Mr. Porter to suggest we dismiss Dr. Allgood from your suit and then pay him to testify as an expert witness for you at trial. I'll inform Mr. Porter to go forward and file his Motion for Summary Judgment."

"But Bridget, we're supposed to go to trial in four months. What in the world is a summary judgment?"

"A Motion for Summary Judgment is made after all discovery has been completed. In other words, because our depositions have been taken and time has been allowed to obtain all records, a Motion for Summary Judgment could be filed. The moving party, which is Porter and Allgood, will submit evidence in their favor to the judge. We will also submit evidence and then the judge will compare both sides. If the judge can determine that a reasonable jury, after looking at the evidence, could only rule one way—for the moving party—he then determines that a jury trial is unnecessary and he enters judgment."

Within the next week, I received a copy of Bridget's response to Mr. Porter's letter. I sat down and opened it. Even though I didn't understand all the court rules and laws, it was clear to me that Bridget wasn't going to play Mr. Porter's games.

Dear Mr. Porter:

In response to your letter of October 23, 1993, I believe you fail to recognize several pertinent points. Perhaps a careful review of Dr. Hughston's records and deposition would assist you.

As you know, the determination of whether the physician/patient relationship has continued is a question of fact and determined by the test set forth in BAJI.

Your threat of malicious prosecution may well be a violation of ethical standards

(See Rules of Professional Conduct, Rule 5-101) and has no merit. Dr. Ulid may have retracted his statements that he made to my client, but there is clearly radiographic, as well as clinical evidence to support his original admission that the February 1977 surgery fell below the standard of care.

Based on the foregoing and all of the evidence disclosed to date, my response to you and your client is to go forward and file your motion for Summary Judgment.

Your claim of clairvoyance with regard to the jury verdict in this case remains to be seen.

Very truly yours,
DUNCAN, BALL, EVANS & UBALDI
A PROFESSIONAL CORPORATION
Bridget C. Halvorson

Obviously, Bridget wasn't going to allow Mr. Porter to intimidate her. Reading her response to Porter and Allgood made my day. At least Bridget understood what had happened to me. At least she was willing to stand up for me, voicing, "What happened to Janet Lynn Mitchell was wrong."

Despite this news, I still fought a depression I couldn't control, and I felt my depression was sure to disappoint God. Each day, it seemed harder and harder to manage my emotions.

Jane saw my sadness. She called me daily. Some days we talked for hours. Others we just sat together in silence, holding the phone.

"Janet," Jane said one day as we sat sipping Diet Cokes in her car, "I think it's time you get some professional help in dealing with your anger. You're not sleeping, and you cry at the drop of a hat. There are physicians who are trained to help people deal with this type of depression."

"That's all I need Jane, another physician. A physician is the reason I'm in this state!"

"I agree, but you must remember that in all professions there are dishonest individuals, but that doesn't mean everyone is bad. Janet, I'll listen and be by your side through this mess, but I'm asking you to seek professional help. It's for your own good, not to mention for Marty and the kids."

I don't know how she did it, but Jane talked me into making an appointment with a psychiatrist. A few days later, Jane came swinging into my driveway, honking her horn. "Come on, Janet Lynn Mitchell," I heard her say as I walked out of my garage. "We wouldn't want to have to explain to the shrink why we're late."

I crawled into her car, and we chatted for the next fifteen minutes until she pulled up in front of a three-story office building. We entered the office and took a seat. Jane looked at me funny as I whispered, "This was your idea, remember?" I then motioned for her to go and sign me in.

Doing so, sitting down next to me, Jane gave me her instructions. "I signed you in, but you have to do the talking with the 'head doctor.' Promise me, Janet, you will talk."

I felt I had no choice. I knew that Jane would be on her feet, ready to speak to the doctor moments after my appointment. I knew that if I didn't at least try to cooperate and get help, Jane would recruit other friends to personally escort me to my next visit. I also knew that I had tried every trick I could think of, recited every verse I felt applied, prayed day and night, and yet I could not help myself.

Dr. John Travis was a cowboy. I knew it the moment I saw his boots and Stetson hanging on the wall. His plaid shirt was neatly tucked in, guarded by a black belt with a large, shiny silver buckle.

He looked to be in his thirties. I was hoping for someone older, someone who had experienced life's travails and the stresses they brought. Instead, young Dr. Travis asked me to take a seat and then introduced himself.

It seemed like one of the longest hours I've ever experienced. I began with my high school years and brought Dr. Travis up to date with both my medical condition and litigation. He asked me several questions, and I answered them the best I could.

"Janet, I'd like for you to stay for another hour to take a few tests. These tests will help me in determining a diagnosis for you, and in setting up your treatment plan," Dr. Travis said.

After approving his plan with Jane, I sat in an empty room holding a number two pencil, coloring in the circles that applied. My ability to concentrate was low. I found myself reading and rereading the same question. When I finally finished, I noted that I had filled in more than one circle on a couple of lines. Not wanting an incorrect diagnosis, I went back to find my errors.

Once finished, I found Jane. She seemed pleased that I had come, cooperated, and was soon going to be told what my problem truly was.

"Janet," she told me, "I spoke to Dr. Travis. He wants you to have some bloodwork. He also wants you to come back next week for the results of the tests you took today. I told him I'd make sure you get here."

Feeling emotionally drained, I gave Jane a hug. "Thanks, friend."

Seven days later I found myself sitting again on the small couch in Dr. Travis's office. "I believe you're suffering from Post-Traumatic Stress Syndrome," he said. "It's a common occurrence when someone has experienced something traumatic. With your recurring dreams of being in a hospital, waking suddenly and feeling as if you're on a gurney being taken to surgery, and your past being played and reviewed in your mind day after day, I think that Post-Traumatic Stress Syndrome is a human, natural response."

*But how can this be?* I thought. *I have God's Spirit living inside of me. Surely God wouldn't give me a task that my body, soul, and mind couldn't withstand.*

Dr. Travis then explained to me in detail the facts surrounding Post-Traumatic Stress. As he talked, I analyzed his words. Yes, I was hurt and angry over something in my past. Yes, learning the truth had been traumatic. And yes, I felt stressed. I concluded that it must be the correct diagnosis.

Surprisingly, I was actually looking forward to my next appointment with Dr. Travis. He planned to discuss my treatment plan with Jane and me. Jane picked me up, and we traveled down the freeway to Dr. Travis's office.

Inside, Mary the receptionist met us, and she was quite distraught. "I'm so sorry," she sobbed. "I meant to call you this morning. You see, Dr. Travis is not able to meet with you today as…" Unable to finish her sentence, she let her face fall into her hands and cried uncontrollably.

"What's wrong?" Jane asked, placing her hand on the receptionist's shoulder. "Is there something we can do for you?"

"I've just had a hard day," she whimpered, trying to stop her tears. "Dr. Travis won't be taking any more appointments. He's dead. He died this morning of a heart attack. And I'm left to inform his patients."

Jane hugged Mary. Bewildered, I took a step back and began to cry. *Dr. Travis dead? Did he have a family? Oh my, he was so young. But he was supposed to tell me what to do about my anger. He was going to give me my treatment plan. He was…*

A few days later Bridget called. "How are you? Do you have a minute?" she asked.

I told Bridget about my trips to the psychiatrist, the Post-Traumatic Stress Syndrome, and, ultimately, Dr. Travis's death. "Maybe I should call you next week to update you on your case. I think life has been a bit too overwhelming these past few weeks," Bridget offered.

I quickly convinced her that I was all right.

"Okay, if you're sure, I'll tell you the latest. Mr. Porter sent me notice that he filed a Motion of Summary Judgment for Dr. Allgood."

"Did we doubt that he would?"

"No, I believe what Carl Kirby, that other victim, said, 'If there's a hurdle to be used, Allgood will use it.' Anyway, the motion is set to be heard on December tenth. I'll file our response and then fly down that morning and state our case. Janet, as I've told you before, I don't believe there's much to worry about. It's Mr. Porter's job to provide satisfactory evidence to convince the judge that you don't have a case, and that absolutely there's not a question for the jury to decide pertaining to the occurrence of fraud and/or concealment."

"Oh," I mumbled while trying to get the gist of what Bridget was saying.

"Simply stated, Janet, the judge will have to decide there is no evidence to be presented to a jury that implicates fraud. Motions of Summary Judgments to dismiss litigation are rarely granted in cases where there's question of fact or an obvious dispute between two parties."

"Bridget, won't this be difficult for Porter to prove, much less to get the judge to rule in his favor? We've got Dr. Ulid's drawing, the missing year, and all the proof in the depositions."

"You're right, Janet. The only thing I see this motion doing is prolonging a trial date. I feel quite confident the judge will deny such a motion. When I spoke to Mr. Keen today, he stated this was a gutsy move on the part of Dr. Allgood. He himself would have never filed this motion."

"I'm sure he wouldn't have. Bridget, just tell me what time your plane will arrive and Marty and I can pick you up. This is a court date we're not going to miss."

---

Two months went by and the day came. Marty and I picked up Bridget at the airport and then drove by to pick up my parents. We were feeling confident about the outcome of the day's motion, yet we still arrived at the courthouse early. I wanted to check out my surroundings, and Bridget wanted to make sure we were in the right place.

Marty, my parents, and I found an empty bench outside Judge Joseph Anthony Higgins's courtroom. We sat down, unloading the documents in our arms. We weren't the only ones who arrived early. Ms. Raddock was dressed for the occasion. She strutted directly past the five of us as if she had never seen us before.

Standing by the door of the courtroom, Ms. Raddock reviewed a list that had just been posted on the wall. Quickly she spun around toward us and grinned. Disturbed by the sudden gleam of happiness, Bridget jumped to her feet and walked over to the notice. She stood reading and running her finger across the page. She looked pale when she turned around. My family and I knew something was wrong. Bridget walked over to Ms. Raddock and to Mr. Porter, who had just arrived. Noting that the doctors had not appeared, I bowed my head and listened closely, trying to eavesdrop on their conversation.

Mr. Porter greeted her with his hand extended. "So Bridget, I see that Judge Higgins evidently sees things the way I do. It's too bad you had to fly down to…"

Red-faced, Bridget glared at Mr. Porter and articulated with great clarity. "Mr. Porter, I want to let you know that I am prepared to ask Judge Higgins to let me be heard."

"Talk all you want, Bridget, but I know this judge. I've been before him many a time, and I know he doesn't change his mind easily."

Bridget, being from out of town, didn't have the advantage Mr. Porter did; he was a familiar face to Judge Higgins. Bridget was the new kid, the foreigner, the stranger.

Lifting my head, I wondered why Ms. Raddock hadn't joined in on the conversation. Instead she stood quietly by in her tightly fitted suit, riding inches above her knees, with her arms folded tightly across her chest and the constant smile of a prom queen.

Bridget soon returned to the bench where my family and I were anxiously waiting. "The preliminary ruling states that the judge plans on granting Dr. Allgood's motion."

"What?" I exclaimed. "What list, what ruling? What does that mean?"

In a whisper, Bridget began to answer me. "Some judges post their preliminary rulings pertaining to the cases calendared for the day. This indicates to the attorneys which way the judge is expected to rule, allowing the lawyers to use any time they have before their case is called to make any necessary changes in their argument. Janet, I am going before the judge today. I'm going to be heard. This ruling is simply wrong!"

There wasn't time for any more discussion. My family sat speechless. The doctors' attorneys walked past us and entered the courtroom, joining several lawyers representing other cases. They all sat in a row facing the judge behind a small podium. My parents, Marty, and I filed in and took seats close to the front, across from some other spectators. Even though I had no idea what the final ruling would be, I wanted Judge Higgins to have to face my family and me while he was making it.

After listening to a few other cases, the judge announced, "Number six, *Mitchell v. Allgood.*" Bridget, Mr. Porter, and Ms. Raddock rose from their chairs and stood a few feet behind the podium, facing the judge.

Using every ounce of charm he possessed, Mr. Porter raced to be the first to greet Judge Higgins. "Your Honor, Alvin Porter for the moving party, defendant Dr. Allgood."

Bridget jumped in next. "Good afternoon Your Honor, Bridget Halvorson on behalf of plaintiff."

Ms. Raddock followed. "Afternoon, Your Honor, Leeza Raddock on behalf of Dr. Ulid."

The judge nodded at each and then turned his face toward Bridget. "You're in trouble," he said with a scowling look.

I slumped in my seat while Bridget stepped forward and centered herself behind the podium. "Your Honor, I did see your tentative ruling that Dr. Allgood's motion had been granted. Yet I would like to be heard."

"Go ahead," he said as he waved his arm, inviting her to speak. "I'm sure you'll appeal me. I'll tell you up front, the appellate court may reverse me because they don't like my ruling. But let me explain to you why, and then you can argue with me.

"There is no credible evidence that the defendants saw or treated the plaintiff professionally after 1978, and I applied the three-year statute of limitation, CCP 340.5. That is for the record, if you don't change my mind and want to appeal. Now you can argue with me."

"Thank you, Your Honor," Bridget said without appearing disconcerted. "I think that it is important for you to know the background of this case." Bridget then spent the next five minutes explaining to the court the summary of my medical treatment, hoping to enlighten the judge. She explained to him the material facts—the concrete evidence and concealment that had been presented to the court in her written declaration regarding this case.

"It is clear that the statute is tolled if there is alleged conceal-ment," Bridget said. "Your Honor, my client presented evidence that there was concealment and that she was not told. In fact, in the case we cited, *Brown v. Blyberg*, the court specifically said that the con-cealment issue tolled the statute, regardless of whether there was a continuing physician/patient relationship. So, I think the defendant is focusing on the wrong issue here. We are asserting in our complaint that there was a concealment, and based on that concealment, the statute is tolled.

"Now, in *Brown v. Blyberg*, the plaintiff sought treatment in 1965 and was told by her doctor that there were tumors that had to be removed, which was why she had this condition in her foot. In 1978, she went to another doctor who, for the first time, told her some bones had been removed. The defendants tried to use the same argument as Drs. Allgood and Ulid in *Brown v. Blyberg*, and the Supreme Court specifically said that when there is alleged concealment, the statute of limitations is tolled."

Taking a deep breath, Bridget continued, "Your Honor, it is their burden to show that there is no triable issue of fact relating to that concealment issue, and they have failed to meet that burden. They kind of skirted around the primary issue of concealment by trying to say that there has to be a continuing physician/patient relationship, and that is not the law's requirement. Your Honor, if you look care-fully at 437 (c), the Summary Judgment section, it requires that all inferences be in the plaintiff's favor or the opposing party's favor."

Bridget concluded and stepped back from the podium. The judge released his fingers that had remained folded together on his desk throughout Bridget's argument. He looked at Mr. Porter and asked with a slight grin, "Do you want to respond to the concealment issue?"

Mr. Porter stepped to the podium and paused. He placed his hands in his pant pockets and stood like someone about to receive an Academy Award.

"Your Honor," he addressed, "I believe that counsel has it wrong as to who has the burden of proof to the defense of the statute of limitations, namely fraud and concealment, for sixteen years or forty years or whatever. We copiously and adequately point out that this case was filed just under sixteen years after the surgery. Also the undisputed statement of facts point out that the plaintiff continued to have enough problems with that right knee so she had three subsequent surgeries on that same knee. The last one, in 1980, was referred to a national expert in Georgia. He continued to see her for years, and she has never seen—there is no evidence whatsoever that she's ever seen the moving party since 1978."

Right away truth was distorted into fiction. Implications were made that Allgood's records existed when in reality they did not. Black and white became gray. Gray became any color Porter wanted it to be. Continuing on, I wondered if Porter forgot for a moment that he was a lawyer working for the result of justice. Rather I viewed him as part of a debate team performing at a contest, trying to persuade the judge in order to become the winner—despite right or wrong, truth or falsehood.

"Janet's admitted that she continued to have pain," Porter boasted. "She claims that her career plans of becoming a nurse were disrupted, so there is no question about her awareness. There is no question that she knew she had a severe problem with her right knee, always did, and probably always will. So the question is: Does the defendant not only have to plead the statute of limitations, but also prove that he did not commit fraud or conceal some facts that would have led the plaintiff to take action?

"I don't believe that is the law, nor could it be the law. Otherwise, a plaintiff could come along forty years later after last seeing the doctor when she's twenty, come along at sixty and say, 'I just talked to another doctor, and he tells me that your doctor did something wrong, and I never found out about it.' So therefore, her argument would be that the doctor would have the burden of proving that he didn't commit fraud, he didn't conceal facts from the plaintiff, which, in fact, in this case is true. There's no showing of it, that Dr. All-good ever concealed any fact or committed any fraud. The plaintiff's entire argument is based on some discussion with a Dr. Ulid in 1992, who was never a partner of Dr. Allgood's. There is no affirmation showing of any concealment or spoilage of records. There's just no proof whatsoever that Dr. Allgood ever committed fraud or conceal-ment. I submit to you, Your Honor, that the party claiming fraud and concealment has the burden; therefore, the three-year portion of the statute should rule the case."

Porter concluded, and the courtroom fell silent. Judge Higgins looked to Leeza Raddock, who stood slightly behind Mr. Porter. "Do you have anything you want to say?" he asked her.

Unlike her performance conducting the depositions, Ms. Raddock looked like a rookie. Taking only a small step forward, not making it to the podium, she replied, "No, I'm just interested to see how you're going to rule."

Bridget returned to the podium. "If I may reply briefly, Your Honor."

"Sure," he answered while leaning forward in his chair.

"I believe the court knows clearly that Summary Judgment is a drastic measure. My client's rights would now be taken away if this were granted. Concealment is a triable issue, Your Honor. Clearly there are triable issues relating to whether my client knew about the injury and its negligent cause. These issues are pointed out by my client's declaration and our statement of disputed facts. There are numerous triable issues of fact relating to that three-year statute.

"I would like the court to read the *Brown v. Blyberg* case. The Supreme Court clearly said in that case that the plaintiff waited thirteen years, and the court overruled the Summary Judgment, and the Supreme Court said that the issue of fact existed relating to the concealment and the one-year statute. And this case is exactly like *Brown v. Blyberg*. Thus, the Summary Judgment is clear that it is the burden of the defendant to prove a complete defense, and they failed to do so."

The judge sat straight up in his chair. "My ruling stands with one addition. The complaint alleges that the concealment was the fact that the doctors did not tell them they had made a mistake during the surgery. I don't think the law requires a surgeon to admit fault to a patient and say, 'I blew it. You can sue me because I screwed up in your osteotomy.' If this is true, then we have a whole new line of cases that are going to make all plaintiffs' attorneys smile big."

One last time Bridget boldly spoke up, trying to persuade the judge. "Your Honor, all of the inferences in this case clearly show there are many triable issues of fact. My client should have the right to present these facts to a jury—"

"I have ruled, ma'am," Judge Higgins declared sternly. "You can appeal and see what they think of it."

"Thank you, Your Honor." Bridget sighed.

And just like that, I had lost. I had lost my right to sue.

*Chapter Fourteen*

# WALKING THROUGH
# THE DARKNESS

I WAS NUMB. Maybe I was afraid to let myself feel, and yet the shock over the outcome of my hearing left me stunned.

Just days after losing my right to sue, I received a letter from Bridget. Enclosed was a copy of a letter she had received from Alvin Porter. Obviously, Mr. Porter had wasted no time and had gone straight from our court hearing to the keyboard. I began to read:

Dear Ms. Halvorson:

This accompanies a copy of the Notice of Entry of Judgment and of our Memorandum of Costs and Disbursements in the amount of $563.50. Rest assured that Dr. Allgood will take whatever steps are necessary to collect these costs and is considering an action for malicious prosecution against you and your client in the belief that you had no basis whatsoever for bringing an action against him in 1993 other than the alleged conversation with Dr. Ulid, who had no records or x-rays before him at the time and who later recanted completely his claim of negligence on the part of Dr. Allgood.

The dam of anger welled up inside me burst, and the resulting scream echoed throughout my empty house. I read the letter again, and I snapped. Emotionally I broke. This thirty-two-cent letter was the excuse I needed. Before I knew it, I was in hysterics, pounding the door of the coat closet. I grabbed my hair, pulling strands through my fingers. "God, help me," I cried. "I can't stand Mr. Porter! I can't stand this man you made in your image! God, You're going to have to change my feelings. I've tried and I can't! God, please show me just one good thing about him!"

I slid to the floor. Through tears that streaked across the letter, I continued reading Porter's composition to Bridget:

> We do not believe that you have the opinion of any qualified expert who, having reviewed the records and x-rays, would be able to express an opinion that Dr. Allgood violated the applicable standard of care in 1977 and we do not believe that your client's statements are sufficient to rely upon in prosecuting this action against Dr. Allgood, which has cost him many thousands of dollars in attorneys fees and much consternation. I should add that your client is extremely fortunate that I begged, borrowed, and "stole" records and copies of depositions in order to minimize Dr. Allgood's costs in this matter, since he had no insurance for the claim and has had financial problems. Had I traveled to Georgia and ordered copies of all of the depositions taken and attended all the depositions taken, Dr. Allgood's claim for reimbursement would be

somewhere in the vicinity of $20,000 (in a
countersuit).

Just as I was calming down from the idea of being sued, I read the next sentence. Porter showed his arrogance as he blatantly offered his own thoughts:

> In my opinion, your client "assaulted" Dr.
> Allgood at a very late date with no proper
> medical support. I think there should be
> a remedy available to him to recoup all of
> his expenses and something for the emo-
> tional trauma, but I cannot assure him
> that there is, except to the extent of the
> recoverable costs.

Emotional trauma? Had he had to learn how to walk again due to someone else's carelessness and concealment? At this point I wasn't sure if I should have laughed or cried. It seemed ridiculous for an attorney to be communicating in such a manner. However, he did conclude his letter with the gracious word sincerely, and his initials were scribbled in thick black pen and covered at least an inch in height. This time his signature wasn't the only thing at the bottom of the page. Porter couldn't help himself from adding a "P.S." regarding his last thoughts to Bridget. "I think you owe it to your client to warn her that she may be a defendant in a counter action before this matter is terminated ultimately."

Just two days after Christmas and Alvin Porter was back to his old tricks. I had a very tough time "liking," much less "loving" this man. In some ways, he was harder to cope with than the doctors. He had no emotional involvement in this case, yet he played with my life like a chess game. This was just another move—checkmate!

I fought the impulse to wad up and heave Porter's letter across the floor. Instead I picked up the phone and called H. Norman Wright, a counselor respected in his field and who had written a book about women being angry called, *Good Women Get Angry: A Woman's Guide to Handling Her Anger, Depression, Anxiety, and Stress.* I knew that I had to get some professional help to sort out my emotions. I spoke to his secretary and made an appointment for the following week.

With a God who now seemed silent, a court system that had failed me, grief that I did not understand, unforgiveness that reeked, and a dead psychiatrist, I found myself sitting across from Norman Wright. Would he be afraid of me when he found out that I was suing my doctors? Would he think I was nuts?

"Janet, my friends call me Norm," he said. "I'd love to see if I could help you."

For the next several minutes I gave Norm a brief history of my medical past and my present emotional status. No, he reassured me, I wasn't nuts. Norm said that my emotions were a signal that something was wrong. For me, therapy would be like open-heart surgery without anesthesia. I would begin to share my pain with another, not worrying that I had to be strong.

"Did you ever think that maybe God did protect you?" Norm questioned. "Maybe the doctors were heading to cut off your entire leg."

At Norm's suggestion, I went home and stood before a full-length mirror and viewed my bare legs. Perhaps this was the first time I had seen them for what they truly were. I was repulsed, so I turned and ran to vomit.

Daily I prayed, "God, help me. I'm crumbling inside. I hate my legs. I can't even describe to you my pain. How am I supposed to feel? You allowed the mistakes in the first place. Then fifteen years later, you allowed me to find out about them. And now, I'm tossed out of court. You've allowed the doctors to hurt me again and again.

They continue the lies, and it seems to be okay with you. Just tell me what I'm supposed to do. If I quit now, the doctors are planning to sue me for their court costs and emotional trauma. If I quit now, others might be injured and find their legs looking like mine."

I hated what was happening in my life. I had been resisting the things God was allowing to occur. Exhausted, I decided to quit my fight and resign my will to God's. I was ready to accept His direction and outcome in my situation. I reminded myself that God had a purpose I didn't understand and might never know. I decided I was going to be faithful—as faithful as I could humanly be.

After receiving Porter's letter, we decided that Bridget would file a motion to reconsider. Surely Judge Higgins was a reasonable man and most likely he had not understood my case. When the day came, Bridget flew back to Orange County and appeared before Judge Higgins. There, she offered additional evidence and again asked the judge for a reversal of the Motion for Summary Judgment. Again, we were told that I didn't have enough evidence to prove fraud and to file a lawsuit.

The disappointment was monumental. I stared out the window as Marty drove me home in silence. An unexplainable peace anchored my emotions. When we got home, Marty looked at me with tears in his eyes and said, "Janet, if the doctors had never made a mistake, I would have never met you." He pulled me close to his chest, and we cried.

That night I tried to reflect on things. I was so confused. I had thought God wanted me to take a stand, to step out and say, "This is wrong; these doctors need to be stopped." Why didn't God stand up for me? In my opinion, God was allowing these doctors to continue to get away with their deceit, lies, and downright cheating, and now I felt as if God were silent.

Even though Randy Worrell, now a pastor and hospital chaplain, reminded me that "one of the greatest tests of a Christian's life is to live with the silence of God," I now wondered if my heart was screaming so loud that I couldn't hear God, or if perhaps God had a special plan in mind for the silence. Was this time of silence God's way of trusting me to live by faith?

"What do I do now?" I asked Norm at my next counseling appointment.

"Grieve," was his simple answer. He was right. I needed to stop putting so much energy into my anger and allow myself to grieve. This was scary because we now hit the nerve that controlled my pain. But how does one grieve? Do you just let yourself feel your pain?

"Grieving is normal," Norm said. "Christians are supposed to grieve when heartache hits. Look at King David. He tore his clothes and fell prostrate on the ground. I'd say that he was upset. Janet, God gave us our emotions so we could use them and grieve."

When I left, I promised Norm I wouldn't stuff my emotions, thus creating an explosion of anger, but I would allow myself the opportunity to feel and grieve. That night Marty found me in our backyard on the wooden swing, sobbing.

"Honey, what's wrong? What are you doing?"

"I'm grieving." Between sobs, I explained to Marty what Norm and I had discussed.

"Well," he replied, "can you let me know what I'm supposed to do when you're grieving?"

My tears turned into laughter. It was obvious this grieving thing was new to both of us. Marty sat by my side, and our discussion led to our new and pending decision. Would we file an appeal with the Appellate Court or resign ourselves that we'd given it our all? Pulling out a letter from Bridget that he had folded and stuck in his pocket, Marty read:

Dear Janet:

Based on the recent rulings of the court we feel it is necessary to set forth our opinion and recommendations for the further handling of this manner.

The court's ruling in favor of both defendants, Allgood and Ulid, on the statute of limitations is a *final* judgment in their favor. The court has ruled that we did not present evidence which established a "triable issue of fact" relating to intentional concealment.

Even though we felt that we submitted sufficient evidence that you asked the doctors about your condition and they gave you a false explanation, the court disagreed.

In discussing this case with our appellate attorney, he tells us that 70% of appellants (the person who appeals) lose. He feels after reviewing your case that you have a 50/50 chance of winning the appeal.

Keep in mind that if we appeal and win at the appellate level, this same issue can be tried before a jury. The jury must find by a "preponderance of the evidence" (a more likely than not standard) that the doctors intentionally concealed this from you. It is a difficult burden, and it is our opinion that you have about a 40% chance of winning that issue at trial.

The judgments by Allgood and Ulid against you entitles them to recover their cost incurred in defending this case from you. Allgood's costs were approximately $500.00. We do not yet have the total amount of Ulid's costs, but will advise immediately upon receipt.

The costs will continue to escalate through the appeal and if the case is taken to trial. Conservatively, you could be looking at total costs from *both* doctors of between $40,000–$50,000 through appeal and trial of this matter. Those costs would be a judgment against you and would not be paid by our firm.

Once you have had an opportunity to review the above, we will need your decision on whether you wish to pursue the appeal and the trial, which may result in a significant cost judgment against you.

Very truly yours,
BRIDGET C. HALVORSON

As soon as Marty had finished reading, he folded the letter and returned it to his pocket. "We'll talk about this later," he said.

"Shall I go back to grieving?" I asked with a giggle.

"Yeah, and maybe I need to join you."

I wasn't sure what to do. Everything inside me told me not to quit, but logic and risk said differently. I thought about how God led the Israelites by fire and a cloud. Now, I felt God was leading me by candlelight, only providing enough light to walk one step or day at a time.

The next week I returned to Norm's office. Hoping he could offer some grand advice regarding the appeal, I sat and listened. "Janet, the appeal is a big decision, but you also have another decision to make."

"What's that?"

"To forgive."

"Forgive?" How could I possibly forgive when I was still over-whelmed with grief? I looked down at my legs and thought of my emotional wounds and physical scars. I remembered the gut-wrench-ing moment when I stood in front of my full-length mirror and crum-bled at the sight of my own legs. My forgiveness would not make these emotions magically disappear. No amount of forgiveness could cover these scars.

Norm was right. My procrastination, unwillingness, or lack of understanding of how to forgive the doctors was destroying me. For my own sake, for my own personal well-being, I had to somehow move on with my life because I was stuck. Deep in my heart I knew forgiveness was my key to moving on. This simply made me mad!

I was grateful that God had forgiven me for my past sins. I also knew that somehow I had to extend the same grace to my doctors.

Through Norm Wright's wisdom, I finally understood that if I did forgive the doctors for their secrets, mistakes, and lies this would in no way minimize what had occurred. My forgiveness would not be ignoring, condoning, or denying their actions. My forgiveness would not offer them an excuse for their medical negligence or lack of integ-rity. It would not require the doctors' involvement whatsoever. I was hoping that once I did the deed and forgave, somehow this would ease my emotions of resentment, grief, loss, anger, and self-pity that I desperately desired not to feel.

During my spring cleaning, I was sorting and stacking things in my closet when I found the remains of the once-beautiful balloon bouquet Annette had so cheerfully brought me. More than three years had passed and while Annette had lived these past three years experiencing all that God had for her, my soul now resembled the balloons: weathered, shriveled, wasted away, and lifeless.

Jolted at my discovery, I phoned Annette to tell her about my find. Annette was positive my next breath needed to be words to my heavenly Father forgiving the men who had hurt me. "Janet, you have no choice. You will live the rest of your life with the consequences of someone else's mistakes and sin. I guess the only choice you have is how you're going to live it."

"Janet," Annette challenged, "don't you remember what Norm Wright told you?"

I thought back to Norm's words: "Christ was able to forgive a wrongful death: his! He clearly understood the emotional distress and physical pain he was about to experience on the cross, yet he forgave. Jesus forgave by speaking words. He didn't wait to forgive until he felt like forgiving. He didn't wait until his pain had eased or reconciliation had occurred. No one had been punished. Christ's forgiveness didn't depend on the repentance of his enemies. It had everything to do with being obedient to his Father."

I sat speechless. I pictured Jesus on the cross, his body throbbing with pain from the piercing of each nail...and it was then that he forgave.

For the past three years Annette and Norm had understood something I did not—forgiveness needs to begin with a decision to forgive. Annette and Norm taught me that forgiveness is a choice, not an emotion. Jesus taught me that it could be done.

At that moment I forgave the men who had hurt me, and I asked God to forgive me for questioning his sovereignty and justice, and then I decided to trust God with all my unanswered questions.

When Sunday came, our family hurried out the door for church with Marty grabbing the umbrellas. After the service we gathered in the fellowship hall. People in our little cluster were drinking coffee and chatting when a friend whispered, "Look out the window. There she is."

"Who?" I whispered.

"Alvin Porter's daughter-in-law."

"Can't be," I blurted, catching the attention of the others. With a slight smile I closed my mouth and paused for a few moments. The group returned to its original conversation and I inconspicuously turned toward my friend. Under my breath I asked, "Are you sure?"

As we whispered like two schoolgirls, my friend told me the story of how a family in our church had a grandpa they loved very much. This grandpa they loved and cared for was the same lawyer I despised.

Suddenly I saw them racing across the patio—Porter's grandchildren trying to duck from the rain pouring off the eaves.

That night I snuggled deep in my covers. I couldn't help thinking about the children I had seen at church dodging the rain. Right then it hit me. Months earlier I had asked God to help me see "one good thing" about Alvin Porter. That day, God showed me one great thing—a grandpa who needed a touch from God. This was the day that God changed my heart toward Alvin Porter. I still did not like him or approve of his professional tactics. I still thought that he was rude and abrasive, but now I was able to see one good thing and to pray for Mr. Porter with sincerity.

After many mealtime discussions, late-night chats, and down-to-the-facts family meetings, the decision was made. Regardless of the odds against us, Marty, my parents, and I decided to file an appeal. Bridget helped us find an appellate specialist, and my parents offered to help finance the costs. A law firm named Rutan and Tucker came to our rescue and assigned Matthew Ross to my case. We understood there was no guarantee of a successful outcome of litigation, but this firm believed that I had been harmed by Drs. Allgood and Ulid, and they believed that Judge Higgins made a terrible mistake in granting the doctors' Motion for Summary Judgment. We began the eighteen-month-long wait for my date with the Court of Appeals. I was not stopping my pursuit for justice.

## Chapter Fifteen

# NOT BY CHANCE

THINGS I HAD NEVER REALIZED about the law, I now knew. I was surprised to discover that it's not against the law for a doctor to make a mistake and not tell the patient. A doctor is not required by law to offer a patient information about a mistake in his treatment *unless* the patient asks the doctor specifically about it. It is, however, against the law for a doctor to *lie* to a patient about a mistake that has occurred. Learning this disturbed me. Patients need to be able to make informed decisions about their health. How could I be assured of doing so with such crazy laws in existence?

"Second opinions" needed to become part of my vocabulary. The doctor I chose for any second opinion would practice "a town away." He wouldn't be in the same medical community where he'd likely be known by my present doctor. I would ask questions and in many different ways.

I would now create my own medical journals for my family members. I would keep records of my children's health history, recording their hospitalizations, medications/doses, and the names of their medical team. This information could prove helpful in dealing with future medical issues. If and when these records didn't seem to add up or prompt me to ask questions, I would ask the doctor's office to provide me with copies of the medical charts. If anyone were to give me a hard time about requesting my records, that would be the red flag telling me to run!

From here on out, I would research and investigate my potential doctors by contacting the medical board of my state. Before any member of my family were to have surgery, I would make sure the surgeon had medical malpractice insurance. I would verify this information in case of an honest mistake or mishap.

Day after day, I read and reread all the information I could find pertaining to medical malpractice. I even had my sister Kathy researching.

"I remember a discussion from one of my nursing classes," she said. "I was told that in the United States there's a one in fifty chance of medical professionals being sued after a medical mistake.[4] Maybe the injured aren't aware that something has happened to them. Maybe they, too, were lied to, or maybe their doctor told them the truth and said that he or she was sorry—then helped them find medical care needed. Maybe the patients don't sue because they understand we all make mistakes."

She told me about a JAMA report that stated: "The patient and/or family was informed of the mistake only 24 percent of the time."[5]

"But I believe patients want to know and deserve to be told when mistakes are made."

"You're not alone. The Archives of Internal Medicine states that 98 percent of the patients surveyed 'desired or expected the physician's active acknowledgement of an error.'[6] I think the reasons doctors and medical professional don't tell is because they're afraid of being sued. Yet statistics show that patients are twice as likely to do so if the mistakes are kept a secret and the patients find out on their own. "

I read her a quote of my own. Doug Wojcieszak of "The Sorry Works! Coalition" states:

```
An apology coupled with fair compensation
stifles anger and the need to file a law-
suit in most cases. Any plaintiffs' lawyer
will tell you the fastest way to defuse a
lawsuit is to be honest, forthright, and
fix peoples' problems. The old axiom of
```

> deny and defend is a tried and failed risk
> management strategy because it increases,
> not decreases, anger with patients and
> families. Deny and defend literally pushes
> patients and families to file a lawsuit.
> Deny and defend also gives the perception
> of a cover up, even when the standard of
> care was met.[7]

"Obviously, the truth is in everyone's best interest," my sister agreed.

More than once Kathy and I chatted on the phone, sharing facts that we at times wished were not true. The more we discovered, the more certain we were as to our need to go through with the appeal.

Within days of this conversation, Matthew Ross filed my appeal. Shortly afterward, Bridget received a letter from Alvin Porter and faxed me a copy. "Bridget, this is some of the best news I've had," I said while talking to her on the phone. Tears of happiness flowed freely while I read and reread the first few lines.

> Dear Ms. Halvorson:
>
> This letter is to inform you that I will
> not be representing Dr. Allgood for the
> appeal. Dr. Allgood does not seem to have
> the funds required to finance an appeal—he
> is no longer in private practice—and I'm
> confident that Mr. Keen will file a brief
> that would cover both defendants.
>
> I have asked Dr. Allgood to obtain new
> counsel for the purpose of the appeal and
> am again recommending that he do so at
> this juncture. However, lacking new coun-
> sel, I am asking him to sign a Substitu-

```
tion  of  Attorney  designating  himself  as
counsel.

Sincerely,
Alvin Porter
```

Yes! The stress and frustration of dealing with Mr. Porter through the appeal had been removed. I now played the waiting game, discovering whom Dr. Allgood would find to represent him or waiting to see if he indeed would represent himself.

Court briefs were filed; additional interrogatories were sent out by Matthew Ross and Michael Keen and returned by all parties involved except Dr. Allgood. He did not file any briefs or complete and submit any interrogatories. I decided he was hanging on to Keen's coattails, gambling the odds that Mr. Keen would win the appeal and we would all go home.

The appellate judge, however, wasn't used to Dr. Allgood's delays. He didn't take lightly to the fact that Dr. Allgood was nonexistent when it came to the appeal.

"Janet," Bridget said one late afternoon, "just opened my mail and thought you might like to see who I received a letter from."

Within seconds, I received her fax. "Yes, Bridget, I see it. It's a letter from the appellate court." I laughed. "I think they've got Allgood's number!"

"At least they know how to play his game," Bridget concluded.

I sat down to read the letter dated October 11, 1994:

```
***  17(b)  NOTICE  TO  RESPONDENT  ***
AS  TO  RESPONDENT  ALBERT  ALLGOOD  ONLY

If respondent's brief is not filed within
15 days from the date of this notice, the
appeal may be submitted for decision upon
```

```
the record and upon appellant's opening
brief unless good cause is shown for re-
lief from default (California Court rule
17(b)). The failure to file a respondent's
brief may be the basis for a reversal.
(Roth v. Keene, 256 Cal. 2D 727, 727-7280.)
No additional 17(b) notices will be issued,
even if further extensions are granted.

State of California, Court of Appeal,
Fourth Appellate District
```

This one piece of paper brought me a glimmer of hope. I grabbed a piece of tape and hung it on my refrigerator for all to see. I counted the days, waiting to hear if Dr. Allgood would ignore his letter, file his brief, or leave town.

Days later, Bridget faxed me another piece of interesting news. Beverly, Dr. Allgood's office manager, had also filed her declaration with the court.

```
I, Beverly Lacasto, declare the following,
I have been an employee of Dr. Albert All-
good for almost fifteen years. I managed
the office portion of Dr. Allgood's prac-
tice in orthopedics and sports medicine.

I recall a young patient by the name of
Janet Hepp, but I have seen that patient,
now Janet Hepp Mitchell, only once since
Dr. Allgood referred her case to Dr. Jack
Hughston in Georgia in 1978. That one oc-
casion was last year, when Janet Mitchell
came to the Newport office and demanded
a copy of her chart in a hostile manner.
Dr. Allgood has never, to my knowledge,
```

treated, examined, or consulted with Janet
Hepp Mitchell since 1978.

When this lawsuit came to life, I was asked
to locate a patient chart for Janet Hepp
and was unable to locate the chart. I cannot recall whether we sent the chart to
Dr. Hughston in Georgia in 1987 or whether
the chart went with Dr. Ryan Ulid when he
left the Fourteenth Street office to set
up his own practice in Orange in the late
seventies or early eighties.

Beverly, too, had betrayed me. Norm's words had come true. I
found myself having to forgive and forgive and forgive again. Beverly's "contradictions of the truth" contributed to the fact that I was
now waiting for an appellate court date. The reality of forgiveness
hit me when I realized I was no longer able to keep an account of
Beverly's or the doctors' wrongs against me. The bookkeeping was
God's department, and so this letter brought me to my knees. I had
one more opportunity to be obedient by forgiving again.

Saturday morning came. Marty was off playing basketball, and the
kids were sleeping in. With no morning rush, I sat down on the couch
with a cup of hot cocoa and opened the newspaper. Staring at me
were seven startling words: "Dead Man's Survivors Sue Doctors and
Hospital." I read the article:

The wife and children of a deceased Lake
Forest man filed a lawsuit Friday alleging
that a hospital and two of its physicians
intentionally concealed his true cause of
death in 1993.

> In court papers filed Friday in Orange
> County Superior Court in Santa Ana, the
> family asserts that Henry C. Fletcher, 61,
> would not have died if doctors had not
> performed surgery while his blood was in
> a dangerous condition. The suit states
> that an anonymous caller reported that
> his death Aug. 11 at St. Ann's in Orange
> County was due to negligence by physicians
> Charles G. Wilcox and Ryan W. Ulid.[8]

I took a couple of deep breaths and burst into tears. An anonymous caller reported the cause of death?

> Further investigation showed that Fletcher
> indeed had not died from a blood clot that
> blocked an artery in his lungs, according
> to the suit.

I wanted to know more. What did the anonymous caller say? Just how did Mr. Fletcher die? How was Mrs. Fletcher? And who in the world was Charles G. Wilcox? My questions were many and my answers few. My calm Saturday had just erupted into an emotional bombshell.

I spent the day sharing the news about Mr. Fletcher and made plans to pick up Jane and head to the courthouse Monday morning the second we dropped our kids off at school. We were going to find the court file for *Fletcher v. Wilcox* and read every page.

Digging through court records this time was more somber than any other that Jane and I had experienced. We knew the system: fill out a card and wait for the file to be brought up from storage. For the next twenty minutes, Jane and I reminisced about our first trip to the courthouse and our scouring through numerous suits. "Remember how shocked we were to find out that Dr. Allgood had been sued for diamond fraud?" Jane whispered.

"Oh, yeah." I giggled.

"Janet Mitchell, your file is ready," the clerk announced.

Jane and I sat side by side and opened the file. Jane used her fingers to trace the words as we read in silence. We were not prepared for what we found.

> Decedent HENRY FLETCHER died on or about August 11, 1993, during the second phase of a two-stage final surgery, which was elective in nature. The surgeon who performed both surgeries was Dr. RYAN ULID. The anesthesiologist for the second surgery, where Mr. Fletcher died, was Dr. CHARLES WILCOX.
>
> Following the patient's death, Dr. Ulid advised Mr. Fletcher's wife and family that Mr. Fletcher had suffered a blood clot, a "pulmonary embolism," and they were unable to revive him. Plaintiffs allege that the family was talked out of requesting an autopsy by the anesthesiologist and by Dr. Ulid, indicating that a pulmonary embolism caused his demise. Further, the family accepted the doctor's explanation and did no further investigation. No autopsy was requested, and the body was cremated.

"Jane, why wouldn't the family have accepted their doctor's explanation? They just didn't know better." My stomach turned in disgust.

"Keep reading. Look at this!" Jane gasped as her finger followed the words along the page.

> In February 1995, Mrs. Fletcher, the wife of the decedent, received, on her voice-

```
mail at home, a message from an "employee"
of St. Ann's Hospital indicating that the
anesthesiologist had "killed" her husband
and he would kill again unless she put
a stop to it. Indeed, without the mys-
terious telephone call, the family would
never have known the cause of death, and
the conspiracy to cover-up the death of
HENRY FLETCHER would have been successful.
The text of this anonymous telephone call
reads in the pertinent part.
```

"Jane, Mrs. Fletcher got this anonymous call eighteen months after her husband's death. What a shock that had to be." I sat restless while Jane began to read in a soft whisper.

```
Mrs. Fletcher, I work at St. Ann's Hospi-
tal. You must hire an attorney and sue the
anesthesiologist who killed your husband.
This is not the first patient whom he has
killed. The hospital is protecting him,
and they are refusing to suspend his priv-
ileges. He is going to kill other people.
Your husband did not have anesthesia; he
was awake and paralyzed. You must hire
an attorney and stop him. The hospital is
protecting him for some reason.
```

"Oh, God, help them!" Jane prayed softly. "Janet, what did the nurses do?" she asked fighting tears. "They must have felt helpless standing by Mr. Fletcher's side, unable to take control."

Jane and I both wiped our tears. "Janet, this is why you can't quit and give up your fight for justice," Jane said firmly. "People are dying. Somehow medical fraud has to be exposed. Somehow you've got to take what you've learned and help educate others."

"I wish I could have done something to save Mr. Fletcher," I quickly remarked. I felt unnerved and very uncomfortable with our newfound information. I thought for a moment and agreed. "You're right, Jane. I can't quit. Giving up will not be in my vocabulary.

"Let's read on so we can get out of here." Page by page we flipped, reading sections that caught our attention. We read them once, then twice.

> The plaintiffs thereafter contacted this law office, the records were reviewed by medical experts, with the result being that it was obvious that the decedent did not die from a pulmonary embolism, but died as a result of gross malpractice by the surgeon and anesthesiologist. Further, that the decedent had died as a result of the stoppage of the heart and due to a lack of oxygen, because they did not infuse any blood, and they knew that decedent's blood levels were insufficient at the start of the surgical procedure. Plaintiff's expert testimony will be that it was obvious what the true nature of the cause of death was that any review by the hospital would have so reflected, and that further, there was a cover-up by the hospital, the orthopedic surgeon, and the anesthesiologist.

"Jane, does this mean Mr. Fletcher didn't have enough blood, so he died?"

"I think so. I've always been told, when preparing a patient for surgery, if they're able, they should be encouraged to donate their own blood. This helps to eliminate problems relating to blood matching and/or transmitting infection."

"Jane, you sound so clinical, just like a nurse."

"I am a nurse," she whispered back. "Regardless if Mr. Fletcher donated his own blood or not—they simply didn't give him any."

> Further, there is clear evidence of fal-
> sification of medical records contained
> within the medical chart of the decedent.
> Attached hereto as Exhibit 'C' is a true
> and correct copy of the 'anesthesia re-
> cord' of the decedent's second surgery.
> Additionally, defendant's subsequent ef-
> forts to conceal from plaintiffs the true
> nature and cause of their husband/father's
> demise, the fraudulent entries in dece-
> dent's medical records, and the hospital's
> failure to disclose information when such
> a duty existed, constitutes fraud, malice,
> and oppression. Defendants' conduct toward
> plaintiffs in this regard entitles plain-
> tiffs to the recovery of punitive damages
> against all defendants.
>
> As can be seen from this medical record,
> although Mr. Fletcher died on the surgical
> table, he is claimed to have returned to
> the recovery room in 'good condition' and
> that his 'reflexes in recovery room' were
> 'responsive.'

"Here we go again, Jane. My records say that I was walking when I was in a wheelchair. Mr. Fletcher's records say he was alive when he was dead."

"And this says that the hospital knew. St. Ann's investigated and knew!" Jane said in a huff.

> Plaintiffs further allege that the hospital conducted certain investigations, discovered both gross negligence and falsification of medical records, and failed to disclose this information to the family or to anyone (plaintiffs include the belated submission of this information to the Medical Board by the hospital in this assertion) in an effort to conceal the true facts.

We turned the page and scanned down. "Look at what Mrs. Fletcher said in her deposition," I whispered. "She sounds just like me. Listen, Dr. Ulid's lawyer asked Mrs. Fletcher, 'Why was it your inclination not to have an autopsy?' Her answer was plain and simple, 'I didn't feel the need to go through that. Dr. Ulid had indicated how my husband had died, and I believed him.'"

"Jane, I believed him, too. All his patients probably believed him."

Jane and I studied the record, discovering one shocking fact after another. "Listen to this!" she said. "'St. Ann's Hospital did not follow its own protocol in investigating Mr. Fletcher's death while his body was still at the hospital, and even after discovering that his death was not the result of a pulmonary embolism, they continued to conceal this information from plaintiffs.'"

Reading on, we found something encouraging. Someone had actually done something right. Following Mr. Fletcher's surgery, Dr. Wilcox's privileges were suspended and then permanently terminated at St. Ann's.

"Yeah, but Jane, what happened to Dr. Ulid? Is concealment and altering medical records an acceptable practice and not one to result in suspension?"

"Don't know," Jane responded in disgust. She turned the page and we came to a section pertaining to Dr. Ulid's deposition.

"Jane, Dr. Ulid was just as defiant in the Fletcher deposition as he was in mine." We continued to read on:

> When plaintiffs' counsel took the deposition of Dr. Ulid on December 11, 1996, attached hereto and incorporated herein by reference, an example of the types of questioning undertaken by plaintiff's counsel and extensively objected to by defense counsel is seen. For example, plaintiff's counsel simply asked '…did you, independent of any hospital committee, conduct any investigation yourself or research yourself as to the cause of the patient's demise?' Following this simple question, it was fully two and a half pages of objections and interpretations later before the witness was finally allowed to answer simply, 'Yes.'

"Jane, look here," I said as I skimmed the following page. I felt my anger boil. "Charles Wilcox filed for protection under the bankruptcy court. I guess Allgood isn't the only doctor who has tried such a scheme. Dr. Allgood's held up my case twice by filing for bankruptcy and then withdrawing the filing."

"I just don't get it. I'll never understand how or why medical malpractice is dismissible in bankruptcy court. Mrs. Fletcher has lost every which way."

"Does it say she's fighting the bankruptcy, like I am with Allgood's?"

"I don't think she is. I wonder if her fight is almost gone."

"Did you see this?" Jane asked, using her finger to mark her spot. "It was after Charles Wilcox 'admitted to falsifying medical records,' that he filed for bankruptcy and received an automatic stay—preventing further court action by the Fletchers."

"Where is the justice?" I moaned.

"Come on, Janet," Jane said as we closed the file. "Let's go sit somewhere, anywhere except here." And with that, Jane and I vowed to pray for the Fletcher family and called our investigation to a close—at least for the day.

Emotionally and mentally drained, I dropped Jane off and went straight home to call Marty at work. "Marty, Mr. Fletcher is dead!" I said gulping back my tears. "He is dead! The court records affirmed it."

The phone was silent except for the sounds of my weeping. After a second or two, Marty delicately said, "I'm sorry, honey, but I can't place who Mr. Fletcher is. Is he a neighbor, someone from church?"

"No! He is the man who died at St. Ann's during his surgery with Dr. Ulid."

"Janet, I am so sorry," he said repeatedly.

"Marty, I'm angry! I'm sad! I'm...All the feelings that I thought I had dealt with have returned. What am I going to do?"

"Honey, I'm not sure what you should do. Yet I think I'll leave work and come home and do it with you. Hey, why don't you say a prayer and then give Norm a call?"

I did say a prayer. Then I set down the phone and crumbled to the floor, curling up into a ball. I rocked myself and prayed, *God, please help me. Please help the Fletcher family.*

I waited until I calmed down before I called Norm. "Janet, your feelings are normal," he assured me. "This is a horrific situation, and you have a right to be angry. If you try to sweep your feelings under the rug, it will just be a matter of time before you'll be tripping over them. It's good you're willing to talk about your feelings. My advice is to keep talking and be honest with God about what you feel."

That night Marty called a family meeting. Marty's aim was to remind his little family of God's sovereignty.

"Guys, I know that things are a little stressful while we're waiting for Mom's next court date. But I want to remind you that God promises to bring good out of any situation. I can't tell you how, but I can tell you it's going to be good."

"I am the good," we heard coming from the couch.

"What?" Jenna blurted.

"I'm the good," six-year-old Joel declared.

"Joel, explain to us…" Marty chuckled.

"Well, if Mommy had never met Dr. Allgood and Dr. Ulid, then she wouldn't have been in the hospital in Georgia. And if Mommy had never been in the hospital in Georgia, she wouldn't have met Daddy. You see, Mommy and Daddy met—and I'm the good."

Marty's lesson came to a quick close. We spent the rest of the night celebrating the good—the creation of the Mitchell family.

Months later, Bridget called and asked me to make another trip to the courthouse—this time to jot down the complaints and bases of all suits filed against Drs. Allgood and Ulid. Not limiting my list to medical malpractice cases, as before, this time I was to make records of all cases. We included breach of contract, tax liens, fraud, and even the "diamond fraud" case filed against Dr. Allgood. Bridget also asked that I note any action pertaining to the Fletcher case.

I rearranged my schedule, summoned Jane, and headed to the courthouse. While sifting through court records and completing the list for Bridget, I decided I'd check to see if any new suits had been filed against the doctors. The clerk happily handed me the half-inch notebook that held the listing of all plaintiffs who had filed suits within the past several months. As I ran my finger down the list of names beginning with the letter *A*, I noticed that Dr. Albert Allgood's name appeared not once but twice. I paused to read the entries.

"Jane," I whispered in astonishment. "Beverly, Dr. Allgood's office manager, is suing Dr. Allgood and so are Allgood's partners."

"What for?" Jane whispered back.

"I don't know, but this is certainly a new twist."

In detective mode, I quickly filled out a file request card and submitted it to the clerk. Within minutes, Jane and I read about Dr. Allgood's not paying his rent for office space and Beverly's complaint. Beverly had filed suit accusing Dr. Allgood of wrongful termination and coercion—requiring Beverly to participate in illegal office practices in order to remain employed. I jotted down the name and phone number of her attorney and went home to call him.

The phone only rang twice before it was answered. "This is Martin Duncan. Yes, I represent Beverly Lacasto."

I spent the next few minutes introducing myself, explaining that I also was in litigation against Dr. Allgood. Thinking fast, I spoke, "Mr. Duncan, could you get a message to Beverly for me?"

Mr. Duncan gave me her number saying, "You'll need to explain to Beverly that I gave you this. She's extremely afraid of Dr. Allgood. In fact, I think I'll give her a call myself and let her know we've talked."

That night I sat down to call Beverly. I wondered if she'd even talk with me or if she believed that I was violent and a threat to her safety? One thing I was sure of—I understood the emotions surrounding Dr. Allgood's betrayal. I dialed the number and left her a message.

The next evening Beverly returned my call. Sounding like the Beverly I once knew, she spoke. "Janet, I can't believe you called me! In the message you left, you said you would pray for me. It's like you're an angel sent from God."

Beverly's voice began to tremble. "Things are really bad. I can't sleep. I cry all the time. I don't have a job. I had to leave Allgood's office. I couldn't do one more illegal thing. Janet, the day I heard him say, 'I can't fire Beverly. She knows too much—I'd have to kill her instead,' I walked away. Yet I find myself looking over my shoulder all the time."

Stunned, I didn't know what to say. I wondered if I, like Beverly, now knew too much. For seconds it was quiet. "God will help you, Beverly. Just as it's impossible for a lifeguard to rescue a man while he's fighting him in the water, you too need to relax, rest in God's arms, and allow Him to carry you to shore."

Through her sobs, Beverly tried to talk. "Janet," she stammered, "I agree. I want God to forgive me and change me."

Beverly and I talked about God's amazing grace for another ten minutes. Her tears ran freely. I didn't understand, nor did I need to understand, the reasons behind them. In Beverly's eyes, I was her heaven-sent encourager.

"Janet," she said right before I said goodbye, "there are a few things I need to tell you. Dr. Allgood has your medical records. He had your chart in the top drawer of his personal file cabinet next to his desk in his office. At one point, I took it over to Alvin Porter's office for review. I know all about your missing medical file. Dr. Allgood has no intention of ever coming clean with it. Today, my best bet would be that the file is back in Allgood's file cabinet or in his storage unit on Elmwood Avenue. Maybe your attorney could send a sheriff in to retrieve it."

"I knew my file had to be somewhere unless it had been destroyed. I'll let my attorney know about this."

"You're right. And you'll never find the x-rays—they're gone—don't know where, but they're gone. Janet, I'm so sorry for the hard time I gave you the day you came in looking for your file. I did know you, and I said I didn't. You were never violent. But Dr. Allgood made me say so. It was all part of keeping my job. Yet, I left Allgood's a few months back. I'm afraid something big is ready to go down, and because of my association and stupidity of doing the things that Allgood made me do, I'll get the blame. You know, nothing is ever Dr. Allgood's fault. It's blamed on anyone and everyone but him."

Not knowing for sure if I really wanted to know what Beverly was referring to when she shared the news, "something big is ready to go down," I paused, kept quiet, and listened.

"Someone is investigating Allgood. They found out about his medical malpractice insurance scheme and informed St. Ann's and the surgical center. That same day, rockets started flying, and Dr. Allgood lost his privileges to perform surgery. The sad thing was, Dr. Allgood didn't seem upset. He looked at me and said, 'I guess today is the day I'll go out on disability.' And he did. He had a doctor friend of his fill out a disability form, and while he no longer performs surgery, he receives $7,000 per month from his private insurance plan. Since that time, he continues to see patients for non-surgical treatment. He just doesn't get it. I think he thinks he's above the law. Whether he believes it or not, what goes around will come around, and he just hasn't been hit with his yet."

Listening to Beverly, my palms turned clammy. I knew that this someone she thought to be investigating was me. I also knew that I wasn't to mention a thing to Beverly without first clearing it with Bridget. Beverly and I ended our conversation with a promise we'd keep in touch.

That night, I fought sleep, anticipating the morning when I could talk with Bridget and Detective Forest. I was now certain that my trip to St. Ann's had brought about good because Dr. Allgood would no longer be performing surgery, and that meant he was no longer able to add another victim to his list.

So full of information, I had to slow my pace when I called Bridget the next day. "Bridget, Beverly's seen my medical chart—see, I'm not crazy. I knew that I had seen my chart!"

"Now, Janet, remember Beverly once said that you too were a threat. We can't believe everything she says verbatim. I think it would be a good idea for you to call Detective Forest and tell him what you have just told me. He'll be interested as he's been monitoring your situation and providing me 'what I need to know.' And, hey, Janet," Bridget said before she ended the call, "I think that it's neat, that of all people, God chose to use you to touch Beverly's life. We should never underestimate the creativity of our God."

*Nope, we shouldn't,* I thought as I hung up. How creative indeed—I was praying with the woman who helped to hide my medical file—the woman who said she never knew me. How truly blessed I was!

A month later Bridget called sounding apologetic, "Janet, I've got another job for you to do. Usually attorneys send a copy service or a paralegal to the courthouse to retrieve information." She then chuckled, "But you're the best service I've ever had."

Actually, Bridget knew the more jobs I had to do, the better.

"Janet," she instructed, "I need you to go back down to the courthouse and look up any progress on the Fletcher case. I'm wondering if they've set a date for trial."

That afternoon I picked up my children, and we all went for an educational ride past city hall to the halls of justice. I promised them that this would be a quick trip. They had heard about the hours Jane and I had spent in the court file room and moaned at the thought of going.

Once inside, I filled out the necessary card, and we sat down to wait for the file.

As we waited, I showed the kids the defendants' notebook. We ran through the *A's* and found nothing pertaining to Dr. Allgood.

"Mom, look up Dr. Ulid," Jason said. As suggested, I turned to the *U's*. "There he is," Jason blurted. "Good old Dr. Ulid is being sued again."

Immediately I looked closer, making sure the case Jason was referring to wasn't the Fletcher case. "*Jillian Winter v. Dr. Ryan Ulid et al*," I read. Right away, I filled out another file request card. "Kids, I have to see who is suing Dr. Ulid and why," I whispered. "This might take a few extra minutes." The three of them sat down at a long table and found a piece of paper. Together they began to play a game of Hangman that I only hoped would last half an hour or more.

Within minutes the Fletcher file was ready. I picked it up, brought it back to the table, and opened it. I wrote down the information Bridget had requested, noted no new information, and returned the file. Shortly after, Dr. Ulid's newest suit was presented to me. "This one is fresh, right off the press," the clerk said. I took the file back to the table where the kids were sitting and sat next to Jenna. I opened it and read the few pages that were there.

Jillian wasn't just suing Dr. Ulid for the same reasons I was. But she was suing his nurse, too, for the role she played —the same nurse who insisted that I couldn't have my medical records. Her words, "You can't have them! I've been told to guard your things with my life," still brought shivers through my body.

I sat and read quietly. "Mom, are you okay?" Jenna asked.

Deep inside I knew that my actions and reactions to life's trials must demonstrate my faith. I also knew that my kids were watching me very closely. What I hoped they were seeing was a mom who loved God and wasn't afraid of digging in her heels and standing up for godly principles. "Sure, I'm fine," I replied with certainty.

"Well then, why are your hands shaking like that if you're fine?" she shot back.

"I think it's the way God made me," I explained. I tried to steady my hand while I took down the same information for this case that I had recorded for others in the past. I was sure that Bridget would be asking me to make another trip to the courthouse for just this purpose.

"We accomplished a lot today," Jenna remarked on our way out to the car.

"Mom, who is Jillian? And what did Dr. Ulid do to her? Do you know, Mom? Huh?" Joel asked over and over again.

"I know Jane will be sorry that she missed this trip," Jason concluded. "Mom, you'd better call her as soon as you get home."

The following day, I met Beverly for lunch and found myself in the middle of a soap opera. "I'm in big trouble," she said. "I was involved in a money scam in which I deposited Dr. Allgood's checks into my bank account. Then in return, I gave Dr. Allgood cash. This was supposedly a scam setup so Allgood wouldn't have to pay taxes. The district attorney is investigating me, but the worse part is, I live with the chilling words of Dr. Allgood, 'I can't fire Beverly. She knows too much. I'd have to kill her!'"

"Beverly, I know I don't know all that has gone on between you and Dr. Allgood, but I do know that now is the time to pray—not panic."

Beverly gave me a hug, thanked me for lunch, and we promised to pray for each other.

---

The next few weeks crept by and Christmas was a week away. Court stipulations were filed, additional interrogatories were completed, and briefs were revised.

Finally the day of the appellate hearing arrived. Marty and I swung by to pick up my parents, and we headed to court. I felt patriotic as we entered the doors. What a privilege it was to be living in America and have another chance to seek justice.

Outside the door of the courtroom I finally met my attorney in person. "You must be Janet," Mr. Ross said as he held out his hand to shake mine.

"I am. And you must be Matthew Ross, the famous appellate attorney," I replied, and then turned to introduce Mr. Ross to Marty and my parents.

Mr. Ross was tall, over six feet, and in his early thirties. His skin was fair, and he wore small wire-rimmed glasses that made him look rather studious.

"Janet, the way I see it," Matthew said, "it's simple. This is not a difficult case to understand. I'm basically going to tell your story and answer any questions."

Twenty minutes passed and we filed into the courtroom. Marty, my parents, and I took our seats on the right, a few rows from the front. Mr. Ross stood in line to check in with the clerk while Leeza Raddock hurried through the doors and stood behind him. A gentleman soon joined Leeza, talking as if they knew each other.

Marty and I wondered why Mr. Keen had not shown up and who the gentleman was talking with Ms. Raddock. Seconds later another man walked through the doors. "There he is," I said to Marty. "I think the man who just walked in is Allgood's friend, the one Beverly told me about. If I'm right and that's Robinson, he's the guy who has been helping Dr. Allgood with his legal troubles."

"The lawyer who was disbarred?" Marty asked.

"Yep, I think that's the one. He fits Beverly's description."

He walked up to the clerk and handed her his business card. The clerk then motioned for the man to take a seat in the back of the courtroom.

The courtroom was quiet. Three judges filed through the door from the side of the room and took their seats across the front.

*God,* I pleaded one more time, *please allow the appellate judges to be shown the truth.* Ultimately I knew that God had my life and this hearing under his complete control.

*Mitchell v. Allgood et al.* was called. Matthew Ross stood and walked to the table front and center. On his right side stood Leeza Raddock and, next to her, the gentleman she had been talking to earlier. One by one, the attorneys introduced themselves to the judges. "My name is Stephen Wiley," the mystery man said. "I work with the firm Keen, Wiley, and Murdock. Mr. Keen has a large caseload, and I'll be taking Mr. Keen's place in this case and will be arguing for Dr. Ulid today along with Mrs. Raddock."

The judge in the middle greeted the three. "Who is representing Dr. Allgood?" he asked. The room remained silent. No one said a thing.

Soon the opening arguments began. Words shot back and forth between the judges and Dr. Ulid's lawyers. Mr. Wiley first stated to the court that no mistake had been made in my original surgery. Within minutes, Ms. Raddock contradicted her partner, blurting out, "Janet Hepp Mitchell knew about the mistake all along! This would cause the statute of limitations to run out a long time ago. We can all go home now," she said with assurance.

I quickly leaned close to Marty and whispered, "You know, you don't know about something—until you find out."

Marty leaned back and mouthed, "Honey, you're profound."

The judge in the middle interrupted Ms. Raddock. "Just tell me, how many angels are you trying to get to dance on the head of a pin?" he asked.

At once, the judge to my left leaned forward, almost rising from the bench. "If I were these doctors," he barked, "I would plead the fifth and run out of town!"

The drama in the courtroom intensified. Knowing this entire act was being played out because of me was hard to fathom. I expected to be nervous and scared; instead, I felt nothing. Numbly, I went through the motion of watching and waiting.

Matthew Ross calmly stated my case. "This case is simple. It's about trust. Janet Mitchell trusted Dr. Allgood and Dr. Ulid," he told the judges. The hearing soon concluded, and we all began the three-month waiting period for the written ruling.

On December 23, 1996, just two weeks after my hearing date, I received a special-delivery letter. My heart pounded as I signed for the envelope. "Thanks," I said while I closed the door and walked into the living room. This was it. I knew the court ruling within these pages would be life altering. Either I would be in great debt due to being sued by the doctors and debating whether to take my case to the California Supreme Court, or I would have won the appeal and be on my way back to the Superior Court for trial.

Luckily for me, my kids were mesmerized, watching the latest Christmas video. Taking a deep breath, I slid the paper out of the envelope and began to read:

Dear Janet Mitchell:

GOOD NEWS! The court of appeal has reversed the judgment. A copy of the opinion is enclosed. The court concluded that
there is an issue of fact as to whether
the statute of limitations was tolled due
to the physicians' fraud and concealment.

```
    I am very happy for you and am pleased
to have been able to argue on your behalf.
Best wishes for a joyous Christmas!

Very truly yours,
Matthew K. Ross
```

God had given me an incredible Christmas present, using extraordinary means to carry out his will. The Court of Appeals of the State of California had reversed the Superior Court's judgment in the case of *Mitchell v. Allgood et al.* I had won!

*Chapter Sixteen*

# BACK ON TRACK

I WAS STILL ON A HIGH from winning my appeal and doubted I'd ever come down. The sting of my past court defeats eased, and I was ready to continue my litigation. Yet it wasn't long until Dr. Allgood played his next hand—filing for bankruptcy a *third* time. Again this placed a "stay" on all legal proceedings pertaining to him—my lawsuit included.

"What goes around comes around." I sighed into the phone. "Jane, Dr. Allgood filed for bankruptcy—again. This time it's not the same type as his last two. He's gone from filing Chapter 13 to filing a Chapter 7."

"What's the difference?"

"In 1994 and in 1995, Allgood filed Chapter 13. Both times a stay was placed on my court proceedings, and I couldn't go forward in litigation against him. Both times, just before his bankruptcy was granted, he sought a discharge, meaning he withdrew his request. People file Chapter 13 when they intend to eventually repay their debts. I'm told all property is kept and the debtor is given three to five years to pay up, using his own income. Chapter 7 is filed when someone wants to wipe out all their debt. It takes no more than half a year and usually takes only one trip to the courthouse to accomplish it."

"Janet, aren't there some rules about this? Can a person play with the court system, continually filing for bankruptcy, then seeking a discharge?"

"Guess so."

"Is there some time limit in filing a Chapter 7 after filing a Chapter 13?"

"Nope. Just as quick as you can blow-dry your hair, as long as the Chapter 13 was withdrawn. Otherwise, it's a six-year wait. Listen, Jane. I've spent the last few hours reviewing Dr. Allgood's submitted petition for Chapter 7, and guess who's listed at the bottom of a page."

"No clue."

"Alvin Porter, attorney at law—duped for a measly $7,069.50."

"You're kidding! Wonder what the fifty cents is for. Remember Mr. Porter wrote he 'begged, borrowed and stole your records' so he could keep his costs down."

"I don't know, but I do know that my attorney fees are mountains higher than his. Yet I only have to pay them out of my winnings— unless, of course, I lose and end up paying the attorney fees for the doctors."

"So, who else has the good old doc included in his bankruptcy?"

"I'm not sure how to read these, but I see a total of over $200,000 listed to the Internal Revenue Service alone. He's got a few other lawsuits listed here from other counties. One's for $23,000 and another for $900. Here's one the plaintiff won, and it's for an estimated $225,000. Dr. Allgood says he sold his country club membership for a grand total of $25,575. 'Impossible,' I was told when I called the country club. 'Memberships are going for well over $100,000.' Yet Dr. Allgood turns around and spends this money, not paying his debtors but for 'bilateral eye connection surgery' for his wife."

"What?" Jane laughed. "I'm a nurse, and I've never heard of this type of surgery."

"I know. I called the physician listed adjacent to the costs. Donna Allgood must have had a plastic surgeon touch up her eyes. At least that's what I was told."

"How's your name listed, Janet? What amount is he exactly trying to discharge?"

"I'm listed all right. I find it absolutely absurd that it's legal for Dr. Allgood to list my name and beside it, in the column stating the amount of claim, he's typed 'unknown.' Dr. Allgood doesn't even know for sure if he owes me or what he owes me, and he's asked for protection under the law."

"Calm down, Janet. Breathe. This is only a petition for bankruptcy. It doesn't mean it will be granted."

"I bet Alvin Porter hopes it's not."

"I think you can rest assured that Alvin Porter won't be reentering your life or representing Dr. Allgood at trial. In fact, maybe he'll come just to watch Dr. Allgood's performance of the century—questioning himself while on the stand."

Late one afternoon a week or so later, the kids were doing their homework and I was sorting laundry when the doorbell rang. Joel raced me to the door and waited like a soldier until I got there to open it. There on my front porch stood a tall, slender woman holding a piece of paper. "My name is Donna Allgood. Are you Janet Hepp Mitchell?"

"I... I am Janet," I said, trying to corral Joel inside the house.

"Mrs. Mitchell, you're presently in a lawsuit against my husband, Albert Allgood. As you know, Albert is representing himself concerning the bankruptcy. He asked me to come by your house and ask you to sign this piece of paper."

I quickly glanced at the paper, noting just a sentence or two with a line for a signature. "Is there a first page to this document? Just what is this? What do you want me to sign?"

"It's a letter to Judge Mayfield, the bankruptcy judge. Albert needs to ask for a continuance regarding the upcoming bankruptcy hearing."

If it truly was a request for a continuance, why didn't Dr. Allgood mail it to my attorneys? "I'm sorry, Mrs. Allgood, but I can't sign anything without contacting my attorney."

"You have an attorney?" she asked, sounding surprised.

"Yes, I do. If you excuse me for a moment, I'll give her a call."

I stepped back inside the house, leaving the door slightly ajar. "What are you going to do, Mom?" Jason asked.

"I'm going to call Bridget and do whatever she tells me to do," I said calmly.

While I placed the call, Jenna grabbed my cell phone and put in a call to Marty. "Dad, Mrs. Allgood is at our door. She gave Mom an almost blank piece of paper with an *X* and a line by it. She wants Mom to put her signature on the line. Mom's on the phone now trying to call Bridget." Jenna informed her father of each movement I made and repeated to him each word I said.

Joel again stood guard by the door while whispering so all could hear, "Mom, is this the woman you're suing?"

Bridget wasn't at work and was not answering her cell phone. The secretary at Duncan, Ball and Evans asked me to remain on the line while they contacted an attorney who could provide immediate counsel.

Within minutes I heard, "Hey, Janet. This is John Ball. Let me get this right. Who's at your door?"

"Mrs. Allgood," I said in a frantic whisper. "And she's still standing there!"

"Janet, don't sign a thing. But I want you to get a copy of the paper she is holding and ask her to give you the first page of the letter so you can see what it is and copy it too. I'll hold on while you see if she has 'page one' with her."

I set the phone down and returned to the door. "Mrs. Allgood," I said, "my attorney would like me to make a copy of the paper requiring my signature and fax it to him. He would also like me to get a copy of the first page. Do you have it with you?"

Mrs. Allgood returned to her car to look while I tried to figure out how to make copies, as I did not own a copier. My quick thinking paid off. My neighbor to the right had a copier, yet she wasn't home. My neighbor to the left knew how to use our neighbor's copier, and I had a key that would let us in. Mrs. Allgood found "page one" and like a parade, Jenna—still on the cell phone—Jason, Joel, my neighbor, and I marched next door to make copies.

"I've got them," I announced to Mr. Ball back on the phone. "I'm faxing them to you as we speak." Music played while I was placed on hold, and Mrs. Allgood walked back to her car and leaned against the door. Several minutes passed before Mr. Ball picked up the phone.

"If Dr. Allgood is truly asking for a continuance, fine—and if not, I'm sure we'll see this paper again." He gave me the go-ahead to sign the document. "And Janet," Mr. Ball added right before we said goodbye, "it's great to finally put a voice with your case. I've been consulting on it from the start. I'm behind you, girl."

Upon hearing John Ball's words, "I'm behind you, girl," I quickly gave way to my emotions. Feeling grateful that a firm known for defending doctors had taken a stand for me, I sat tearfully trying to find the words to thank him.

Days later, I was relaxing on the couch, munching on popcorn, when Joel ran in with the mail. After separating the ads from the bills, I noticed a letter from Duncan, Ball and Evans.

Opening it, I read the letter once and then again. Cheering as if I had won a sweepstakes, I immediately called Marty at work. "Marty," I squealed. "Alvin Porter tossed in the towel for good! He quit. He won't be coming back at all. Dr. Allgood had to find himself a new attorney. And guess who he picked?"

"Slow down, Janet. Start from the beginning..."

"Okay," I said and took a deep breath. "Today I received a letter from Bridget's law firm. Enclosed was a copy of a letter written to them from Mr. Porter. The greatest part of the letter is when Porter states, 'I am no longer representing Dr. Allgood in *Mitchell v. Allgood*. Dr. Allgood and I have not made our peace on fees for my service, and I am quite allergic to representing bare doctors on open credit.'"

"How ironic," Marty chuckled. "Dr. Allgood needs a new lawyer. Maybe he should try paying the next guy he hires."

"Well he got one—himself!"

"Janet, you've got to be kidding. Dr. Allgood's going to represent himself? Through trial?"

"That's what Mr. Porter says."

"This I've got to see!" Marty concluded.

---

A month later, it was the day before Beverly Lacasto's arraignment. She had been arrested and bail had been set. Yet tomorrow, she would be formally charged with a crime. Marty and I had taken our boys out of school for the week, sending them on a trip with my parents. Jenna stayed home with us as she had been waiting for months for her appointment at the hospital with the diabetic team.

The morning of Beverly's arraignment, Jenna and I awakened early since she had to be at the hospital by 7:00 a.m. for her blood work. Afterward, I planned to take her to school and then swing by to pick up my neighbor Lorraine. Jane had recently moved to northern

California, Marty was working, and my dad was on "vacation," so Lorraine had offered to accompany me to the courthouse.

Jenna gave blood without a flinch. Then we hopped into our van, I started the engine, and I pulled out far enough to know we had trouble. Within seconds, Jenna and I were standing outside the van looking at the flattest tire we'd ever seen. I quickly phoned the automobile club, and they came to save two damsels in distress.

"I don't know who doesn't want you going where," the tow-truck driver spat out. "But, ma'am, I do believe that someone has slashed your tire. We best call the hospital security."

"Mamma," Jenna said under her breath. "Maybe you shouldn't go to court today. Maybe this kind man should just tow us home."

"You'll think up almost anything to stay home from school," I teased Jenna, trying to lighten the moment.

Half an hour later Jenna and I sat at a tire shop watching the van being hoisted high while a young man mounted a new tire.

"A few more minutes and I should be done," he said. "If it wasn't an ice pick, you had to have picked up a nail, and a mighty long one at that."

Late and a tad shaken, I dropped Jenna off at school and headed to Lorraine's. Without a minute to spare, we entered the courtroom and sat behind Beverly's family and friends.

*Where's Dr. Allgood?* I wondered as I quickly scanned the room.

"Janet," a voice whispered, "remember me? I'm Elaine. I was Dr. Allgood's nurse during the years you had your surgeries. I haven't seen you in years. I retired several years ago, but I've kept in touch with the gals in the office and the other docs. I've been following your case—unbelievable. I hope you get him. Janet, you know Dr. Allgood thinks he's above the law!"

The doors of the courtroom then swung open. In late but fashionable style, Donna Allgood entered, followed by Dr. Allgood and the district attorney. Within seconds, all three had filed straight past my seat, making their way to the front. Mrs. Allgood glanced my way and then took a double take as if she had just placed me. Dr. Allgood caught my eye. He glared with his lips pulled tight as he walked by, clearly provoked by my presence.

I returned a slight smile in exchange for his piercing stare. This was the first time I had seen Dr. Allgood since I had won the appeal. In fact, five or more years had passed since I'd seen him dancing through his deposition.

The court came to order. Judge Joseph P. Simmons called Beverly to the podium placed front and center. Beverly had opted not to have a jury trial, meaning she had chosen to be tried by a judge rather than a jury of her peers. Right away I recognized that Judge Joseph P. Simmons was very different from Judge Joseph Anthony Higgins, who had granted Dr. Allgood's Motion of Summary Judgment. The kindness, compassion, and respect Judge Simmons demonstrated was a definite contrast to the former judge's abruptness and lack of compassion.

"Beverly Lacasto, you are aware of the charges filed against you. How do you wish to plea?"

The courtroom was silent. Tension filled the room. Looking down at the floor, Beverly answered with hesitation and a sigh, "Guilty, Your Honor."

"Mrs. Lacasto, do you understand the implications of a guilty plea?"

"I think so," Beverly said timidly.

"I'd like to give you the opportunity to withdraw your guilty plea and replace it with *nolo contendere*."

Beverly's attorneys requested that they be given time to confer with their client. For the next few moments Lorraine and I tried to overhear her lawyer's explanations. "A guilty plea means you're admitting fault to the charges," Beverly's attorney explained. "*Nolo contendere* means that you're not admitting fault but that you're not contesting the charges either."

The emergency conference concluded, and Beverly moved back to the podium. "*Nolo contendere,*" she confidently announced. "I plead *nolo contendere.*"

It was strange. Court was not what I had envisioned. There was no jury, no great deliberations, not even a motion or two. After additional statements by the judge, a few words by Beverly's lawyer, and a mouthful from the district attorney, witnesses were called on Beverly's behalf.

Elaine walked to the podium and paused to gather her composure. She licked her bottom lip while she gazed somberly around the courtroom. After one last stare at the doctor who had employed her for more than a decade, she recited her declaration:

Your Honor, I have known Beverly Lacasto since May of 1979. We worked together in a doctor's office with several physicians, Dr. Allgood and Dr. Ulid to name a few. I was the office nurse and Beverly was the office manager. I have been asked to come today and share with you information about the environment in which I worked.

I found it very difficult working for Dr. Allgood. His office staff was constantly riding the wave of his personal life while trying to perform their jobs. It seemed that Dr. Allgood always had a deal in the works that was going to close on Friday.

At one point, Dr. Allgood invested in a silver mine in Idaho. He told us that we would be getting shares in the mine. It was supposed to be a big producer of silver, yet we never saw our shares.

Another venture we rode was when Dr. Allgood insisted on keeping a *lot* of loose diamonds in the office safe. Believe me, this caused many tense moments. Part of Beverly's new job description was to photocopy all the certificates for each stone. In fact, Beverly was often expected to perform tasks which she was not comfortable doing.

Years back, Dr. Allgood invested in some boxers—boxing at the stadium. We saw them as patients for physicals and injuries. Dr. Allgood had Beverly sign a document as Donna Allgood and then took Beverly to the fight as his wife.

Beverly did a lot of things that she was uncomfortable doing and was constantly forced to smooth things over with the other docs in the practice when Dr. Allgood couldn't pay. There were numerous times Dr. Allgood didn't have money in his account to meet payroll. Beverly would make daily trips to the bank with checks from the day's mail. I am aware that Beverly even worked with no salary for a few months. She's even told me that her husband loaned Dr. Allgood money on a few occasions. The other doctors in the practice finally got tired of Dr. Allgood's excuses and prom-

ises never kept and asked Dr. Allgood to
leave. It's been in the last year or so
that Dr. Allgood took Beverly with him and
joined a walk-in clinic.

I longed for Elaine to tell the judge that Dr. Allgood filed for bankruptcy and included his $15,000 debt owed to his partners. I wanted him to know that Allgood's total liabilities listed in his bankruptcy, excluding the amounts "unknown," were listed at $1,135,371.89.

When Elaine returned to her seat, Beverly's daughter made her way to the podium. Full of confidence, she engulfed herself in her mother's defense.

The judge never wavered. He sat intently listening to the monologue taking place before him. When Beverly's daughter returned to her seat, the judge leaned forward, folding his hands. "This trial is not about Dr. Allgood and his wrongdoing. That would be for a different court at a different time. Today we are here to address the state's charges against Beverly Lacasto for the embezzlement of Dr. Allgood's funds. Beverly has pleaded *nolo contendere*, and I hereby deem this court concluded for the day."

Looking directly at Beverly, the judge added one last detail, "Beverly, you will return to this court February 7, 1996, at 9:00 a.m. for sentencing."

Like that, it was over. Beverly was certain to be spending some time in jail. She could get up to seven years for the charges against her. Though she swore that she was not guilty of all the charges, she had taken responsibility for those she admitted to and would be paying her debt to society. She would also be forced to reimburse Dr. Allgood from her monthly prison earnings, whatever they might be.

Dr. Allgood left the court all smiles but with a glare sent in my direction. I'm sure Dr. Allgood felt that Beverly had robbed him, but it appeared that he found great pleasure in being "redeemed."

One afternoon the following week, I got a phone call. "Say, Janet, this is John Ball from Duncan, Ball and Evans. I've got some news to share with you. Bridget's had a family emergency, and she had to take a leave of absence from the firm. I'll be taking over your case and taking it to trial. As you know, Bridget had planned to fly down early tomorrow morning to represent you in bankruptcy court regarding Dr. Allgood's bankruptcy. She can't and something has come up, so I can't come either. I'm required to be in court up here in Sacramento tomorrow."

"Well, what am I supposed to do?" I asked perplexed.

"Janet, I'm going to fax you a paper. This paper is what we call a Substitution of Attorney. You must file it first thing tomorrow morning. It will allow you to substitute as your own attorney, and then you can ask for a continuance."

"A continuance?"

"Don't be worried," Mr. Ball counseled. "Tomorrow, go to court and state to Judge Mayfield you're appearing to request a continuance, a time extension. Explain that I was required to be in court in Sacramento. Judge Mayfield will understand that I cannot be in two places at once. Janet, if I didn't believe you were capable, I wouldn't be asking you to do this."

"But, Mr. Ball, who is Judge Mayfield? What do you know about him?"

"First of all, he's a she. Her name is Judge Ruby Mayfield. Otherwise known as Your Honor. Truthfully, I knew nothing about her until I placed some calls to law firms down by you. I'm told she's the perfect judge for you to appear before. She's kind, sensitive, and firm."

My heart sank at the thought of representing myself. I remembered the piercing stare Dr. Allgood sent my way at Beverly's arraignment.

*Only a fool hires himself as his own attorney,* I thought. I guess I was one step ahead. I'd not hired myself, but was assigned to the task.

Moments after I ended my conversation with Mr. Ball, I called my dad to inform him of my new assignment. Trying to sound upbeat about the matter, I asked, "Are you ready, Dad? Marty has an important meeting at work tomorrow. Can you escort me to court?"

"Sure," he said then questioned me about the whys.

Next, in not such an optimistic tone, I called Norm Wright. "I don't think I can do this," I confessed. "Norm, I don't even know which side of the courtroom I should stand on, much less how to address the judge or know when to sit or stand. I'm not sure that I'm ready to face Dr. Allgood without representation. Remember he, too, will be there representing himself."

"First of all, Janet, you can do this! Scripture says you can do all things through Christ who strengthens you. It's your responsibility to obey what you feel God has asked you to do. It's Christ's responsibility to strengthen you. Quit looking to find courage and strength within yourself. Start expecting Christ to supply it to you, and at just the right time."

"Well, don't you think now's the time?"

"Janet, the time will be the moment you walk through the courtroom doors."

Somewhat hoping that Norm would give me permission not to show up the following morning, I quieted down and listened.

"Now for the logistics," he said. "Don't go alone. When you get there, explain your situation to the clerk of the court. I'm sure you're not the first person this has happened to. The court is well prepared for such an occasion. When you see Dr. Allgood, don't look him in the eye. Keep your eyes focused on the judge. Allow the doctor to choose his side of the courtroom and take his seat. You obviously take the other side. Janet, don't give Dr. Allgood an opportunity to intimidate you. You have to stand firm and fight this bankruptcy. You cannot just walk away, allowing the doctor to get away with what he has done. Janet, God will be with you, and remember, he will strengthen you—at just the right time."

Knowing that the right time would be nine o'clock the following morning, I listened to my last-minute instructions and thanked Norm for being available to talk with me. I made dinner, then gathered every important document pertaining to my case that I could find. I tucked the pages into a manila file folder and set them by my purse to take to court. Marty cleaned the dishes and helped the kids with their homework, sending me upstairs for a relaxing bath. *God,* I prayed while soaking in bubbles, *thanks for promising me that you'll meet my every need. And tomorrow, I'll be counting on your strength and wisdom.*

The moment I prayed, James 1:5 came to mind, "If any of you needs wisdom to know what you should do, you should ask God, and he will give it to you. God is generous to everyone and doesn't find fault with them." I can ask God for wisdom in how to handle my situation, and he will give it to me. I needed to doubt my doubts, forget my feelings, and pray for wisdom.

The morning came, and my father and I were off to the courthouse. We got there early to file the proper paperwork informing the court that I was temporarily representing myself. The court clerk was more than helpful. She listened to my predicament and gave me directions as to where to file my Substitution of Attorney. Minutes later we made our way back up the elevator and into the courtroom.

The court clerk motioned for us to take seats to the right with several others who had cases being heard. Five or so minutes passed before the courtroom doors opened again. I turned my head far enough to see that it was Dr. Allgood entering.

Judge Mayfield made her appearance. Her gray hair shone in a tightly knotted bun. Promptly, she took her seat and called the court to order. "Good morning, Ladies and Gentlemen. I'd like to welcome you to my courtroom," she greeted. One by one, Judge Mayfield called cases to appear before her. Each one was short and to the point, apprising her on the progress of the lawsuit they represented.

"Case number nine, *Mitchell v. Allgood*," Judge Mayfield called.

Immediately I stood with my file folder in hand. Pausing for a moment or two, I allowed Dr. Allgood to make his way to the front of the courtroom and take his position on the left side of a bar-height table. The judge motioned for me to follow Dr. Allgood, and so there we were, plaintiff and defendant, standing side by side in Federal Bankruptcy Court.

"Mrs. Mitchell, I have seen your Substitution of Attorney and understand it's your desire to ask for a continuance. I will grant you this request, yet I would like you to state your position pertaining to Dr. Allgood's bankruptcy."

It was twenty minutes past nine, and God wasn't a minute late! Confidently, I addressed the judge while Dr. Allgood stood silently staring off into the air.

"Your Honor, in 1992, I filed a lawsuit against Dr. Allgood. This suit was for professional negligence, negligent misrepresentation, fraud, and concealment. I believe I have proof to convince a jury that Dr. Allgood concealed facts pertaining to my medical care. In 1994, a Motion for Summary Judgment was granted in Dr. Allgood's behalf. In 1995, Dr. Allgood filed for bankruptcy in your court and included his possible upcoming debt owed to me, if I did indeed win my suit. This bankruptcy froze all of Dr. Allgood's other legal proceedings, making it necessary for my attorney to obtain your permission to proceed with an appeal. When permission was granted, Dr. Allgood asked you for a dismissal of his bankruptcy, and it was granted.

"In 1996, the Fourth District Appellate Court overruled Dr. Allgood's Motion of Summary Judgment and granted me the right to sue. Shortly after, Dr. Allgood again filed for bankruptcy, including my name, thus placing a stay on all his legal proceedings and preventing me from going forward in litigation against him. Today I am requesting that you withhold my name from Dr. Allgood's bankruptcy, allowing me to return to Superior Court to obtain a verdict."

Nodding as if she understood my reasoning and request, Judge Mayfield looked to Dr. Allgood and asked for his response.

"Judge Mayfield," Dr. Allgood replied, "I find no reason for you to grant Janet's request of removing her name from my bankruptcy. I have filed for bankruptcy within the provisions of the law and feel that you need to approve my request. "

"Dr. Allgood," Judge Mayfield addressed. "I believe you need to remove the 'stay' and allow Janet to proceed in her suit against you."

"I'm not going to do that," he exploded. "Why would I do this?"

Sternly Judge Mayfield articulated her words. "Dr. Allgood, I suggest you remove the stay on Janet's civil case, thus permitting her to proceed against you in civil court."

"And what if I don't?"

Immediately Judge Mayfield's eyebrows rose. Maintaining her tactful manner, she spoke. "Dr. Allgood, if you do not remove the stay and allow *Mitchell v. Allgood* to go forward, then you will be sued in state court and in federal court!"

And with that, she thanked me for my time and instructed me to return to her court when a verdict had been reached. I was once again back on track and off to trial!

"Dad, what did she mean?" I whispered. "How would Dr. Allgood be sued in state and federal court? Would I be suing him?"

"I have no idea, Janet, you fooled me. I thought you knew exactly what Judge Mayfield was talking about."

We waited until the courtroom was almost empty before we left. We wanted Dr. Allgood to be gone before we made our exit. My dad pushed the door to the courtroom open, and to our surprise, Dr. Allgood grabbed the door, holding it open for us to walk through.

"I'm going to sue you!" he hollered, waving his arms at me. "Janet Hepp Mitchell, I'm going to sue you in state and federal court. I'm going to sue you for all you have!"

At once my father and I walked back into the safety of the courtroom. The court clerk had heard the commotion and called for an officer. Dr. Allgood went on his way.

"I bet you're ready for lunch," my dad said as we waited, giving the doctor a few moments to find his car.

"Well, if you're not in a hurry, can we stop by the file room in the Superior Court?"

We walked out of the building and into the next, down a long hall to the last room on the right. I went to the clerk's window, filled out request cards for the two cases, and gave them to the clerk.

"So this is where you and Jane have spent hours snooping through files. This is the room that holds the evidence," my dad teased.

My father followed me over to the table holding the "who's suing who" notebooks. I pulled out the large notebook that listed defendants whose names started with *T-W* sued during the past ten years or so. Turning the pages to the back of the book, I found the letter *U.* "Here it is, Dad. Look how many times Dr. Ulid has been sued," I said in a whisper.

"Gee whiz, Janet, that's about twenty-something too many." My dad ran his index finger down the list. "What about this case, Janet? What happened to Mr. Anderson?"

"I'm not sure what the outcome was. The last time Jane and I were here, they couldn't find the file. I do know it's a medical malpractice case."

"Can we check on it now? Let's see if they've found it."

I filled out another request card and waited. Meanwhile, my father played detective, looking up Dr. Allgood's name in the defendant's books. He even looked up his own name. "Nope, my name's not listed," he said jokingly as I returned with one file. "Where's the Anderson case? You went for three files and came back with one."

"The Winter case is dismissed. I think they settled."

"Well, where's the other one?"

"It's gone."

"It's gone? Where? How?" my dad quizzed, assuming I knew the answers.

"The entire file has been discarded," I said disgustedly.

"How can that be?" my dad fired back.

"Easy," I said taking a small piece of paper from my pocket. The clerk wrote it down for me. "Government code GC 68152 provides for the destruction of case files that have been settled or dismissed. Jillian Winter's file will probably be the next to go. Dad, this makes me so angry! People can't even depend on court files when they need to check out a prospective doctor. When someone settles a medical malpractice case, the details of what happened to them just disappear. It's not always chiseled in stone at the medical board or here at the courthouse for all to see!" I ranted in a rare public display of anger.

"Janet, calm down," my dad said, placing his hand on mine. "Maybe we need to go somewhere to eat lunch and leave the Fletcher file for later."

When I convinced him that I was okay, mad but "okay," my dad agreed to stay a few more minutes and read of any recent happenings in the Fletcher case.

First, we noted that the Fletchers' motion for punitive damages had been granted. These damages were awarded with the intent to punish someone for an intentional or malicious act.

"Dad, look. Their trial is set for February 16, 1999. Mine is to start February 14. How can Dr. Ulid have two trials running at the same time?"

"I have no idea. But I wouldn't want to have both of you women after me, especially during the same month!" He chuckled.

Reading on, we were stunned. The lawyers for the Fletchers had served defendant Ryan Ulid with a "Request for Admissions." After taking a deep breath, my dad began to read to me in a whisper:

> The Requests for Admissions are very specific to the allegations of this action. Note the following:
>
> REQUEST NO. 1:
> Admit that you, (Defendant Ulid) were aware of prior complaints concerning the medical competency of Defendant Dr. Charles Wilcox before the death of Henry Fletcher.
>
> REQUEST NO. 2:
> Admit that immediately following the death of Henry Fletcher, defendants Ulid and Wilcox had a physical altercation outside the surgical suites.
>
> REQUEST NO. 3:
> Admit that immediately following the death of Henry Fletcher, defendant Dr. Ulid verbally threatened to kill defendant Dr. Wilcox.

REQUEST NO. 4:
Admit that at the time of signing the death certificate of Henry Fletcher, there was no reasonable medical belief that Mr. Fletcher's demise was a result of a "pulmonary embolism."

REQUEST NO. 5:
Admit that the failure to inform Carolyn Fletcher that Henry Fletcher's death was not a result of a pulmonary embolism was a breach of your (Dr. Ulid's) fiduciary duty.

REQUEST NO. 6:
Admit that you (Dr. Ulid) knew, prior to August 11, 1993, that Defendant Charles Wilcox was referred to as "the murderer."

REQUEST NO. 7:
Admit that you (Dr. Ulid) refused to work with Charles Wilcox prior to August 11, 1993.

REQUEST NO. 8:
Admit that you (Dr. Ulid) questioned defendant Dr. Charles Wilcox's medical competency prior to August 11, 1993.

These requests for admissions are clearly designed to narrow the issues in this case. Plaintiff's request is an easy one—admit or deny.

It is apparent that the requests for admissions are "reasonably calculated to lead

```
to the discovery of admissible evidence"
as they ask for an admission of facts that
will be used...
```

"We've read enough!" my dad fumed and closed the file. Obviously shaken, he steepled his hands against his chin and looked off into the distance. "Janet, we're leaving." Abruptly he rose to his feet to return the file. He stopped and turned his head. "Are you coming?"

I sat frozen to my chair, with tears streaming down my face. "Dad," I cried, forgetting to whisper. "This says that Dr. Ulid knew of the complaints concerning Charles Wilcox's medical competency. He knew Wilcox was known at the hospital as 'the murderer.' He had refused to work with Dr. Wilcox until August 11, 1993—the day Mr. Fletcher died. Why did he have to pick that day to say it was okay? Don't you see, Dad? Mr. Fletcher would still be alive if they had checked his blood count prior to surgery."

"No, Janet, you're wrong," my dad said, placing his arm around my shoulder. "Mr. Fletcher's death was evidently the fault of many. St. Ann's 'made mistakes,' Dr. Ulid 'messed up,' and Mr. Fletcher had 'the murderer' on his case."

I was certain my dad and I had created a scene in the file room. A room that displayed no wallpaper or pictures held enough visualization and excitement of its own.

"Come on, honey. Let's go."

With a slight wave to our spectators, I grabbed my file and purse and followed my dad out the door.

*Chapter Seventeen*

# STANDING FIRM

I WASN'T SURE WHY I'd signed up for the women's retreat, except for a strong feeling that I was supposed to be there. With Annette working full time and Jane living so far away, I figured it was time to let down the wall I had carefully constructed around myself and interact with people.

Agnes, Marty's mom, flew in the morning I was to leave. "It's only you and the roosters that would get up this early," I chatted as I picked her up at the airport. We spent the day together, stopping to get breakfast and shopping at the mall. After we picked up the kids from school, I jumped in the church van heading to the mountains for the women's retreat. *God, what am I doing here?* I prayed. I wasn't sure I was ready to be around so many people.

That first evening I ate dinner with the ladies and then excused myself to find a pay phone to call home. "Marty, what am I doing here?" I cried, trying not to be noticed by the women standing nearby.

"If you don't know, you can come home."

"Marty, I just know I'm supposed to be here, but I don't know why."

Marty tried to comfort me. He then promised to come and rescue me on a moment's notice. We said our goodbyes, I hung up the phone, and I returned to my room.

The next morning I woke up rested and ready for the day. On my way to breakfast I passed a group of women in the hall.

"Say, Janet," one woman called out, "I'm Marjorie Day. You contacted me and my law firm several years ago regarding a med-mal case. How did it turn out?"

I remembered Marjorie. I'd taken the drawing that Dr. Ulid drew of my knee to her. She was interested in my case, yet at the time, she couldn't represent me due to a conflict of interest. She was involved in litigation where Dr. Ulid was an expert.

"My case is heading for trial in a couple of weeks," I said shyly.

"What? You're just getting to trial? What's taken so long?" Marjorie asked, moving closer to provide for a more private conversation.

"I won my appeal December of 1996, and it's taken almost two years to get a court date."

"An appeal? You've been to the appellate court? Oh, my dear girl."

The next few minutes I gave Marjorie a quick synopsis of my case.

"Unbelievable," she uttered more than once. "Who is representing you, Janet?"

"Duncan, Ball and Evans."

"Who are they?" she said with uncertainty. "I can't place them."

"They aren't from around here. They're a defense firm in Sacramento. They're looking for a local firm to work with them and help try my case."

Laying her hand on my shoulder, Marjorie spoke softly. "Janet, you call my office Monday morning. I'd like to speak with your attorney."

"Sure," I replied.

Marjorie looked the same as when I first met her six years earlier. Her petite stature, blonde hair, and poise make her quite an impressive lady. From what I could remember, Marjorie had been practicing law for about thirty years. To date, her most legendary case was in

1984, when she won the largest verdict in the history of California at that time.

*God,* I prayed, *If you want Marjorie to be involved with my case, and if you want me to call her Monday morning, please confirm this to me. Then I'll know you're behind the plan.*

The next morning I got up, packed my things, and headed to breakfast. There was no Marjorie Day waiting for me in the hallway. I ventured to the dining hall, ate with the gals, and noticed that Marjorie was nowhere to be seen. Maybe she had left early and gone home.

Later, I took a seat near the back of the room for the last morning worship service. Glancing around, I spotted Marjorie off to my right, singing praises to God. Many women rose and shared their testimonies while I sat as if I were glued to my chair. After additional songs and a devotional, the weekend was brought to a close. Women stood or moved about the room, arranging transportation, and saying their goodbyes.

I made my way across the room to exit when I felt a hand grab my arm. It was Marjorie. She put her hand on my shoulder, shaking me gently. "Now, Janet, remember, you're going to call me first thing tomorrow morning."

That was just the confirmation I needed.

As I sat near my telephone Monday morning waiting until the law office opened to call, my phone rang. "Say, Janet, this is Marjorie Day. I've just had a wonderful chat with Bridget."

"Bridget?"

"Yes, I phoned the office and spoke to John Ball. He then gave me Bridget's home number. John said, 'If you're interested in the Mitchell case, you need to talk with Bridget. She knows this case inside and out.' Bridget gave me an update and told me about your bumps and hurdles to trial. Sounds painful," Marjorie said with a chuckle. "Janet, I've told Bridget I'd like to try your case with her firm. Is this all right with you?"

"All right with me? It's more than all right. It's wonderful!"

We talked a few more minutes and set a date to get together to discuss my case. We said goodbye, and I phoned my dad.

"Dad," I hollered through the telephone receiver. "I've got myself a plaintiff attorney and a defense attorney to represent me at trial. What could be better than one of each?"

"How did you accomplish this, Janet?"

"I didn't find her. God brought her to me," I answered and then told him about the retreat.

"You mean Marjorie Day, the elder from our church?"

"Yep. I mean Marjorie Day, elder at church, attorney at law, and friend of the needy."

A couple of days later I stood at the doors of the Day and Day Law Firm. Once inside, I was greeted by Marjorie, who led me up the stairs to a large conference room. "That's my desk over there." She pointed to the corner. "I gave my office to my son Chris when he took over my practice, so I sit up here," she said happily. "I'm seventy-six years old and basically retired, yet I still piddle around finding odds and ends to put my fingers into."

"Would you classify my case in the odd section?" I joked.

"Janet, in all my years of litigation, I don't think I've represented a more worthy cause. I thought I had tried my last case. It'd have to be something remarkable to keep me off the golf courses and sitting in this chair."

Changing the subject, Marjorie told me of her morning conversation with John Ball. "I told him I'd need a couple of months to pull things together at my end." John agreed and took care of getting us a new trial date."

"So when's the date?"

"March fifteenth," Marjorie replied. "It's not the two months that I asked for, but we'll be ready."

For the next several hours Marjorie and I worked. She wrote as I talked. I presented her with my three four-inch notebooks that held every correspondence, motion, and paper pertaining to my case. We reviewed copies of my medical records. Page by page, hour by hour, and day by day we sat and prepared for trial.

"Janet," Marjorie said when she called a week later. "We've got to line up our experts for trial. Is Norm Wright available if we need to call him to the stand?"

"I see him on Thursday. I can ask him, but I'm sure he is."

"I'd like to find a local medical expert to testify. There's no reason to import the expert from Sacramento if we can find one down here."

"And don't forget we have the videotape of Dr. Hughston's deposition," I added. "Too bad he's not physically up to coming."

"Janet, I plan to call Jackie from the rehabilitation center. I can't wait for the jury to hear the results from her week-long evaluation of you. 'Tough poise' were her exact words."

Following Marjorie's directions, I wrote down the name and address of the doctor she wanted me to see. "Dr. Lewis is a local doctor whom I've used several times when needing an expert witness. In fact, I've made you an appointment," she said. "I'll be out of town that day, but I'm sure you can handle the appointment alone. I've sent him a letter explaining your case. You just need to show up and let the doctor take a look."

I arrived a few minutes early to my assigned appointment with Dr. Lewis. Within minutes he entered the room, closed the door, and took a seat. Without any eye contact he spoke. "Mrs. Mitchell, I understand you're in a lawsuit involving Drs. Ulid and Allgood."

"Yes, sir, I am."

Dr. Lewis stood and stepped up to the examining table. There I sat wearing a pair of rolled-up sweats with my legs dangling off the side. He picked up my right leg and looked it over. Placing his hand in his pocket, he drew out a measuring tape and measured each and every scar.

"Stand up for me, please. Does your knee go out on you, collapse, or slip?"

I answered yes to all the above. The doctor continued to examine the instability of my knee. "Are you in therapy?" he asked.

"Yes, sir, physical therapy three times per week," I replied.

When he was finished, he fiercely recorded all of his measurements, jotted down some additional notes, and placed his hand on the doorknob to leave.

Turning so that I could see his icy stare, he announced, "I know Dr. Ulid, and you have no business suing him or Dr. Allgood. Good day, Mrs. Mitchell."

Marjorie had told this doctor about my case and the names of the doctors I was suing, so I wondered why he even agreed to see me since he felt this way. Maybe he just wanted to see me for himself.

"Janet," Marjorie said when I answered the phone the following morning, "I'm back in town. It's nine o'clock, rise and shine."

"I'm up," I replied while trying to sound awake. The reality was I was exhausted. I had already played taxi driver, dropping my kids off at three different schools and immediately afterward found my way back to bed. "I went to see your expert," I said.

"Already heard," Marjorie replied, not sounding bothered by the news. "Janet, there are plenty of experts. I'm setting you up to see another one, this time in Los Angeles in a completely different medical community than Dr. Ulid and Dr. Allgood. You need to understand that many doctors choose to remain silent regarding mistakes and misdiagnoses made by their peers. A doctor from a different medical community might be more comfortable and willing to expose the mistakes or misdiagnoses of their colleagues."

"I see. Just let me know when and where, and I'll be off to Los Angeles."

"Janet, while we're on the phone, I want to tell you that the Fletcher case settled yesterday. They had won, and it was on appeal, set for trial next week. Still, Mrs. Fletcher and her children decided enough was enough and settled."

"I don't blame her," I moaned. "I'd be too tired to face an appeal, too. What happens next? Now that they've settled, will the medical board investigate?"

"Only the medical board knows, and we won't," stated Marjorie. "Remember the medical boards of each state don't inform the public of complaints and out-of-court settlements concerning a physician unless it, the medical board, has filed formal charges, and formal charges require months of investigation.

"Janet, most plaintiffs who settle a court case sign a confidentiality agreement not to talk about their case, people involved, or their settlement. At the time they settle, they're so relieved that their fight is over that they don't even think about the confidentiality agreement preventing them from filing a complaint with the medical board. This might be true with Mrs. Fletcher."

"I agree," I said sympathetically.

"Perhaps the Fletchers filed their case with the medical board early on, and an investigation is already taking place."

"Marjorie, I hope you're right."

That night the kids were playing an intense game of Monopoly, and Marty was relaxing in a chair when I slipped away to make a call. The next day Beverly was to arrive at Judge Simmons's court by 9:00 and turn herself in. From there, she would be admonished by the judge, handcuffed, and placed on a bus, beginning the first day of her two-year sentence. "Beverly," I said as she answered the phone, "how are you doing? Are you sure you want to go alone? I'd be glad to go to the courthouse to be with you and pray with you before…"

"No. I need to do this alone," she replied.

"You take care and know you're in my prayers," I said before we ended our call.

"The same to you. And don't forget to write me and let me know how your trial goes."

Early the following afternoon Joel came running in with the mail. "Mom, Dr. Ulid's office sent you a letter," he yelled, waving the envelope. I met Joel in the hallway as he handed me the letter and ran off to play.

"Dear Mrs. Mitchell, This is to inform you that your outstanding balance of $4.50 has been sent to collections."

I laughed. What nerve! I paid my co-pay. I'd never received a bill and my last visit to Dr. Ulid was more than seven years ago. And now they'd sent me to collections for $4.50?

I immediately called Marjorie.

"You're kidding," she said when she heard the news. "Just pay the bill and file the letter. When the check clears, file it too."

"This isn't adding insult to injury. It's more like a comedy act," I remarked.

"I agree," Marjorie said with a chuckle. "But say, Janet, I was just about to call you. I'm wondering if you could come by the office."

"Now?"

"Sure."

There was a sound of excitement in Marjorie's voice, so I grabbed my keys and drove right over. I was led up to her corner where she was hard at work.

"I'm glad you could come." Marjorie smiled. "I've got something to show you." Looking through a stack of papers, Marjorie continued. "Here it is. I subscribe to a newspaper for attorneys. It's a daily legal briefing that keeps attorneys up to date on the latest legal rulings. Today when my copy arrived, I saw this."

I reached over and took the paper. "Do you notice Judge Mayfield?" she asked. I couldn't help but notice. There on the front page was a five-by-seven photo of Judge Ruby Mayfield, Dr. Allgood's bankruptcy judge. The bold black title above the photo read, "Bankruptcy Judge Gains Reputation as a Fraud-Buster."

Marjorie chuckled. "I thought this might make you smile."

Right away I sat down and began reading the article. "Judge Mayfield is one of the most gracious, polite, and caring judges in her district." This did not surprise me at all as I had seen those qualities while representing myself in her court. The next several lines brought me great pleasure. "It would be hard to find a judge more supportive and empathetic. On the other hand, if she suspects you've committed some type of fraud—you're in trouble!"

"Hey, Marjorie, do you think Allgood's newly hired bankruptcy lawyer has read this? This article says, 'If you are a crooked attorney, you'll have trouble, too!' I wonder what happens when you're an okay attorney who just so happens to be representing a crooked client?"

"Well then, I believe, you're about to be surprised and about to be in trouble too!" Then, Marjorie added in a serious tone, "Do you understand that medical malpractice judgments are dismissible in bankruptcy? It's legal in the state of California to make a medical error and have it discharged in bankruptcy. It's also legal for a doctor not to carry medical malpractice insurance and then discharge any past or future judgments through bankruptcy."

I drew a deep breath and replied, "Does this mean after I win in Superior Court I'll need to—"

Interrupting me, Marjorie finished my sentence. "After we have a judgment of concealment and medical negligence in Superior Court, we'll need to go before Judge Mayfield and ask to be permanently removed from Dr. Allgood's bankruptcy. Janet, this could end up in another trial, but this time it will be in Federal Bankruptcy Court."

Marjorie's words hit me like a tidal wave. "How long would that take?" I asked. "Who would represent me there? What would we have to prove in order to win?"

"Slow down, Janet. Let's take one step at a time. I'll stand with you through this entire litigation. We might need help, since I'm not a bankruptcy attorney and don't claim that I know all that bankruptcy involves. But I do know that we would have to prove fraud in order to win."

"Well isn't concealment fraud?"

"Yes, it's a form of fraud, but there are five elements that constitute fraud, and we'll have to prove each and every one of them. I made you a copy of the rule. It says in order to establish a fraudulent representation under 532(a)(2)(A):

> A creditor must successfully demonstrate five elements: (1) The debtor must have made a representation; (2) at the time the representation was made the debtor must have known it was false; (3) it must have been made with the intention and purpose of deceiving the creditor; (4) the creditor must have relied on the representation; and (5) the creditor must have sustained damage because of that as a proximate cause.
>
> Lee-Benner v. Gergely (In re Gergely), 110 F.3d 1448, 1453 (9th Cir. 1997).

"Well, this doesn't seem overly difficult to prove," I replied.

"In your case, Dr. Allgood's conduct is squarely within the realm of this section. The way I see it, Allgood acted on false pretenses and made fraudulent representations by failing to disclose and intentionally concealing material information regarding your surgeries and condition. Janet, there is no doubt in my mind that at the time of the mistake Dr. Allgood concealed and knowingly misrepresented the actual cause of your condition. Plus he acted in willful disregard of this knowledge by failing to disclose material information. I believe that Dr. Allgood intended to deceive you and your parents so he could, at the least, avoid liability for his negligence. And you all relied on his representations in making decisions concerning your medical treatment. And as a result of Dr. Allgood's fraudulent representations, you suffered damage. You see, all five elements are here. But don't be thinking that Allgood won't put up a good fight."

"Don't you think it's odd that Dr. Allgood hired a high-priced attorney to fight his bankruptcy, trying to protect his money, rather than hiring an attorney to defend his reputation regarding medical fraud and concealment? I want him stopped. I want him exposed so that—"

"I know you do, Janet. I want him exposed, too—and I'm going to do it."

Driving home, I began mentally listing additional fraudulent facts. After my list grew to more than ten, I was certain that five elements should not be difficult to prove. My thoughts flashed back to the article. Judge Mayfield would see through Dr. Allgood's bankruptcy. It all seemed so simple. A doctor should not be able to lie about a patient's condition, cover it up, and then continue to practice as if nothing happened. Seeing this article assured me that others felt that Judge Mayfield seemed fair, honest, and out to seek the truth. After my experiences with Judge Higgins and being tossed out of court, I didn't have the same trust in the court system I once had. I did, however, trust in a God who, without my understanding or okay, had chosen both judges to rule on my behalf.

The day came when I was to be seen by Marjorie's expert in Los Angeles—Dr. Walter Burg, orthopedic specialist at Cedars-Sinai Medical Center. My mother accompanied me as I drove to meet with him. "What do you think he'll be like?" I asked my mom.

"I'm not sure, honey. Let's hope he's not another friend of Drs. Allgood or Ulid."

It took us a couple of hours to get there and find the office. Right away, I was taken back for x-rays. I slipped into a pair of sweat pants, rolled up my pant legs, and hopped up on the x-ray table.

"What happened to you?" the technician asked while positioning my leg.

"Met up with the wrong doctors, I'm afraid."

"I thought you might have met up with a football team or the ski patrol. Are you here to see Dr. Burg?"

"Yes. We're thinking of using him as an expert witness in my case."

"I've heard he's great. Never seen him on the witness stand, but he's been the expert behind many winning cases."

After my x-rays were developed, I was taken across the hall, into the examining room where my mother was waiting. Within minutes, Dr. Walter Burg stepped in and introduced himself.

"Mrs. Mitchell, I've reviewed your medical chart. At least the parts of it that are still existing." Flipping to Dr. Allgood's entry of my first right-leg surgery, Dr. Burg mouthed facts like he was preparing a timeline. "See you had hip surgery…"

"No, sir, I don't believe those records are accurate."

"That's what they say," he blurted. "'The patient underwent surgery at St. Ann's on February ninth where internal derotational osteotomy of the right hip was done. The patient tolerated the procedure well.' Mrs. Mitchell, are you saying that you did not tolerate the procedure?"

"No, sir. I didn't have the procedure."

My mother and I were confused. We had no idea if Dr. Burg actually thought I had had this so-called hip surgery, or if he was preparing for his performance at trial.

We reviewed pages of my medical chart pertaining to my office visits with Drs. Allgood and Ulid. My knees were evaluated, measured, and scrutinized carefully. "See you at trial," Dr. Burg said. "You've got yourself an expert!"

Two more weeks went by. It was time for all parties involved in my case to gather at the courthouse and try to come to some sort of a settlement. For most, settling a court case is a treat, yet in my case I saw it as a mistake. I didn't want *Mitchell v. Allgood et al.* to be added to the thousands of medical malpractice cases that settle and never get the attention of the medical board. I would not sign a confidentiality agreement, pretending that nothing ever occurred. Despite my insistence not to settle and the doctors' complete apathy, all parties were required by the court to attend the settlement hearings.

Marty, my parents, and I sat on the benches outside Judge Vincent J. Fragassi's courtroom. Stephen Wiley and Marjorie Day met with the judge in his chambers, discussing the whereabouts of Dr. Allgood. "No settlement can be entertained without Dr. Allgood present," Judge Fragassi insisted.

Marjorie appeared through the double doors of the courtroom. "The judge isn't playing Allgood's game. This time, he's even sending Dr. Allgood a letter threatening to order a contempt citation."

"What's that?" I asked.

"It means there will be a warrant out for his arrest if he doesn't show up May first," Marjorie answered.

"If Allgood's not careful," Marty pointed out, "he's going to pave his way right to jail."

"Janet," Marjorie said, "I'm going back to the office to spend some extra time preparing. Since I don't have a secretary, why don't you come along? I've got some work you can help me with. I haven't had time to organize your file. It was sent down from Duncan, Ball and Evans in boxes—many boxes."

While Marjorie worked on her opening statement to the jury, I sat and sorted bills and medical records, making a dated list. We visualized cross-examinations. We tried to imagine each question the opposing side could come up with. We made plans to meet regularly and continue preparing for trial.

"Janet, whenever possible, I'll be asking questions that I already know the answers to. I don't like surprises during trial," Marjorie exclaimed.

Jane's and my trip years ago to Dr. Ulid's office came up in conversation. "Marjorie, we took the file after Rhonda said she was to guard my things with her life. Why don't we want to offer the evidence that we took the file?"

"My dear, I know that you gals took the file. Yet if the other side knows about this, they're likely to say that you and Jane removed the missing year from the file. And there we'd be, spending a day of trial trying to clarify that point. Janet, at trial, only answer the questions asked. Never offer information—unless we find some tidbit that the other side must know."

That night I pulled my flip book from my purse. Starting from the front, I read note card after note card, trying to think of anything other than the trial. I felt there was very little that was actually in my control. But then I remembered, *Janet, you're not supposed to be in control—that's God's job.* With that thought, I grabbed a pen and made a list of "my absolutes." Using the fronts and backs of several cards, I wrote down things that I absolutely knew to be true. Over the next few days I added more thoughts to the list. I made a copy of it, posting it on my refrigerator for all to see. Some of it read:

### My Absolutes

- God loves me!

- God likes to make the impossible possible.

- God will defend me. (He will do it in His way!)

- God will judge, and vengeance belongs to Him alone.

- God's Word says that a false witness will be found out.

- God handpicked my attorneys. He chose them to represent me.

- God has chosen me for this situation. His purposes will be fulfilled.

- God owns the cattle on the hillside. He will provide for all my needs.

- God will reward me, as I have fought the good fight and remained faithful.

- God instructs me to patiently wait for Him, expecting that He will intervene.

- God is greater than anything my enemies bring against me. (This is the best incentive I have to hold my head up, walk straight ahead, and face my opposition.)

- God is trustworthy. He can be trusted with my life. He has never forsaken those who trust in Him.

- God deserves the best I have to offer. (My behavior through this trial will be honoring to Him.)

- God is a fair and just God. He delights in justice. He promises me justice, if not on earth, in heaven.

- God's Word is a lamp unto my feet. He will direct me and provide me wisdom so that I will know how to respond to each and every situation.

- God knows all. (He even knows the whereabouts of Dr. Allgood's medical records and Dr. Hughston's missing x-ray.)

So, what do I have to be afraid of? Nothing, absolutely nothing!

---

Two days later, Bridget called. It was great to hear her voice. "I've called to tell you the latest. John Ball has a calendar conflict, two trials scheduled for the same week. Marjorie did her best and talked me into returning to work and trying your case with her. Your trial date of this Monday has been rescheduled for April 29. I've got some catching up to do, and this will give me time to do it."

"Marjorie didn't tell me that you were back on the job."

"She wanted it to be a surprise. Marjorie's been working on me for some time. You know, it's only right that I'm there. I've dealt with these characters from the beginning, and I'd love the opportunity to see them sweat under direct examination. Marjorie invited me to stay with her. I think it's a great idea, as it'll give us extra time to discuss trial strategies. I'll fly down each Sunday night and fly home Thursday evenings. Court is closed on Fridays. That way, I'll get a three-day weekend before heading back to Orange County."

The thought of my attorneys going home together each night of my trial tickled me. Who'd have thought I'd go from not being able to find representation to having two women lawyers sharing tea each evening?

Over the next few weeks, I spent my days helping Marjorie, looking for evidence, and talking to other victims. After a day at the courthouse searching through records, I raced home and called Jane.

"Hey, going to the courthouse without you seemed strange."

"Well, tell me girl. What did you find out?"

"Are you sitting down? Three more suits have been filed against Dr. Ulid."

"Oh, no," Jane moaned.

"The first is *Reynolds v. Ulid*. It's a medical malpractice case. They're saying Dr. Ulid performed surgery on the wrong location, the wrong site."

"What did he do, operate on the wrong leg?"

"I'm not sure. I didn't have the time to read the file."

"You know this happens, Janet. I've heard that one out of every four orthopedic surgeons has or will accidentally operate on the wrong limb at some point in his career. It's called wrong-site surgery. It's not just an orthopedic problem. Wrong kidneys and breasts have also been mistakenly removed. Guess it pays to examine the surgery consent forms before you sign them. You might even be able to catch an early error."

"Yeah, like your wrong leg scheduled for surgery," I chuckled painfully. I paused for a moment and took a sip of water. "This second case was filed two months after the wrong-site surgery. It's a med-mal case, and again, I didn't have time to review the file."

"So tell me about number three."

Unexpectedly, tears filled my eyes, and my lips quivered. "Jane," I tried to steady my voice. "*Peterson v. Ulid* is another wrongful death case."

"Wow, Janet, you did discover a lot without me."

"I know more."

"What could be more than a wrong-site surgery and a wrongful death?"

"A lot," I murmured under my breath. "Yesterday I received the packet of information I ordered from the California Medical Board regarding Dr. Charles Wilcox—stipulation for surrender of license, dated April 1, 1998."

"Wow, Henry Fletcher's anesthesiologist lost his medical license."

"Not before people lost their lives," I added. "What confuses me and makes my blood boil is that all four complaints and accusations attached to this stipulation occurred in 1993. The complaints read: 'gross negligence' and 'repeated negligent acts.' Unfortunately, it took the medical board until 1998 to pull the doctor's license."

Jane and I continued our conversation. She tried to console me while I grieved for the families that had felt the sting of Dr. Charles

Wilcox. "You know," Jane said, "in a lot of ways you're kind of like a hero."

"What?"

"You've spent the last seven-plus years trying to expose medical concealment and fraud. You've refused to quit and stay quiet."

"Jane, silence kills," I half whispered. "I guess I've been more afraid to turn my back on what I know than to face the system head-on."

"I think it's a God thing. God chose you, 'cause he knew you'd follow through."

Jane continued her "lift-me-up" session while I tried my best to talk her into flying down for a weekend.

"I'll be there for your trial. Before you know it, I'll be on the witness stand, wearing my new outfit!"

"And I'll be seated among the lawyers looking straight at you," I giggled. "And I'll be thinking what a lucky gal I am to have you as my friend."

"Ditto," Jane said.

After years of waiting, my trial was finally within reach. Even so, the next few weeks crept by. Each day I placed an *X* on the calendar, crossing out one more day along the road to waiting.

Friday night came and, as usual, the Treasure Seekers, a small-group Bible study consisting of my daughter Jenna and ten other junior high girls, gathered in our home. Even though my trial was just three days away, I wanted to meet with these young girls one more time before we took a "trial break." Following tradition, we gathered in the backyard and ended our meeting with a candle-lighting ceremony and prayer time. We had an open-eye policy during prayer since earlier in the year, one of our treasure seekers had lit her hair on fire. After a great time of sharing and praying, we committed to God all that concerned us. As in weeks past, we concluded the ceremony by singing our theme song and holding our candles toward heaven. It was then we heard "Bang! Bang! Bang!"

"Gunfire!" the girls screamed.

Immediately candles flew into the air. Girls dodged flames while they ran for cover into the house.

Probably just backfire, I concluded as I followed them inside trying to calm them.

"Someone shot up the next-door neighbor's house," Marty reported when he walked through the front door. "The windows are shattered. Glass is everywhere."

"Is anyone hurt?" I asked.

"Doesn't appear that anyone was home," Marty replied.

Who did it and why? Who were the bullets intended for? Would the shooters return? I silently wondered. I tried to stop my imagination from fearing the worst.

The shooting at Columbine High School three days earlier had us all on edge. During the Bible study time, I had given each girl a name of an injured Columbine student that I had cut from the newspaper. For more than an hour, we discussed our fears and worries concerning the tragedy. "What can we do to help?" the girls asked over and over.

"Pray," was my consistent answer.

But now, one hour later, police cars lined our street. The girls, Marty, Jason, Joel, Agnes, and I had experienced the sounds of gunfire and threat of violence ourselves.

"What should we do?" the girls asked.

"Pray," was my firm answer.

The girls' parents arrived to pick up their daughters. Yellow caution tape ran down the sidewalk, and officers sorted through broken glass looking for bullets. "Not a common sight in our neighborhood," I said lightheartedly to one of the moms.

That night sleep did not come easily. The "what ifs" ran through my mind. What if the family had been home? Would they have been injured? What if the shooters come back? *God, thank you that no one was injured tonight. Thank you for watching over us.* And with that thought, I turned over and went to sleep.

The next morning I rolled out of bed and began to do what most moms would do who planned to be "preoccupied" for a month. The prepared meals were stacked high in the freezer, chore lists were made, and clothes were in the wash. Agnes and I sat down and made the last-minute grocery list.

"Janet, I don't believe you know what groceries you have. I know you've been preparing for this trial for months, but, girl, I've counted eighteen boxes of cereal in your outside pantry."

"Guess we don't need cereal," I replied.

Saturday flew by. That night, Agnes popped corn, the kids picked out a movie, and we all gathered together for family fun.

Sunday morning came early. Marty sat blowing the horn until we all crammed into the van ready for church. "Just one more minute, and you would have been left," Marty teased as I fastened my seatbelt.

"Just one more day until Mom meets the judge," Joel blurted.

"No, I think it's one more day until the jury meets Dr. Allgood!" Jason laughed.

Unable to resist adding to the fun, Agnes playfully concluded, "Just one more day, and you'll all be eating cereal for dinner."

I was at peace. I knew I had done all I could to prepare myself for this day. I had researched, found courage I didn't know existed, and refused to quit. I'd planned ahead—my home was ready.

The night before the trial, we ate dinner and then gathered our family in the living room. It was time to check in with the kids, offering some last-minute instructions and words of wisdom. Agnes and I sat side by side on the love seat with our backs to the front window. The kids sat in a row on the couch next to Marty in the wingback chair.

"Guys, I want you to listen to me," Marty said. "Mom's trial starts tomorrow, and we're told it could last a month. Yes, the opportunity we've prayed for has come. Now we'll all need to keep up with our individual family chores, work together, and help each other out when needed."

At once, the kids gave their word, and Marty moved on to the serious stuff. "I want you all to understand," he said, looking into the eyes of each child one by one, "I want you to know that no matter what happens during this next month and no matter what the trial outcome is, God is still in control of our lives. By filing a lawsuit, our family took a stand and did what we believe God asked us to do..."

Marty stopped mid-sentence. He jumped to his feet, pulled back the sheers, and stared out the window. "Kids, the next four weeks and the verdict are in God's hands. Win or lose—God is God."

Releasing the sheers, Marty flipped around. "Janet, do you know why the Orange County bomb squad has just pulled up in front of our house?"

The bomb squad? I was too frightened to speak.

"The bomb squad?" the kids yelled at once, leaping from the couch.

Grabbing the sheers, I saw the vehicle, too, along with six police cars that now lined our quiet street. Officers swarmed the neighborhood.

Before we could evaluate the situation we heard a knock on the door. Marty ordered the kids upstairs with Grandma. In seconds we stood face to face with two police officers. When we stepped outside, our neighbors joined our foursome.

"We told them about your trial starting," my neighbor said.

"Sir, a bomb-like explosive has been found fifteen feet or so from your home. It's got enough power to take out at least four homes—yours being one of them," the officer announced.

Questions were asked and answered. I gave the officers a summary regarding my upcoming trial while curious neighbors looked on from the sidewalk across the street. Some even parked themselves along the curb as if they were waiting to watch a firework show. In minutes, yellow caution tape secured the area. It didn't take long before the onlookers realized their front-row seats might not be the safest place to watch the action.

Men in protective gear arrived armed with special canisters to aid in the removal of the bomb-like substance. Officers combed the neighborhood looking for additional dangers, and others questioned neighbors, seeking any information pertaining to the explosives.

Knowing it was the perfect time to vacate the neighborhood, Marty assembled our kids, his mom, and me, and we headed out for ice cream. We all thought going for ice cream sounded like a great idea since none of us wanted to be around to see our neighborhood blown to bits.

"Dad, I'm afraid," Jenna, now fifteen, whimpered from the back of the van.

"If our house explodes, where will we live?" asked nine-year-old Joel.

I gulped. "Marty, maybe we shouldn't go to trial. Maybe this is a sign that we should—"

Before Marty could speak, Jason did. "Have you all forgotten about our family mission statement? Have you forgotten about the promises we made?"

Out of the mouth of my thirteen-year-old son, words came that helped me gain perspective. A year earlier, our family had spent several nights together answering questions and writing a family mission statement. We had written down who we are, what we believe, and where we're headed.

"Mom," Jason quizzed while mentally reviewing our mission statement, "did you forget the part that says, 'We, the Mitchells, will honor God by standing up for what is right and by standing up against what is wrong'? Or how about the part that says, 'We will honor God with our persistence,' and 'When something is hard, we will dig in and not give up'?"

That night, the ice cream tasted ever so sweet. For even though Marty and I were alarmed and worried, totally unaware of who placed the explosives in our neighborhood and why, we knew our children realized that no matter what, God is God, and he is in control.

When we returned home, the neighborhood was once again quiet. Marty tucked the kids in bed while I placed a call to Marjorie. I informed her of the night's excitement and then laid out my "trial clothes" for the following morning. The police promised to patrol our neighborhood throughout the night and in days to come, yet Marty and I were still frightened of the unknown.

I prayed while I tossed in bed, *Lord, five hours ago, I thought I was ready for trial. But tonight fear grips me. My energy is depleted. If you want my trial to start tomorrow, I'm counting on you to sustain and protect us.*

The big day arrived. Everyone was up and getting ready when the phone rang.

"I've got news," Marjorie said when I answered the phone. "Stephen Wiley is sick. His partner phoned the court early this morning and pled for a continuance. The judge granted his request." Marjorie chuckled. "Trial's delayed!"

I thanked Marjorie and hung up. Then I burst into laughter and tears. I knew this news meant the immediate stress would be lessened, but now it was back to the waiting game.

"Janet Lynn, I've flown to California three times to attend your trial. And each time something comes up," Agnes joked in obvious relief.

I spent the next few weeks helping Marjorie and finishing some last-minute detective work on my own. Using the Internet, I found the phone number of Jillian Winter, another person suing Dr. Ulid, and called her.

"Yes, Jillian is here, but she can't come to the phone. She's sleeping," I was told.

"Can you tell her I called?"

"Sure I will. She did get your letter; she just hasn't been up to responding."

"Is she okay?"

"Janet, Jillian lost her fight. No matter what they did, her new doctors could not save her leg. The damage was too great."

"What?"

"Her leg has been amputated. She's experiencing phantom pains as if it still exists. She takes high doses of pain meds and sleeps most of the time."

"I'm so sorry," I said as tears stung my eyes.

"You know, Jillian's leg could have been saved if she had been told the truth after the initial error and then received proper medical care. Yep, if she had known seven months ago that she was going to lose her leg, she would have never settled her lawsuit. Who would have guessed her elective knee surgery would have brought her such problems?"

"Please let her know I'm truly sorry. Let her know I'm going all the way. A jury is going to hear my story."

"Go for it. Don't let anything stop you from exposing Dr. Ulid!"

I cried for days after hearing the news about Jillian. It all seemed so senseless. Jillian was thirty-two years old and without a leg. What had Dr. Ulid gained for keeping such a secret? I now felt an even greater purpose for going to trial.

"Janet," Marjorie said when I called to tell her the news about Jillian, "I'm sorry for Jillian too. But you must remember, just as Beverly Lacasto's trial was about Beverly and her wrongdoing—and not the outlandish lifestyle of Dr. Allgood or what he had done to her—your trial is about what the doctors did to you, not about their horrific adventures or medical blunders concerning others. I doubt we'll even have the opportunity to inform the jury about Beverly, Dr. Allgood's threats, or his many lawsuits."

"Well, what about Mr. Fletcher and Jillian? Jillian just lost her leg, you know."

"Janet, your trial has to be won on its own merit, showing that the doctors fraudulently concealed their medical negligence pertaining to your right leg."

What a disappointment! I wanted the jury to know about the several lives the doctors had upset by their lack of integrity and/or lack of skill. I wanted them to know that this was Dr. Ulid's third time in this courthouse in the past nine months. Instead, I swallowed what I knew.

## Chapter Eighteen

# IN HOPES OF JUSTICE

TWENTY-TWO YEARS after my botched surgery, the day of my trial had finally arrived.

"Janet, this is your day!" Bridget said as we met in the hallway outside Judge Fragassi's courtroom.

In minutes Marjorie and her husband, Will, walked up beside us.

"I wouldn't miss seeing my wife in action," Will said. "This is sure to be one of the highlights of her career." Being a lawyer himself, Will understood it all and was proud of Marjorie and her many accomplishments.

Bridget, Marjorie, Will, my parents, and I sat down on the benches against the wall. "I'm glad Marty went in to work today. We'll probably spend all day selecting a jury," Marjorie said. "Your trial could start as early as tomorrow." We spent the next few minutes chatting about the trial and then in the distance noticed Stephen Wiley and Dr. Allgood walking off the elevator.

"Dr. Allgood looks like he's heading for the gym," my dad said with a chuckle. "Just look at him—no sport coat or jacket, and he's carrying a bright turquoise gym bag." Dr. Allgood did resemble a golfer rather than a doctor who was acting in his own defense.

"You know, Bridget," Marjorie said, "Dr. Allgood is fully aware of proper courtroom etiquette and attire. He's an expert witness for Social Security hearings and appeals. In fact, he even tried to delay this trial due to his heavy court schedule."

"Where's Dr. Ulid?" I asked, noting he wasn't with his lawyer.

"He probably won't show up until the jury's picked and opening statements have concluded," Marjorie explained. "He'll do his best to stay at work and let his attorney handle things here."

Soon Mr. Wiley and Dr. Allgood made their way down the hall and walked past the six of us. Dr. Allgood made sure we felt his displeasure at being there by the scowling look he offered. "I don't think he expected to see you," I whispered to Bridget.

"I think he's in store for a few surprises," Bridget replied. "And, Janet, don't you let him intimidate you."

"Yeah, show him your briefcase," my dad said, breaking the tension and causing a laugh.

Within minutes, the elevators opened again. Each one was packed with potential jurors on their way to Judge Fragassi's courtroom. Like a herd, they made their way down the hall past us, sitting inconspicuously against the wall. The bailiff stepped out of the courtroom, and the potential jurors gathered around him. He then assigned each person a number. Numbers one through fourteen were instructed to enter the courtroom and take their seats in the jury box. The remaining ones entered and took seats as tentative trial observers.

We waited until the last juror had entered and then made our way through the doors. My dad gave me a hug right before he, my mother, and Will sat down behind the potential jurors. I followed Marjorie and took a seat between her and Bridget at the L-shaped counsel table made of mahogany.

I looked around the room where I would spend the next few weeks. The jury box was to my right. Next to it stood a wooden podium. I looked straight ahead and up the wall. My eyes stopped at the Great Seal of California. I didn't think I'd ever seen one so large. I followed the wall back down and noted the empty chair that would, in moments, be filled by Judge Fragassi. To the right sat the witness stand that would soon be my seat. *I can do this,* I reminded myself.

Mr. Wiley and Dr. Allgood entered the courtroom and took their seats at the same counsel table—too close for comfort. One chair remained. It would sit empty until Dr. Ulid made his grand entrance. While Bridget, Marjorie, and I all faced the judge, the defense team had a face-to-face view of the jury. And with a slight movement of their eyes, they could watch every expression I made.

The room grew quiet as the bailiff walked to the front. "All rise," he commanded as Judge Fragassi entered the courtroom.

"You may be seated," the judge announced. "Good morning, ladies and gentlemen. Welcome." Right away he explained to the jury the awesome responsibilities and privileges of their roles. Then he gave a brief overview of my case and explained his method in selecting a jury.

At the conclusion of Judge Fragassi's remarks, he asked Mrs. Day to take the podium. Marjorie stood in her tailored pastel suit with matching shoes. In the style of a classy grandma, she introduced herself to the jury. "Good morning, ladies and gentlemen. My name is Marjorie Day, and I represent Janet Mitchell in this case..."

Mr. Wiley was next to go to the podium. He introduced himself and informed the jury briefly about the client he represented. Dr. Allgood followed suit.

Individual jurors were then questioned. Marjorie and Mr. Wiley used their limited number of challenges to remove undesired candidates. Judge Fragassi even removed a few on his own, citing "for cause." Dr. Allgood, however, did not choose to eliminate any. I wondered if it was his trial strategy to come across as "Mr. Friendly." It took a day, but the jury was finally selected and court was dismissed. The twelve jurors, two alternates, and all parties involved were told to report back the following morning by nine o'clock sharp.

The next morning Marty, my parents, and I met Bridget, Marjorie, and Will outside the courtroom. "Have a few boxes?" I asked Will when I noticed two luggage carts stacked high.

"It's all yours, Janet. With six years of legal proceedings, the paperwork adds up," Marjorie replied.

Within moments, my aunts and cousins arrived. They were my moral support for the day because if all went as planned I'd be testifying. Since Marty and my parents were all witnesses, they had to remain in the hall outside the courtroom until they had their turn to take the stand.

It was soon time to take our seats. Marjorie opened the courtroom doors for me to enter. Halfway through, she grabbed my arm and stopped me. "Janet," she whispered, "I'm seventy-six years old, and I doubt the doctors know what's gonna hit them."

We resumed the same seats as the day before except for my family members and Will, who now sat in the front row. Marjorie and Bridget joined Mr. Wiley, who had arrived earlier and was busy sorting papers. While the lawyers prepared, I ran my hand gently across the tabletop. Yes, it was true. I was finally going to have my day in court! I smiled. I knew whether I won or lost, I would be able to sit and receive God's protection and provisions.

Just moments before nine o'clock, Dr. Allgood arrived. Still without a suit jacket and carrying his gym bag, he seemed eager to defend himself. The court came to order, and the room echoed a loud silence. Judge Fragassi greeted the jury. "Good morning, ladies and gentlemen. This trial will be conducted in two phases. In the first part, you will decide the issue of whether or not the plaintiff filed suit within the time frame provided by law. The law provides that the time period may be extended if Plaintiff provides proof of fraud or intentional concealment. Defendants deny that there was any concealment or fraud to extend the statute of limitations. All right. Counsel," he said as he turned toward Marjorie, "do you wish to give an opening statement?"

Marjorie nodded and walked to the podium. She set down her legal pad and then dragged the podium a few feet, angling it so that she could face the judge and look the jurors in their eyes. Once situated, she greeted the jury with a smile. I wondered if she then whispered a silent prayer. I watched her as she made eye contact with each juror. After acknowledging each one, she began a monologue that I knew she had rehearsed many times. As she spoke, I looked up and felt all eyes of the jury on me. Not knowing how I should respond, I gave them the nicest smile I could muster.

"My name is Marjorie Day, and I represent Janet Hepp Mitchell, who is sitting to my left. The purpose of this preliminary talk is not to give you evidence, but it's to give you the picture on the jigsaw puzzle box. Anybody do jigsaw puzzles? The picture shows what you get when you've put all the pieces together. I think by the time we're through you'll be able to see the whole picture. This picture is something that the doctors did to Janet. We believe the evidence will signify to you that Drs. Allgood and Ulid made a conscious decision between themselves and successfully covered up a very serious medical mistake—and for a number of years.

"Recently, a doctor friend of mine gave me this rather tattered model of the knee," Marjorie said while holding up the model for the jury to see. For the next few minutes, she scientifically, yet in layman's terms, communicated and demonstrated my congenital problems. "A terrible mistake was made during Janet's first surgery on her right leg. Her doctors cut her bone at the wrong angle, the wrong degree. If you can imagine a broomstick and you cut it at an angle and try to rotate it forty-five degrees, you can see that the sides wouldn't fit.

"Now, Dr. Allgood will tell you that Dr. Ulid was assisting him during this surgery. Dr. Allgood will also tell you that Dr. Ulid had done the surgery before, and that Dr. Ulid was going to sort of walk Dr. Allgood through it. The consent form that was signed by Janet's parents named four doctors as the surgeons. I think something was said about Dr. Allgood's qualifications and he said, 'Well, I am the Dr. Kerlan of Orange County,' so Janet and her parents had a lot of confidence in him, and that will be made known to you by the writings of the defendants themselves."

With a pause, Marjorie scanned the jury. She placed one hand on her hip and with the other she motioned toward Dr. Allgood. "The one thing that the 'Dr. Kerlan of Orange County' neglected to tell Janet or her parents was that he had never in his life performed this operation on anyone! This was the first fact that the doctors did not disclose to Janet and her parents."

Obviously feeling at home in front of a jury, Marjorie left the podium and crossed the jury box, acting as if she were having a private chat with each juror. "Expert doctors will be brought in here to tell you about these things and why the mistake happened. We know why. We know the mistake was done. We also know the doctors had to have known about it. After Janet's surgery, Drs. Allgood and Ulid told Janet and her parents that everything was fine. This was the second concealment made by the doctors."

Not stopping to review her notes, Marjorie continued on while I watched the jury from the corners of my eyes. "This 'successful' operation put Janet in a wheelchair and led to six additional surgeries. 'What happened to me?' Janet asked the doctors many times. 'Well,' Dr. Allgood said, 'that's just the way God made you.' And at another time Dr. Ulid said, 'Well, that's the way you were made in your mother's womb.' This," Marjorie declared, "was, of course, the third concealment. Every day the truth wasn't disclosed to Janet was a lie. Every day!" Marjorie repeated. "And that started in 1977.

"Then in January of 1978, they opened her knee again. Dr. Allgood suggested they 'ought to go in with an arthroscope.' That's a little hole they put a scope in to remove the torn cartilage Janet was told she had. Well, the operation report that was prepared by Dr. Allgood says that yes, they did find a torn cartilage, but that he didn't remove it. He then told Janet and her parents that they would remove the cartilage the following month and told them that it was necessary to turn her tibia a little more. Fourth lie!" Marjorie exclaimed as both the jury and Mr. Wiley fiercely took notes. Dr. Allgood remained motionless.

"Well, in fact," Marjorie continued, "we believe you will reach the inevitable conclusion that the arthroscopy surgery was a sham, and that they performed it to look inside and see how much damage had been done. Further records will indeed show that Janet's cartilage was not torn. Evidence will prove this surgery was needed so the defendants could plan the additional surgery to repair the damage that they caused—again hiding it.

"Unfortunately, Janet did not improve with each surgical attempt. So her parents found a world-renowned doctor named Dr. Hughston in Columbus, Georgia. He was known for his ability to repair knees. In any case, Dr. Allgood wrote Dr. Hughston a referral letter and admitted to him that a mistake had been made. You will see that letter before this part of trial is over. Interestingly, the last line of that letter says, 'I hope you can help her,' or words to that effect. 'These are very nice people and very trusting of our profession.' Dr. Allgood had a good reason to believe that Janet and her family were trusting because they had gone through all the surgeries and accepted the explanation that God did it and even allowed Dr. Allgood to operate again."

I again looked over at Dr. Allgood. There he sat looking ever so self-assured. He caught my eye and smiled slightly while his lips remained sealed tight.

Marjorie kept her momentum and continued her monologue. "Dr. Hughston performed three surgeries on Janet, but he was not able to reconstruct the knee. Because of the sham—the 'torn cartilage' that wasn't ever torn, and the surgery that followed—so much scar tissue was created by Drs. Allgood and Ulid that Dr. Hughston had to make tendons, so he jury-rigged support for the knee as only one with his experience could do."

Marjorie spoke for the next hour, briefly touching on it all. "When you see these letters and records that we have," she said, "and when you've heard the witnesses, I think you will agree that there has been a deliberate concealment, and that concealment is what excuses Janet's failure to file a lawsuit any sooner than she did. Thank you," Marjorie concluded while offering her appreciation to the jury for their attentiveness. She then took her seat and poured herself a glass of water. I smiled at her for a job well done.

Immediately Mr. Wiley stood and was on his way to give his opening. I leaned back in my chair and took a deep breath. I wondered what he could say that was any different.

"Good morning, ladies and gentlemen. As you know, I am Stephen Wiley, and this is my chance to give you an overview of what I believe the evidence is going to show during trial. The first phase of the trial will involve the statute of limitations. Essentially what you're going to be called upon to do is to decide when the plaintiff was aware of an injury from treatment received from the defendants and when a reasonable person would have a suspicion of wrongdoing. And the last issue would be whether there was an intentional fraudulent concealment, an actual act of concealment of an injury or the cause of the injury, that would cause the statute of limitations to be tolled or extended in this particular case."

Mr. Wiley appeared calm and credible. Methodically he explained the facts concerning my condition and medical history. "The plaintiff's primary theory in this case is that Dr. Allgood cut Janet's tibia up at an angle and went into the knee joint, damaging ligaments and other soft tissues. We believe the evidence will be clear at the end of this case that this did not happen, and that the doctor acted within the standard of care, and that the cut did not damage any of those structures. Unfortunately, despite the doctor's best efforts, things did not get better for Ms. Mitchell. I am confident," he said, establishing eye contact with each juror, "that when all the evidence has been presented in this case, you'll conclude that Dr. Ulid, and for that matter Dr. Allgood, didn't do anything wrong at the time of the February 9, 1977, surgery. However, if the plaintiff was going to sue, we believe that the evidence is clear that she was aware of her poor outcome as of 1977, and certainly by 1978, and she knew she had a bad result. Yet this lawsuit was not filed until 1993, more than fifteen years following the first surgery."

Stepping back from the podium, Mr. Wiley stood resolute. In the tone of an army commander speaking with certainty, he continued, "We believe the evidence in this case will show that there was no intentional concealment, there is no fraud, and there is no cover-up. Not at all! In fact, just the opposite. I think the evidence will show that the doctors were always honest and open, always providing their opinions to the patient as to what they thought was happening with the knee.

"Yes, I believe Dr. Ulid told Janet some things that were just flat out wrong, and he'll be here to testify. He told her that the backside of her knee had been injured by the osteotomy cut and that there may have been ligament damage as a result. The evidence will show

how the very next day, the very next day, Ms. Mitchell went to see a lawyer."

*God, you know this isn't true. Stop him!* I prayed as I squirmed in my seat.

Bridget could tell that I was irate. She wrote a quick note on her legal pad and slid it toward me. "You're okay," it read.

Mr. Wiley paused for a moment and took a sip of water. "So we believe the evidence will show as far as the statute of limitations is concerned, by 1977, certainly by 1978, Ms. Mitchell was aware there was a problem, that she had an injury, it was an unexpected bad result, and that any reasonable person in that position, if they were thinking about a lawsuit, would explore it at that point in time. And lastly, there was no concealment. There was no intentional concealment of anything in this case. In fact, I think just the opposite is true. Thank you for listening."

Mr. Wiley took his seat, and I took a deep breath. I wasn't afraid of the truth, but the nonfactual damning of my character created a knot within my stomach. *I'm not a gold digger! I prayed and received counsel from many before I filed this suit. Maybe Stephen Wiley needs to have a heart-to-heart talk with his client—this time with Dr. Ulid hooked up to a lie detector,* I thought. *Maybe, Mr. Wiley, believes what he's been told, like I did.*

A morning recess was granted. We had fifteen minutes to wait until Dr. Allgood would be given his turn at the podium. "Janet," my dad whispered when I walked back to where he was seated, "you look like one of them."

"Who?" I asked jokingly. "A doctor or a lawyer?"

"Definitely the lawyer," my dad answered. "You've got the briefcase to prove it! What do you have in there anyway?"

"Copies of everything. Letters to and from the doctors, a ten-page list of important dates with records to support it, and copies of other lawsuits filed against Dr. Ulid and Allgood. All in all, I'm ready."

Fifteen minutes later, court resumed. I was eager to hear Dr. Allgood's side of things, yet I braced myself for whatever he might say. Without greeting the jury, Dr. Allgood stood at the podium and began speaking. "A doctor who treats himself is a fool and has a fool for a doctor. A lawyer who treats himself is a fool and has a fool for a lawyer. And a doctor defending himself in the law may be the lowest of the bunch as far as being a fool. Because this case is twenty-three years old and because the anatomy of the knee is involved, I felt that I could explain the anatomy, the function, and the surgeries as well as anyone.

"Like I stated yesterday during jury selection, if you can accept objective findings and make your decision on objective findings, I think everyone will be happy. I would like to show as we go through the jigsaw puzzle and fill in the pieces that there are objective evidences in our records. Now, before I get myself into the anatomy, I would like to give a small bio of myself being described as the Dr. Kerlan of Orange County."

"Sir," the judge interrupted, "during the opening statement you need not do that. You will be able to give your biography during testimony. All right?"

"All right. That's fine," Dr. Allgood replied while he studied his notes.

"Sir, the opening statement is to tell the jury what the evidence is going to show in regards to the issues that are before them. And that's the time limitation period," Judge Fragassi added.

For the next hour, Dr. Allgood reviewed my medical history. It was somewhat the same history that Marjorie had shared hours earlier, except great detail was given to each surgery, facts were left out, and some were misconstrued. Medical terminology was used, certainly adding confusion for the jurors.

"I don't feel there was any concealment," Dr. Allgood said. "When Janet went to Georgia, I sent Dr. Hughston all my x-rays. He saw the osteotomy cut. We'll go through, and we'll show you that there's no concealment on our part. I wanted Janet to get well as much as anyone."

Standing confidently in front of the jury, Dr. Allgood took a stab at Marjorie. "Well, my 'sham operation'...it was not meant to be a surgery of any kind. It was called a diagnostic arthroscopy. When we got to the back of Janet's knee, we found the cartilage was attached so we left it. And it's still there today."

*That's not true! I left college for surgery!* I thought. *The operation report supplied by St. Ann's confirmed what I had been told: surgical diagnosis—a torn cartilage.*

Dr. Allgood talked for another half hour. I was sure the jury had to be feeling restless since the opening statements had taken their toll on even me. Finally, he came to a conclusion. Using every bit of his charismatic personality, he gave his own instructions to the jury. "Look for the objective findings. If we cannot follow up in the chart with a note or an objective finding, then you should disregard it. If we can, then it must be accepted. I don't think we ever hid anything or threw away records. We just didn't get the result we wanted, the two groups of physicians, our group here in California and Dr. Hughston's in Georgia. Thank you."

"Thank you, sir," Judge Fragassi said to Dr. Allgood. He admonished the jury not to speak about the case, court was adjourned, and we all headed home.

That night I curled up in bed and thanked God for my first day in court—a system he created to help bring justice to many.

Bright-eyed, my family made our way back into the courtroom the following morning. I was prepared, as prepared as one could be, for my name to be called as the first witness of the day. Little did I know, I'd be on the stand most of the day.

"Call your first witness, Mrs. Day."

Immediately Marjorie signaled for Marty and my parents to exit the courtroom. "Yes, I call Janet Hepp Mitchell to the stand."

Before I had time to fret, I was standing with my right hand raised and being sworn in. Marjorie walked to the podium with her yellow pad, and I found my way to the witness box. For a moment, Marjorie and I paused, communicating in a way only a lawyer and client can. We both grinned at each other. I took a breath, and Marjorie began her questioning.

Marjorie spent the first half hour asking me about when I first met Dr. Allgood and my reasons for seeing him. I told of the night in the hospital when Dr. Allgood made his great discovery—my "congenital problems" that had gone unnoticed by him for two years. We reviewed when I met Dr. Ulid and how I understood that he and Dr. Allgood would perform my surgeries as a team.

"Did you trust your doctors?" Marjorie asked.

"Absolutely."

"Did anyone ever tell you anything that made you doubt the professional ability of your doctors?"

"Not until August 4, 1992, the day Dr. Ulid divulged the secret."

"Janet, from your point of view, was your first surgery on your right leg successful?"

"No, ma'am, it wasn't."

"What happened?"

"My knee had problems. It would give way and collapse. I also noticed that the outside of my leg had a bow shape to it."

"Did you talk to the doctors about this?"

"Absolutely. I asked them, 'Why is my leg this way? What has happened to me? How did this happen?' I asked probably every question a girl at that age would have known to ask."

"And tell us the answers you received."

"Well, the doctors were very compassionate. Dr. Allgood knew of my Christian faith, and he told me that I had to accept my condition. He explained my condition was a congenital result of the way God had made me. Dr. Ulid gave me a similar answer. He said it was a congenital result, not the one he wanted, not one that any of us wanted, but that it was a result of the way I was made in my mother's womb."

"And Janet, did you believe them?"

"I did. I never had any reason to doubt my doctors."

Marjorie then walked me through every surgery. She questioned me regarding the procedures, their outcomes, and the physical pain and emotional stress each one brought.

"Janet, when you went to Georgia the first time, did Drs. Ulid or Allgood give you anything to take with you?"

"We were given some x-rays from Dr. Ulid to take—none from Dr. Allgood. But when I gave them to Dr. Hughston, he said that they really didn't show him much because they were x-rays taken after my third right knee surgery, not the first."

"Did Dr. Hughston ever suggest to you that your previous doctors had goofed?"

"Absolutely not."

"Did he ever voice any criticism of them at all?"

"No, not at that time."

Marjorie's questioning soon brought us to my fall at the airport and my visits with Dr. Ulid that followed. I was pleased that Dr. Ulid had arrived at the start of my testimony, abruptly taking his seat at the counsel table. To my surprise I wasn't nervous. Instead, I quickly remembered the Henry Fletchers of Dr. Ulid's past. I sat up straight, holding my shoulders back. With a tilt of my head, I faced Dr. Ulid and reiterated his confession, as though it had happened yesterday. "Dr. Ulid said it was time I knew."

Hearing these words, Dr. Ulid's head sank. His face turned a deep shade of red. I wasn't sure if this was due to embarrassment or anger, but it didn't really matter. What did matter was that he appeared to recall what he had said. The jury sat silently and watched as I faced Dr. Ulid and answered each of Marjorie's questions.

"Janet, what did you leave with Dr. Ulid after he told you of the mistake?"

"The x-rays I had just received from Dr. Hughston. Dr. Ulid said he wanted to evaluate them, and he would then return them to me."

"Did Dr. Ulid ever do that? Return the x-rays?"

"No," I replied. "They've disappeared."

"Janet, you wrote a note to Dr. Ulid. Did you not?"

"Yes, I did."

"Do you see this?" Marjorie pointed to a three-by-four-foot reproduction of my letter. "This is Exhibit 9 marked for identification," Marjorie informed the court while placing the letter on the chart board. "Janet, would you be kind enough to read it?"

For the next few minutes, the jury read along and wrote fiercely while I read into the microphone. "Dear Dr. Ulid, I want to thank you for your honesty in telling me the truth about my right knee..."

"I'd ask that Exhibit 9 be admitted into evidence," Marjorie stated.

"No objection," Mr. Wiley said with a sigh.

Marjorie moved right along. She did not slow her pace in questioning or presenting the evidence, including Dr. Ulid's drawing.

"Janet, you use a cane when you're going to do any extended walking, is that correct?"

"I use a cane when I'm on this type of flooring. I use a brace sometimes. I also have a wheelchair, and sometimes I just walk. It depends on where I'm going, how long I'm going to be gone, and what type of floor I think I'm going to be walking on."

"Did you recommend Drs. Ulid and Allgood to others?"

"Yes. I took my children to see Dr. Ulid. My aunt, husband, and friends have seen Dr. Ulid. Dr. Allgood performed two hip replacements on my grandmother."

"So you continued to believe and trust these doctors. Is that right?"

"Yes, ma'am, I did."

"I have nothing further at this time," Marjorie concluded.

Judge Fragassi leaned forward and pulled his glasses from his face. He ordered a fifteen-minute break and admonished the jury not to discuss the case with anyone.

I took a drink, chatted with Bridget, and then walked over to talk with my parents. Not long after, I once again took my seat on the witness stand and looked to Marjorie. She knew I was ready for the fight and gave me a wink. I turned to Bridget; she stared back at me. "You can do this, Janet," I imagined her saying.

Mr. Wiley stood at the podium. "Good afternoon, Ms. Mitchell."

"Good afternoon," I replied.

Promptly he began questioning me about my past medical condition—what I knew and when.

"Ms. Mitchell, what risks do you remember either Dr. Ulid or Dr. Allgood informing you about prior to the first surgery on your right leg?"

"I don't remember Dr. Allgood discussing much about risk, other than saying, 'Kiddo, don't you worry about it. I'm going to take care of you. You're going to be fine.' However, I remember I did discuss some risks with Dr. Ulid. We talked about infection because I was concerned about it. Dr. Ulid told me he would give me an IV that would help prevent infection. I did ask him about nerve damage. He told me that this wasn't real common and that he would be careful."

"Ms. Mitchell," Mr. Wiley said sharply. "I would like you to read from your deposition, page 103, line 21 to page 104, line 25."

What could I have said any different? He's trying to discredit me. Taking a breath and saying a quick prayer, I turned to the page, steadied my voice, and read out loud:

> *Question.* What did Dr. Allgood tell you during the pre-op conversation with him?
>
> *Answer.* That my surgery date was set and "we're going to do it kiddo."
>
> *Question.* Did Dr. Allgood go over any risks and complications with you?
>
> *Answer.* No, he did not and that's why I asked about infection.
>
> *Question.* Did you ask Dr. Allgood about any of the other risks and complications in addition to the infection?
>
> *Answer.* You mean nerve damage?
>
> Question. Yes.
>
> *Answer.* I don't believe that I asked Dr. Allgood about that because he had told me not to worry that there were no problems related to this surgery. He put my mind at ease.

I finished reading and looked up, joining the jurors who were looking at Mr. Wiley.

"Ms. Mitchell, that was your testimony, correct?"

"Yes, sir."

Then without a flinch, Mr. Wiley replied, "Okay," and continued his questioning. Time and time again questions were asked, followed by the same time-consuming event requiring me to read out loud from my own deposition. I felt as if Mr. Wiley was trying to trap me in my own words, yet nothing great or too controversial was noted. For the next hour, I was grilled about each surgery and its outcome, what the doctors told me and what I had understood. Despite the tension mounting, I prayed that I would remember all that was needed and that I would communicate effectively.

"Ms. Mitchell," Mr. Wiley said, "let's focus on your conversation with Dr. Ulid. This you say was the first time it ever entered into your mind that something wrong may have been done at the time of the first surgery?"

"Yes. I never thought that my doctors had made a surgical mistake. Mr. Wiley, I never suspected that what I had been told was a lie. I relied on my doctors' words."

Pausing for a moment, Mr. Wiley glanced toward the jury, probably noting that all eyes were focused on me. "Ms. Mitchell," he said with disgust, "can you remember word for word everything that Dr. Ulid said to you during that conversation?"

"Mr. Wiley, I'm sure there are several words that I've forgotten, but there are also some words that Dr. Ulid said that I will never forget. That's why I wrote Dr. Ulid the letter—the ballerina card. I wanted to say back to him what I had heard him say, to give him a chance to tell me whatever he needed to."

"Ms. Mitchell, during the time you were under Dr. Ulid's care, he never talked to you about this letter?"

"No, sir, he didn't."

"For example, Ms. Mitchell, when you came back in on September first, he didn't say, 'I received your letter, and this is what I think'? Nothing like that ever happened? Correct?"

"No," I repeated. "Dr. Ulid never acknowledged my letter."

"Okay, during your discussion with Dr. Ulid, he talked to you about the posterior cruciate ligament being cut during that first operation, didn't he?"

"Dr. Ulid talked about a lot of ligaments being cut. He mentioned the posterior cruciate ligament. I don't recall if he said it was cut or if it wasn't cut."

"Ms. Mitchell, let me read from your deposition, page 216 to page 217, line 10:

> *Question.* Did Dr. Ulid tell you that it was the posterior cruciate ligament which had been cut or so he thought during the 1977 surgery?
>
> *Answer.* I don't—I don't recall which. He drew lines back and forth on the drawing. He said, "These are the ligaments that were cut." He mentioned the posterior cruciate, posterior lateral. I don't recall what all he said. I know when I got to my car, I wrote down the only ligament that I could remember.
>
> *Question.* And that was the posterior cruciate ligament?
>
> Answer. Yes.

"Excuse me," Judge Fragassi interrupted. "You said, 'Wrote it down.' Where did you write it down?"

"I wrote it down on the original picture that Dr. Ulid had drawn for me, Your Honor."

"Are you speaking of Exhibit 9 or 10?"

Seeing that she could quickly clarify the situation, Marjorie stood. "Excuse me, Your Honor. Perhaps I can clear this up. I thought the original drawing had been marred. I whited out the words Janet said she wrote and then made a replica of what Dr. Ulid had drawn. Dr. Ulid has seen this reproduction and has said yes, this is the drawing he made. The drawing that is attached to Dr. Ulid's deposition has Janet's writing on it."

Time continued to pass. With each question, the gray areas became either black or white. "I have no further questions of this witness," Mr. Wiley concluded.

A recess was granted. I waited for the jury to exit the courtroom. Then I stepped down from the witness stand, walked out into the hallway, and melted into my father's arms.

"I'm sure you were great, honey. I'm sure you didn't back down once," he said.

"But Dad, he sure tried his best to get me to agree to things that didn't happen."

"I think the worst is over, Janet," Marjorie chimed in. "Being questioned by Dr. Allgood won't be nearly as difficult for you since he's an amateur at cross-examination."

After the break, Dr. Allgood began his questioning of me, and Marjorie's words became true. Oddly, it seemed as if several of his questions were to answer his own curiosity rather than add any vital information for the jury to process. Dr. Allgood brought out Dr. Ulid's copy of my medical records that included several of my visits with Dr. Allgood. "Janet, how much walking were you doing between coming out of the cast on your right and the next left-leg surgery two to three weeks later?"

"I was using crutches. I did not put full weight on my leg at home or coming into your office or leaving it."

"Okay. And then you had your surgery, and you were going to be in a cast for six weeks on your left leg. What was your form of ambulation?"

"Dr. Allgood, I was in a wheelchair," I answered, hoping to jar his memory.

"In the progress notes here, there's a notation that you were walking on both your legs and you were very pleased. There were no signs of any instability. Janet, would you say that Dr. Ulid and I conspired to hide the reality of how you were doing?"

"I don't—I've never seen your records, Dr. Allgood. Dr. Ulid's records state that I was doing fine, and then a whole year is missing in which I had four surgeries. It's obvious to me that I wasn't doing fine. I don't know how to respond to your statement, Dr. Allgood. Why did I make the appointment with Dr. Hughston clear across the country if I was doing so well?"

After several more minutes of persistent questioning followed by firm, confident answers, Dr. Allgood set down his notes and called it quits. "Okay, very good," he said. "That's all I have. Thank you."

I felt exhausted. Court was over for the day. Marjorie, Bridget, Will, my parents and I sat together in the courtroom while Marjorie laid out her master plan for the following day. "George, you and Mary Lou will take the stand tomorrow," Marjorie told my parents. "And Jane is flying in tonight, isn't she?"

"Yes, Jane and Marty will be here tomorrow, ready to steal the show," I said.

"I don't know," Bridget chuckled. "Janet, you're going to be a hard act to follow."

## Chapter Nineteen

# EXPOSING THE TRUTH

JANE FLEW IN about seven o'clock that evening. As tired as I was, I was on an adrenaline high. I picked her up at the airport, not wanting to miss a second of being with her. We chattered nonstop for the rest of the evening. "Janet Lynn, I never thought I'd be dragged into court, and here I am going with you."

The following morning Marty, Jane, and I drove to my parents' house and picked them up. We traveled to the courthouse with great anticipation, knowing that they would be called to the witness stand before the end of the day.

Once there, we saw my aunts and cousins who had returned to see the action. Jane was the first to be summoned from the hall. Sitting between Marjorie and Bridget, I had a full view of Jane on the stand. She looked nervous. I gave her a nod of "Go for it, girl," when she looked my way.

"Raise your right hand please...Called as a witness on behalf of the plaintiff, please state your name for the record."

Jane spoke, spelled her name, and began answering Bridget's questions.

"What is your occupation, Mrs. Hall?"

"I am a registered nurse."

"Are you a friend of Janet Mitchell's?"

"I'd say she is my best friend."

"Mrs. Hall, in 1992 did you go with Janet to Dr. Ulid's office?"

"Yes, I did."

"What, if anything, did you hear Janet say during that visit?"

"We were standing at the receptionist window and she said, 'I'm Janet Hepp Mitchell, and I've come to pick up my x-rays.'"

"And was there a response?" Bridget asked.

"I'm going to object, Your Honor," Mr. Wiley proclaimed. "This is hearsay."

"Overruled," Judge Fragassi shot back with his eyes closed as if he were trying to follow Jane's story.

"Was there a response, Mrs. Hall?"

"They weren't able to locate them at that time."

"Move to strike. Hearsay," Mr. Wiley interrupted again.

"Not on that ground," the judge replied.

Calmly Bridget tried again. "Mrs. Hall, do you remember the gist of what the receptionist said?"

"Objection!" Mr. Wiley hollered. "Hearsay!"

Once again Judge Fragassi was right behind him. "Overruled."

"Mrs. Hall, what did she say?"

"She said we couldn't pick up the x-rays that day."

Upon hearing Jane's conclusion, Mr. Wiley looked relieved. All the "objections" and "hearsays" appeared ridiculous when such insignificant information was brought to light. Jane took a deep breath, as though she were getting ready for round two.

"Mrs. Hall, did you return with Janet to Dr. Ulid's office?"

"Yes."

"And to whom did Janet speak?"

"Originally, the receptionist."

"And what, if anything, did the receptionist say?"

"I'll object!" Mr. Wiley again spouted. "It's irrelevant and hearsay."

"Overruled on both grounds," Judge Fragassi stated firmly.

Jane looked to Bridget and waited for her nod. When she saw it, she continued, "The receptionist told us to go inside the office and speak with Dr. Ulid's nurse."

"And what, if anything, did the nurse say?"

"First, Janet said, 'I'm Janet Hepp Mitchell, and I'm here to pick up my x-rays.' The nurse said, 'I'm not sure you can do that.' And Janet said, 'Yes, I can. They're mine.' The nurse asked Janet, 'What are you going to do with them? Are you taking them to another doctor's office?' And Janet said, 'I need them. They're mine.' So then the nurse went off to look for them and eventually came back and said, 'I can't find them.' But then something came to her mind. She said, 'Wait a minute. I think they're back on my desk.' After returning empty-handed she told us, 'I was told to guard your x-rays with my life.'"

"And did she come back with the x-rays?"

"No, she did not."

"I have nothing further, Your Honor."

Like a child begging for one more try, Mr. Wiley stood to his feet. "Your Honor, I would move to strike the testimony of the receptionist or the comments made by the receptionist in the office as hearsay and irrelevant."

"Mr. Wiley, I overruled that," Judge Fragassi said, sliding his glasses off his nose and eyeing the persistent attorney.

"Okay," Mr. Wiley said in an undertone. "I have no questions of this witness."

I figured Mr. Wiley was probably afraid of what Jane knew and he didn't. Jane therefore didn't have to worry about answering any questions about the "hot medical file." Surely the jury could tell that Mr. Wiley did his best to prevent them from hearing Jane's testimony. Way to go, Jane!

Thinking that she had finished and could leave the witness stand, Jane was stopped as Dr. Allgood approached the podium. *Oh, this could last forever,* I moaned silently. But I was wrong. He asked Jane only one question—the date of our visits to Dr. Ulid's to pick up the x-rays.

Jane left the stand and took a seat as an observer while the bailiff went to retrieve my mother, who was the next to testify. She was asked several questions about my medical care and my previous appointments and surgeries with the doctors.

"Mrs. Hepp, at any point in time from the time Janet had the surgery in February of 1977 until August of 1992, did any doctor ever tell you that a mistake had occurred in that February 1977 surgery?"

"No doctor ever indicated any kind of mistake whatsoever. I never would have let them operate on Janet's grandmother, my mother, if they had!"

"And during that time, did you ever suspect a mistake had occurred in that February 1977 surgery?"

"No, ma'am. We trusted them completely."

Bridget finished her questioning in about fifteen minutes. This time both Mr. Wiley and Dr. Allgood passed up their opportunity to question the witness. My mother stepped down from the stand and walked over and sat down next to Jane. "Mary Lou, you had it easy," I heard Jane whisper. "I was objected to several times."

My dad was brought in from the hall. Right away, I could tell that this wasn't a comfortable situation for him, yet I knew he would do anything necessary to expose the deceit he had experienced.

Within minutes, he was sworn in and sitting in the witness box. Bridget took the podium and began the questioning. She asked him a few basic questions pertaining to his family and his past employment before venturing into the questions about my medical care with Drs.

Ulid and Allgood. "Mr. Hepp, this isn't a very good copy, but this is a Consent to Operate. Is this your signature at the bottom?"

"Yes, ma'am, it is."

"Will you read the names of the first two surgeons listed?"

"Yes, Dr. Allgood and Dr. Ulid."

"Okay, and it was your understanding that Dr. Allgood and Dr. Ulid would be Janet's surgeons?"

"Yes."

"Now, after Janet's right leg surgery, did the doctors tell you how it went?"

"Well, yes," my dad said with assurance. "I can't remember the exact words, but they conveyed to me that everything went fine, just as they had expected."

"And as time progressed and Janet had the same surgery on her left knee, did she begin having problems with her right leg?" Bridget asked.

"After she was able to stand up and start walking, she would fall down quite a bit. I know that because I had to pick her up several times," my dad answered.

"Did you ever go with Janet and ask the doctors something like, 'What's going on? Is there something wrong here?'"

"Well, I don't remember going in and actually collaring them on this problem, but they explained to us, 'Hey, we've got a congenital problem here. We're fighting nature. This is the way God made her...'" Wiping tears from his eyes, my dad looked down as he fought for composure. Moments later he lifted his head, unable to stop the flow of tears. "That's what we were up against," he uttered.

"You seem a little upset. Do you feel like maybe, you know...?" Bridget said, and then paused while my father reached for a box of tissues.

"I'll be all right," he replied, trying to sound convincing.

I'm sure Bridget jumped at the opportunity. My dad was truly vulnerable, and this was a chance to show the jury the pain the doctors' lies had created. "Mr. Hepp," Bridget said with compassion, "do you blame yourself somewhat for this?"

"Objection," shouted Mr. Wiley. "That's irrelevant!"

"Overruled," Judge Fragassi said, then turned to my father, looking for the answer.

"Yeah," my dad mumbled as he tried to pull himself together.

I wiped my tears with the palm of my hand. I heard sniffling coming from the jury box and weeping from my family sitting to my back. Yet my eyes were glued on my father, a man who had given me his all—financial support, love, and encouragement—reaching for the stars with me—and now he said he blamed himself for my troubles. I didn't care who was watching me. I cried like a baby.

"Is your answer no?" Bridget questioned, as if she had not understood.

"No," my dad said curtly. He then turned his head away from Bridget, staring Dr. Allgood down. Trembling, he half stood and leaned over the witness stand. "I do blame myself," he stammered. Then looking deep into the eyes of Dr. Allgood and pointing his index finger at him, he spouted, "I do blame myself! Because it was my decision to hire that man!"

Immediately Mr. Wiley stood and addressed the judge. "I would move to strike the last part of the response as nonresponsive."

"Sustained," ruled the judge.

Nevertheless, the jury had seen and heard my dad's testimony. I watched them from the corner of my eye and noticed that a few were wiping away tears. Bridget paused for a moment and let everyone settle down.

"Mr. Hepp," Bridget continued, "at any time, from the day Janet had her surgery up until August fourth of 1992, the day Dr. Ulid confessed, did any doctor ever tell you that there was a mistake made in that February 1977 surgery?"

"No, ma'am."

"Did you suspect it at all?"

"No, I didn't suspect it a bit."

"That's all I have. Thank you," Bridget said as she completed her short, yet insightful, questioning of my father.

The judge then turned to Mr. Wiley. "Counsel, any questions?"

"No questions," Mr. Wiley replied, while observing tender emotions coming from the jury.

"Sir, do you have any questions of this witness?" the judge asked Dr. Allgood.

"I have one, Your Honor."

Dr. Allgood smiled, seemly unaffected by the testimony he had just witnessed. He sprang to the podium to question the man whom he had betrayed. Still trying to find a way out of assuming his responsibilities, he questioned my dad regarding what he knew and when. Dr. Allgood's goal was to prove that we knew a mistake had been made so he could prevail on the statute of limitations issue. "Mr. Hepp, did Dr. Hughston discuss with you what he thought was wrong with Janet's leg?"

"No. He told me he thought he could fix it, and that made me feel real good."

Dr. Allgood's one question quickly turned into three, still with the intent of trying to establish that my father must have had some idea that I had been injured. Hearing the same type of answer over and over again, Dr. Allgood called it quits. "Oh, I see. Thank you," he said and walked back to his seat.

Bridget had an opportunity to ask a few more questions on redirect. She clarified a few facts, then politely thanked my father and returned to her seat.

"Thank you, Mr. Hepp," Judge Fragassi said. "You may return to your seat."

Lunchtime had arrived. The jury filed out, and my family sat quietly with puffy eyes and tear-streaked faces. While my aunt passed around the last of her tissues, Marjorie, Bridget, Will, and I joined my family in the back of the courtroom.

"George, we couldn't have planned it better," Marjorie cheered, trying to ease the tension. "I deem you the star witness of the day!"

The following day we were all back in court. "Good morning, ladies and gentlemen, counsel. Let the record reflect—the jury is impaneled. Sir, if you'll take the stand," Judge Fragassi requested as he nodded to Dr. Allgood.

Dr. Allgood rose from his chair. He forgot the etiquette of the court as he crossed in front of the counsel table and headed straight toward the judge. Immediately the bailiff left his position and headed toward Dr. Allgood, ready to grab the doctor to stop him, when the judge spoke sternly into his microphone, "This makes my bailiff nervous."

Dr. Allgood realized the commotion he'd created by walking toward the judge. He quickly turned and headed back to the counsel table, crossing it from behind, and then walked directly in front of the jury to the witness stand. As if nothing had happened, he took his seat and confidently smiled.

Across the room, Marjorie stood at the podium and returned a smile. "Good morning, Doctor."

"Good morning, Marjorie," he replied as though they were best friends.

"Dr. Allgood, in your opening statement, you admonished the jury to pay attention to our records. Do you have any medical records regarding Janet?"

"Yes."

*What? In Allgood's deposition he had said that he had no records, and the previous day in his opening he said, "There are objective evidences in our records that show each step along the way."* "Dr. Allgood, where are they?"

"Here," Dr. Allgood replied, pointing to the small stack of papers he had emptied from his gym bag.

"Were they made available to us when we asked for them?"

"Oh, these records? The records? You say, do I have any? Yes," he said nodding. "When Dr. Ulid and I were treating her together before 1978."

"Actually, those are the records that were produced by Dr. Ulid in response to a subpoena; is this correct?" Marjorie challenged.

"Yes," Dr. Allgood replied without a flinch.

"But you produced nothing in response to a subpoena; is that correct?"

Again I thought about my records that Beverly had seen so neatly stored in Allgood's personal filing cabinet.

"Dr. Allgood, do you have, or does your office have, a policy as to how long you keep records?"

"Yes, there's a policy."

"And what was the policy at that time, do you recall?"

"Well, I have records of patients from 1972, when I began my practice. I think the policy is, if the patient has not been seen between five and ten years, the records can be put in storage or discarded. And I believe with the x-rays…there is a legal statute on that. I don't know what it is. But I would say because there's nothing in my records pertaining to Janet, that I had since '78, my records would have…" Not making sense and without finishing his sentences, he stumbled to the next. Mumbling to himself, he looked into the air as if the answers to this question would be flying by at any time.

"Well, you're speculating now. I didn't want you to speculate. I just wanted to ask what your policy was."

"Yes. My policy is that they would then discard them if they hadn't been seen."

"Dr. Allgood, when was the last time that you recall seeing Janet?"

"I would say around September of '78."

Changing her stance and shifting her weight to one foot, Marjorie counterattacked. "Do you recall writing a prescription in January of '81 for an exercise bike?"

"No."

"If you don't recall a letter from Dr. Hughston back in 1980, do you recall a letter from Dr. Hughston in 1987 reporting to you on Janet's condition?"

Quickly defending himself since moments earlier he had told the court he'd last seen me in September of 1978, he now said, "In reviewing Dr. Hughston's record I see correspondence to Dr. Allgood, but I don't recall ever seeing that letter or acting on it, no."

"Dr. Allgood, you wrote Janet a referral letter and sent it to Dr. Hughston, did you not?"

"Yes."

"Exhibit 7 for identification, September 6, 1978, letter from Allgood to Hughston. Doctor, would you read that letter out loud?"

Dr. Allgood read the letter.

"Now Dr. Allgood, in this letter you wrote, 'We feel that the posterior lateral capsule of the knee has been involved in the osteotomy.' What does the word *involved* mean?"

Dr. Allgood leaned back in his chair and gave an explanation I doubt even his colleagues could follow. Indeed, Marjorie did not even want to touch it.

"Doctor, have you read Dr. Hughston's deposition?"

"No," Dr. Allgood replied.

"Have you read the deposition of Dr. Walter Burg?"

"No."

"Have you read the deposition of Dr. Wilbert Gillian?"

"No."

"Well, would it surprise you to know that every one of these doctors says the word *involved* means you cut it? Is this an unusual interpretation for the word *involved*?"

"Cut could be part of this, yes."

"Okay. You testified that you had never performed Janet's surgery before. Is this correct?"

Dr. Allgood glanced toward the jury. With a look of helplessness as if he were somehow now the victim, he nodded his head. "Correct, but I had told Janet's parents that."

"Doctor, in your deposition you stated, 'I definitely wouldn't have performed Janet's surgery without Dr. Ulid because he recommended the surgery. Dr. Ulid was going to show me how to do it, but he felt I should still continue managing the patient. That's very common even today, surgeries that I know and my colleagues will say, "You take the patient, I will come in. We'll do it together and we will continue managing them." So there's nothing untoward, but I would have never done it without Dr. Ulid because he was good at this.' Is this testimony still your testimony today?"

"Yes."

"Were you counting on Dr. Ulid to do the surgery, actually wield the saw, or were you counting on him to walk you through it kind of step by step?"

"The latter."

"Did you ever tell Dr. Ulid that you had never performed this surgery before?"

Dr. Allgood shifted in his seat as if trying to communicate that he might need a break from the questioning, yet, having no representation to suggest this for him, he sighed. "Oh, I'm sure I did. I'm sure that I told him. I'm sure I said, 'Why don't you do the surgery and I'll watch,' and he said, 'No, you'll be able to do it.'"

I was off in my own thoughts when I heard Marjorie clear her throat and ask, "Dr. Allgood, did you discuss with Janet and her parents any of the problems or the risks associated with the surgery which you planned to do?"

"My routine discussion with a patient is—"

"Doctor, let me interrupt you for a moment," Marjorie said while scribbling a note and then reworded her question. "What routine do you generally follow?"

This question seemed to excite Dr. Allgood, and he quickly began to answer it with arrogance. "In the 1970s and actually in the 1980s there was a thing called an informed consent. An informed consent is where everything from death to pulmonary embolus to a million problems should be told to the patient. I'd never followed that in my career. I felt I would spend more time explaining the surgery, what our plans were and what our post-op plans were...I would say that we did not discuss all of the possible complications that occurred."

"Well, Doctor, isn't it the standard of practice that a patient must be informed of the possible risks and hazards? Not to say if you take a vitamin pill today you might die two-weeks from now, but of the recognized risks; isn't that a standard of care question?"

"Well, I think you should tell the patient what your plans are. Seven days you're going to really hurt. Some people hurt, some people don't hurt. But I would say that I explain to them the major parts of the surgeries that I do."

Obviously getting frustrated and tired of Dr. Allgood's "trips around town" to answer one direct question, Marjorie placed her hands on her hips. "Excuse me, Doctor!"

Looking sheepish Dr. Allgood admitted, "I wouldn't say that I did the total informed consent, no."

Informed consent is a law; I knew it, and Marjorie knew it. It's every patient's right to be informed and then to consent to this knowledge and understanding, so with her hand firmly anchored to her hips and looking Dr. Allgood straight in the eye, Marjorie asked, "Isn't that below the standard of care, not to give the patient informed consent?"

"No," Dr. Allgood responded.

Not taking her eyes off him, Marjorie spurred Allgood's memory. "Actually, you testified in your deposition about that very subject, didn't you?"

"I don't know. Maybe. I'm sure I did. What page?" Dr. Allgood sputtered.

Bridget found the page, stood before the court, and clearly and articulately she read:

> Question: Do you recall, in 1976, was it your practice to go through with a patient, and the family in this case because she was a minor, the risks of the procedure you were planning to do?

> Answer: My philosophy since 1972 has been to try to describe to the patient the anatomy of what their injury is by showing them models. I would try to show them what we're going to do at surgery and the postoperative care.

Pausing as to emphasize what lay before her eyes, she then continued reading from Dr. Allgood's deposition: "I never since 1972 said to my patients, 'You could die, you could get infections,' I never have gone along with the informed consent. I've gone along with trying to have the patient understand it, and I still do it today."

Bridget took the silent direction from the judge and sat back in her chair.

Marjorie cleared her throat. "Doctor, you heard Janet testify that when she asked you why she was having all the trouble after that first surgery you told her that God had made her that way. Do you recall this?"

"I don't know when I talked to her about that, whether it was after the second surgery or what, but I do remember saying, 'I believe it's because of the functional pathomechanics of the walking that it's stretching this capsule each time.'"

He had just testified that when he communicated with his patients he used words they'd understand. Did he truly think I'd have understood "functional pathomechanics" at seventeen?

"Move to strike the answer as nonresponsive," Marjorie pled.

The judge looked over and faced Dr. Allgood. "Sustained. Listen to the question."

Again Marjorie quizzed, "This is a yes-or-no question, Dr. Allgood. Tell me, at any time did you tell Janet that God had made her that way and that this was the reason for the complications?"

"I can't see me saying, 'God made you that way,' but if she said it that way, that's fine."

"Did you intend that to comfort her?"

"No. I don't think my job is to be a comforter."

"Dr. Allgood, was there anything that should have tipped Janet and her parents off that something had gone wrong in Janet's first right-leg surgery?"

"What?" he asked looking confused.

"That somebody made a mistake or had done something wrong?"

"Well, I don't know of any mistake in those surgeries that I did that I can say would have caused this problem."

Convinced she had gotten the answers that she had needed and hoped for, Marjorie ended her examination. "I have no further questions of this witness."

I thought for a moment that we would all have a break. That we could go off into some corner and hear of Marjorie's conquest. Instead, the judge kept things moving. With his arm extending outward toward the counsel side of the table, he motioned for Mr. Wiley to take the podium. It was now time for him to chisel away the evidence in his cross-examination of Dr. Allgood.

"Good morning, Dr. Allgood," Mr. Wiley said.

"Good morning, John," Dr. Allgood returned.

For the next half hour, Dr. Allgood did what he did best. He charmed the jury while describing his background and expertise in orthopedic surgery. From being a physician for several professional sports teams to treating at least twenty Olympic athletes, Dr. Allgood drenched the jury with his background.

For two hours, the court sat and listened to Mr. Wiley and Dr. Allgood discuss my condition and go page by page through Dr. Ulid's medical records of my care. While questions were asked and answered, Dr. Ulid sat at the counsel table and, like he did at his deposition, began playing with a paper clip. For an hour he twisted, turned, and slid the clip around the table. I wondered if he had helped prepare questions for Mr. Wiley to address with Dr. Allgood. I wondered how hard it was for him to be sitting there watching his ex-friend, ex-associate, yet "partner in secrecy," being questioned by his attorney.

"Dr. Allgood, take a look at Exhibit 14 in the blue binder. Is this the report that you dictated on the day of Janet's first right knee surgery dated 2-9-77?"

"Yes."

"And this is an accurate account of what happened during the course of the surgery as best as you can recall?"

"Yes."

"Did you enter the posterior aspect of Janet's knee joint during this surgery?"

"No."

"If you had entered it during the surgery, would that have been something you would have included in your report?" Mr. Wiley asked assuredly.

"Definitely."

"Is this something you would have told the patient about?"

"Definitely," Dr. Allgood repeated with confidence.

"Is this part of your training, to tell patients the truth about what happens during surgeries?"

"Part of my training? No. No," Dr. Allgood stammered.

With such an unexpected answer, Mr. Wiley quickly continued on. "Dr. Allgood, you mentioned yesterday records being missing or lost. Is there a time frame when there are some records that you believe are missing?"

"I would say that there's a year missing, from January to December of 1988, 1989."

"And that's because those records were destroyed or...?" Mr. Wiley stuttered while appearing to think twice about his question.

"Well, they were probably discarded," Dr. Allgood clarified.

"Dr. Allgood, did you ever conceal any information from Janet Mitchell about her medical condition, what had happened during any of the surgeries?"

"No, I don't think so."

After asking additional questions, Mr. Wiley concluded, "That's all I have, Your Honor. Thanks."

"Counsel?"

"I don't have anything else at this time, Your Honor," Marjorie stated.

"Now, Dr. Allgood," Judge Fragassi said. "You may testify at this time if you so wish, but you don't need to because you've been called under evidence code 776. So you don't need to testify at this time in any way. All right? Do you understand?"

"Yes, Your Honor," Dr. Allgood replied. "I think it's been covered very well. I mean it would just be redundancy."

After the lunch break we were seated back in the courtroom. All eyes were on Dr. Ulid as he took the seat at the witness stand.

"Good afternoon, Doctor," Marjorie said as she stood at the podium.

"Good afternoon," he replied, obviously not happy about being there.

Right away Marjorie began her questioning. Soon she got to my appointment on August fourth—the day Dr. Ulid confessed.

"Dr. Ulid. Do you have any independent recollection of your conversation?"

"Other than what is written in the chart, I do not."

"Have you read Janet's deposition?"

"No, I have not."

"Are you aware that she was alleging that you told her that there had been a mistake in her first surgery?"

"What I told her was from my recollections which, when we get into this, we will find that my recollection was wrong. I had said that the osteotomy cut had possibly entered the posterior aspect of the knee joint and damaged a posterior cruciate ligament. My recollection was wrong."

"Dr. Ulid, you thought it had damaged the posterior cruciate ligament?"

"I already testified to that, yes."

"And now you're saying that there was never any damage, any untoward damage, inflicted anyplace around the knee at the time of her surgery?"

"My answer is a resounding 'no.'"

"And what do you base your now so-called erroneous conclusion on that there had been damage?"

"I believe that I answered that, Counsel. I had a 'wrong memory synapse' and my memory synapse made an incorrect joining, so to speak."

My Aunt Margaret chuckled, and giggles were heard throughout the courtroom. One juror sat perplexed, shaking her head; another's mouth dropped open, as if in disbelief.

Marjorie paused for a moment to allow Dr. Ulid's words to sink in. She then resumed asking several questions about the anatomy of the knee, concentrating on the details of my medical records. I watched the jury. They took notes and listened intently.

"Dr. Ulid, Janet wrote you a letter on August eighth and apparently you now believe that you were incorrect and that the allegations made as repeated in the questions were also incorrect. Did you know that Janet was very upset over the things that you told her?"

"I think when you tell people they've got a significant problem, it would be very unusual not to be upset. I would be upset. If she wasn't upset, then I'd walk out of the room scratching my head and saying 'Gee, what a funny reaction.'"

"So," Marjorie said while changing her stance, "you knew she was upset and you got the letter. And you didn't call her and tell her that you were wrong, that you had made a mistake, that she shouldn't be upset anymore. Dr. Ulid, you received that letter in August and sometime in October you received a letter advising you that Janet was contemplating filing a lawsuit. Now, it was three more months before a lawsuit was filed. Did you at any time, either after you reviewed the chart, after you got her letter, after you got the letter giving you three months to think about it, did you ever call and say, 'Janet, I'm so sorry. I made a terrible mistake. I've upset you for nothing'? Did you ever do that? And the answer is yes or no."

There was no "yes" or "no" answer, but a lengthy monologue instead.

"Move to strike that answer as nonresponsive," Marjorie demanded.

"Sustained," Judge Fragassi barked. "Do you understand what the question is, sir? Did you ever call her up and say, 'What I told you about the wrong cut on the bone, that's in error'? Did you ever call her and tell her?"

I sat perched waiting to hear his answer. The jury sat amazed. "No, I didn't," Dr. Ulid replied.

"I don't have anything further at this time," Marjorie concluded.

As Marjorie sat down, Mr. Wiley took to the podium for the cross-examination. Immediately he began with a review of Dr. Ulid's résumé. From the schools attended to thirty-five years in practice, details were shared. It was made clear to the jury that Dr. Ulid had been the assistant surgeon during the first surgery in question and that he had no recollection of a mistake being made. It was apparent that Dr. Ulid was relieved when the questioning was over for him—at least for the day.

Marty was to be the next person called to the stand. I could tell that he was more than ready to speak his mind and tell this court what he knew. I sat across from him during our lunch break. He, Marjorie,

Will, Bridget, and my parents were all involved in a lengthy conversation. Instead of joining in, I sat and marveled at my husband. How blessed I was that years ago Marty walked into my hospital room to cheer up some gals he didn't even know!

Once on the witness stand, Marty cleared his throat and one by one began answering Bridget's questions. He sounded as if he were a native Californian because his southern accent had diminished over the years and only returned when he spoke to his family, visited the South, or called me darlin'.

"Mr. Mitchell, do you recall what Dr. Ulid said the day he drew the picture of Janet's knee?"

"Yes. He told me that in the first surgery on Janet's right knee, they had incorrectly cut the bone. And he actually drew a picture showing that the cut should have been parallel, not on an angle, and that this is what caused Janet's disability."

"And up until that time had Janet ever suggested to you that Dr. Ulid or Dr. Allgood had ever done anything wrong?"

"No."

"Mr. Mitchell, were you with Janet at the appointment when she first learned about the mistakes?"

"No, I was not. I saw her later that evening."

"And what did she tell you?"

"She was crying. She told me that Dr. Ulid had explained to her about her bone being cut wrong in the first surgery. She was very upset."

"And what did you do?"

"I just held her."

After several minutes of questioning, Bridget concluded, "I have no further questions of this witness, Your Honor."

"Counsel?" Judge Fragassi stated, waiting for a response from Mr. Wiley.

"Yes, Your Honor, I have two questions for Mr. Mitchell."

Each question that followed referred to Exhibit 10, the large replica of Dr. Ulid's artwork. It really seemed to bother Mr. Wiley that I had written "posterior cruciate ligament" on the side of the original drawing. He just didn't want to accept the fact that Dr. Ulid mentioned to Marty and me that several ligaments had been cut. He, on the other hand, wanted to believe and prove that Dr. Ulid specifically informed us that the mistake he thought had occurred cut only the posterior cruciate ligament.

Marty was then excused from the stand. He walked by me, giving me a quick pat on the shoulder, and then took his seat next to my father.

"We are right at the hour," Judge Fragassi announced. "Ladies and Gentlemen, court is adjourned until 9:00 a.m. tomorrow morning. Please recall my admonishment; don't discuss the case among yourselves or form any opinion on the case until it's submitted to you for decision."

We all said our goodbyes. All of us were tired, and yet we knew that when my family went home, Bridget, Marjorie, and Will would still be preparing for another day of trial.

## Chapter Twenty

# THE VERDICT

WE ENTERED THE COURTROOM to face another day. The jury took their seats, surely wondering what surprises this day might hold.

With a smile, Marjorie took to the podium, ready to question Mr. Borst, the radiologist from St. Ann's Hospital. She greeted him in her cheerful manner and then began her questioning. After a half hour or so, the testimony got interesting.

"Mr. Borst, you were only shown two MRIs pertaining to Janet; is this correct?"

"Correct."

*Two? But, I had three MRIs, in three different years,* I thought.

"You were also shown x-rays dated 6-29-92; is this correct?"

"Correct."

"So, Dr. Borst, you can't possibly correlate the MRIs then with any x-rays, or can you?"

Immediately, Mr. Wiley took to his feet. "Your Honor, I don't have the June 29, 1992, x-rays here today. I didn't plan on using them, and I didn't bring them."

"Counsel," Judge Fragassi responded, "you don't have the x-rays in your possession?"

"No, Your Honor," Mr. Wiley confessed.

"Excuse me, Your Honor," Marjorie suggested. "Perhaps Counsel would be kind enough to bring those tomorrow?"

"I'm not sure if the witness is available tomorrow," Mr. Wiley responded.

"Well, in any case, Doctor," Marjorie continued, asking one more question, "can you tell me from these films if Janet's tibia was cut above or below the tibia tubercle?"

"Below, ma'am," Mr. Borst answered.

"Thank you, Doctor. I don't have anything further, Your Honor," Marjorie said and then returned to her seat.

"All right. Dr. Allgood?" Judge Fragassi said, motioning for him to take the podium. Then looking toward Dr. Borst, Judge Fragassi explained, "Dr. Allgood is representing himself."

"I'm Dr. Allgood. Dr. Borst, in *pro per* [meaning representing himself]. Would you please go over your last statement again pertaining to the level of the osteotomy cut?"

"To be very honest, I don't think I can tell if the cut was on top of or below the tibia tubercle. It's going to be in the vicinity."

For the next twenty minutes Dr. Allgood asked questions regarding the location of the osteotomy cut, the status of my ligaments, my degenerative joint disease, my joint space narrowing, and the loose bony fragments floating throughout my knee.

"Would you show us the anterior cruciate ligament?" Dr. Allgood asked, walking over to the MRIs.

"There's not a normal anterior cruciate ligament here," Dr. Borst replied.

"Very good," Dr. Allgood said, sounding like a teacher. "Now, would you grade the amount of degenerative arthritis that you see in this knee?"

"Sir, I need to know how old the patient was at the time this film was taken."

"Your Honor," Marjorie interjected, "I believe Janet was thirty-two."

"This knee is very advanced for a thirty-two-year-old woman."

"That's all. Thank you. Very good," Dr. Allgood uttered as he finished his questioning.

"Counsel, any further questions?" Judge Fragassi asked.

With nothing further, my MRI films were submitted into evidence. Dr. Borst left the stand and Dr. Kent, the defense's next witness, was summoned from the hall.

Once he was sworn in, the medical expert for the defense made his way to the witness stand and Mr. Wiley walked to the podium.

"Good afternoon, Dr. Kent. You're a medical doctor?"

"That is correct, an orthopedic surgeon." With the question asked, Dr. Kent outlined his prestigious education and wide experience in orthopedics. "I've been in private practice for forty-two years. I've written in the area of orthopedics, taught, and was the chief of orthopedics at Hoag Hospital."

"Dr. Kent, are you familiar with the performance of derotational osteotomies of the tibia?"

"Yes, sir. I have performed up to twenty of them."

"Have you reviewed films in this case?"

"Yes, sir. The July of 1992."

"As far as the MRI, you mentioned the film led you to the conclusion that the osteotomy cut did not enter the knee joint; is that true?"

"Yes, sir. I reviewed the MRI and I see two cuts. Both of these lines level horizontally."

*But there were three cuts. Where's the third one, Dr. Kent? Look beyond the scar tissue.*

For the next forty-five minutes Mr. Wiley and Dr. Kent discussed my MRI and the assumed facts surrounding my surgeries. While they talked, Marjorie and Bridget jotted down statements made by Dr. Kent. Selected x-rays were shown, and finally Mr. Wiley asked the question I had been waiting for. "Dr. Kent, how many osteotomy cuts do you see in these films?"

"I see two," Dr. Kent promptly replied.

I flinched, wanting to scream, *Where's the third?* I looked at Bridget and caught her eye. Quickly she passed a note with the number two crossed out and the number three circled many times.

The questioning continued, and Mr. Wiley soon came to his grand finale. "Dr. Kent, based on your review of the deposition testimony and the medical records, operative reports, MRI, study, do you see any evidence from a medical standpoint that suggests to you that the osteotomy cut made in February of 1977 entered Mrs. Mitchell's joint space?"

"I see no evidence that it did."

"That's all I have," Mr. Wiley concluded. "Thank you."

"Cross-examination," Judge Fragassi stated without offering a break.

Quickly Bridget passed her freshly written notes to Marjorie. Marjorie added them to hers and walked to the podium.

"Hello, Doctor." Marjorie smiled. "I wasn't expecting the pleasure of your company today, and I don't have your deposition here."

Immediately Mr. Wiley handed Marjorie his copy of Dr. Kent's deposition.

"Thank you, Counsel," Marjorie said while finding her desired spot in the deposition. "Dr. Kent, the court has already instructed the jury that a deposition is evidence taken under oath. Doctor, on page 44, I asked you, 'Do you have an opinion as to the reason for Janet's subsequent problems?' And of course we're talking about subsequent to the first surgery."

"I'm with you."

"Okay. And you said, 'Yes ma'am.' And I asked 'What is that opinion?' and you said, 'At this point I will continue to use the word *assume*, but I think we can point out why my assumption is correct. I will continue to say that the osteotomy cut was horizontal. That's because, one, the surgical report says that it was horizontal, and two, it's in the proper place.' The proper place for what, Doctor? You were just going by the operative report, right?"

"That is correct, Mrs. Day."

"Now, I believe you also said, 'With two doctors watching the saw' during Janet's first right-knee surgery, 'it would be very apparent if the saw were to be angulated enough to depart from the horizontal.' Is that correct?"

"That is correct."

"They would have had to have known?"

"Yes, ma'am."

"Doctor, reading the documents that we reviewed this morning, the referral letter that Dr. Allgood wrote to Dr. Hughston, and the note that Dr. Ulid made in Janet's medical chart fifteen years later, do they both say essentially the same thing, that Janet's ligaments had been invaded?"

"Yes, ma'am."

"Now, Dr. Allgood stated here that the posterior lateral capsule, the ligaments of the knee, have been involved in the osteotomy. *Involved* means cut or damaged in some way; isn't that true?"

"I'm not quite sure what it means. To me this is ambiguous. We would have to ask Dr. Allgood what he meant."

"In your deposition on page 57, line 12, you interpreted *involved* to mean that it certainly appeared to indicate that the posterior lateral capsule of the knee was somehow invaded in the first osteotomy."

"Okay. So you changed the word from *involved* to *invaded*. I am simply saying—I'm not quite sure what Dr. Allgood means by that."

"Did you sign your deposition, Doctor?"

"Yes, I did."

"Doctor, is it within the standard of care to invade the posterior capsule ligaments?"

"That's vague and ambiguous, incomplete and hypothetical!" Mr. Wiley sputtered.

"Sustained," Judge Fragassi ruled.

"How do you interpret *invade*, Doctor?"

"I don't see the word *invade* here."

"Dr. Kent, I am just asking you to interpret the word *invade*."

"All right. *Invade* would have to mean going into the structure."

"Okay. How would one go into the structure when doing an osteotomy?"

"When doing an osteotomy we would expect if you use the word *invade* and you accept that it would have to be with one of the instruments."

"So you would have to use either a saw or an osteotome or something like that to invade that capsule, wouldn't you?"

"Yes, ma'am."

"Dr. Kent, would such an invasion be below the standard of care?"

"Objection. Vague and ambiguous. Incomplete. Hypothetical!" Mr. Wiley spouted.

"Overruled. Sir, you may answer the question."

"Yes, I would say that would be below the standard of care."

"Dr. Kent, if such a surgical error or mistake happened, should it be disclosed to the patient at the first opportunity?"

"Yes, ma'am."

"Is failure to disclose this to a patient below the standard of care?"

"Yes, ma'am."

Marjorie walked over to the x-rays positioned near the jury. One by one she reviewed each x-ray with Dr. Kent. "So the second and third osteotomy cuts are visible?" Marjorie asked.

"The second is visible here, and we see what appears to be a ghost of it here and the third osteotomy."

"But we can't see the first osteotomy; can we, Doctor?"

"No."

"So there were three osteotomies done on this patient's leg, were there not?"

"Yes."

"Dr. Kent, you've never examined Mrs. Mitchell, have you?"

"No, I have not."

"Your Honor, I have no further questions of this witness."

As Marjorie took her seat, Dr. Allgood walked to the podium. "I only have one question," he said. Immediately his question was objected to by Marjorie, sustained by Judge Fragassi, leading to more questions asked by Dr. Allgood. Mr. Wiley was then given time for his redirect while Bridget and Marjorie took notes. Soon another day in court was over and the thoughts of a four-day weekend were welcomed.

Court resumed on Tuesday, the day after Memorial Day. I was rested and knew what the day would bring. I would again be called to the witness stand and have to face Drs. Allgood and Ulid. After six years of waiting, I was ready. But first, we'd hear from Dr. Burg, my expert witness.

"Good morning, Ladies and Gentlemen. Let the record reflect—the jury is impaneled and all are present. Counsel, call your witness," Judge Fragassi instructed.

"Yes, Your Honor," Marjorie stated as she turned to the back of the courtroom. "Plaintiff calls their medical expert, Dr. Walter Burg."

Within minutes, Dr. Burg was sworn in and seated in the witness box. It had been just weeks since my mother and I had traveled into Los Angeles and met with him.

Marjorie began by asking Dr. Burg about his education and training. He told about his prestigious associations and his current status as a professor of orthopedics and position of chief of staff at Cedars-Sinai Medical Center.

"Doctor, you've actually examined Janet Mitchell, have you not?"

"Yes, ma'am."

"Can you tell me from your review of Janet's medical records and x-rays how many osteotomy cuts were performed in all?"

"Looking at the x-rays, there were three osteotomy cuts on her right leg. Unfortunately, the films that were taken after Janet's first surgery are lost...or at least they're not available."

Marjorie proceeded to place x-rays up on the light box for the doctor to review. One by one he pointed to each of the osteotomy cuts that were shadowed across my tibia.

"Doctor, after reviewing the records, did you find any obvious causes for Janet's ligament instability?"

"No, I searched for it. If this patient had had instability prior to her first right-leg surgery, that would have accounted for it. But according to the records, she had a stable knee, and following the surgical procedure, she had this instability."

"Doctor, in the blue book you should have in front of you, would you please look at Exhibit 43."

"Your Honor," Mr. Wiley suddenly interrupted, "may we approach?"

The next thing I knew, the judge ordered an early morning break. As Dr. Burg left the stand, the jury walked out into the hallway. I walked back to where my parents were seated and sat next to them, waiting and listening. The court reporter and all the attorneys gathered around the judge. I didn't know what all the commotion was about. Exhibit 43 was a letter written from Dr. Hughston to Dr. Allgood describing the locations of the three osteotomy cuts on my right leg.

"Your Honor," Mr. Wiley began, "I'm not aware that Dr. Burg has reviewed this document. I've read his deposition in this case, and it's never referenced by anyone anywhere."

"He has read the letter, Your Honor," Marjorie stated. "He's reviewed all of Dr. Hughston's records."

"Where did you get Dr. Hughston's records?" Judge Fragassi asked.

"From Dr. Hughston," Marjorie, Bridget, and Mr. Wiley stated in unison as Dr. Allgood remained silent.

"Your Honor," Marjorie said, "this exhibit is a letter to Dr. Allgood from Dr. Hughston, and Dr. Allgood should have had the letter. He should have seen it."

"That's a letter written to me in 1978, Your Honor," Dr. Allgood stated. "It's just that my records are gone because I haven't seen the patient since then. I didn't see anything in the letter that was bothersome, but I haven't seen it before this morning."

"Dr. Allgood, you purged your records," Judge Fragassi reminded.

"Your Honor," Mr. Wiley said, "this is a substantive letter. There are things in it that are going to have an impact on issues in the case. That's why I'm bringing it up. I've never seen it, and I took his deposition."

"Mr. Wiley," Judge Fragassi replied, "let's look at the letter and see if there's anything that bothers you. Now I look at it and..."

"Well, Your Honor," Mr. Wiley sighed. "The issue, as far as where the osteotomy was performed by Dr. Hughston, that's important in terms of looking at the x-rays and the MRIs."

"Well, he says where he performed it," Judge Fragassi sternly replied.

"Dr. Hughston says that he performed it between the other two," Marjorie added.

"And that's an issue in the case," Mr. Wiley said.

"What do you mean?" Judge Fragassi asked. "Whether Dr. Hughston performed his osteotomy cut between the other two?"

"Right," Mr. Wiley stated. "And the MRIs interpreted by my experts show that the osteotomy cut by Dr. Hughston was in the same location as the original one performed by Dr. Allgood. The plaintiff's assumption, however, is that the cuts are in different locations."

"Your Honor," Marjorie said, slightly disgusted, "there were two other MRIs performed. They only gave Dr. Borst one MRI. There are forty x-rays out there that they've never showed to Dr. Borst."

"That's another issue," Mr. Wiley spouted. "What I'm concerned about is this document."

"Mr. Wiley," Judge Fragassi ruled, "if Dr. Burg has reviewed this record—that's what he'll testify to."

Dr. Burg did testify to the facts surrounding Mr. Wiley's "questionable document." After the break, Marjorie finished her questioning, and my stomach turned as Mr. Wiley ruthlessly questioned Dr. Burg. An hour or two later, Dr. Allgood found his way to the podium, ready to tackle my expert witness.

"Objection, Your Honor," Marjorie said more than once. "Dr. Allgood is testifying again."

"Just ask questions, Doctor. You're arguing with the witness," Judge Fragassi stated.

"Dr. Allgood," Dr. Burg said, perplexed, "what I don't understand from all your questioning of me is why is Janet's left knee perfect and the right one isn't. Answer that if you can. Answer that and you have solved my problem. You've got a knee that has so much trouble—I just don't understand."

Dr. Allgood did his best and used complex medical terminology—certainly to confuse the jury. He wasn't as patient as the other lawyers had been during their questioning. At one point, he tried to grab a model of the knee right out of Dr. Burg's hand as Dr. Burg waved his arm in the air making it impossible.

Another break was granted, and I tried to focus my thoughts on what was to come. This was my last chance to state my case through Marjorie's questioning. I would answer her questions and trust God to handle the rest.

Once court resumed, Bridget gave me a nod and I stood, my head held high, and made my way to the witness stand. Marjorie paused and then began her questioning. She asked me about my visits with Dr. Ulid and his great confession. We reviewed my trip to Dr. Allgood's office when I'd been told that they did not know a Janet Hepp Mitchell. From my accident in Mexico to my college years and my many days in the hospital in Georgia, she quizzed. After an hour or so, Marjorie finished, and Mr. Wiley took her place for his cross-examination.

Mr. Wiley began by saying he had just a few questions. Many began with, "Janet, did Dr. Hughston ever tell you...?" Questions continued, trying to pinpoint just when I was told I had degenerative arthritis. Within a few minutes, it seemed I gave him the information he was seeking as he said, "Thank you, Your Honor, that's all I have."

Dr. Allgood declined his last chance to question me. The judge turned to Marjorie.

"Plaintiff rests as to this phase of the trial," Marjorie said politely, folding her hands on top of the counsel table.

Exhibits were then moved into evidence, and Judge Fragassi recited his instructions to the jury: "Ladies and gentlemen of the jury, it is now my duty to instruct you on the law that applies to this case. It is your duty to follow the law. As jurors, it is your duty to determine the effect and value of the evidence and to decide all questions of fact. You may not be influenced by sympathy, prejudice, or passion...The verdict form that will be submitted to you has one question. You will also receive three copies of the instructions I've just read. At this time I'll stop and allow counsel to make their last arguments."

Marjorie calmly walked to the podium. "Thank you, Your Honor. May it please the court, in my opening statement to you, I told you what I thought the evidence would prove. Now it's time to reflect on what we've presented and then you're to decide if we have, in fact, proven our case. The question that you will answer is, 'Did Dr. Albert Allgood and/or Dr. Ryan Ulid intentionally conceal from plaintiff material information concerning Janet Hepp Mitchell's medical care or treatment?' Unquestionably mistakes were made in plaintiff's medical care. Let's review the testimony of Dr. Borst, the defendant's radiologist. And what did he see in the films of Janet's knee? He saw two osteotomy cuts. But how many were there? Three! Three osteotomy cuts *did not* show up on the MRI that was shown to Dr. Borst. Why? Dr. Borst was shown the MRI from 1992. Not the MRI from 1991 taken in Dr. Allgood's office that disappeared with Dr. Allgood's medical file. Out of the forty x-rays we had available, Dr. Borst was given the MRI from 1992, which Dr. Ulid had ordered. That's all Dr. Borst was given. He's a fine radiologist. Had he been given all of the evidence, he might have had something more to testify to."

Systematically Marjorie then reviewed each detail, from the day Dr. Ulid confessed to the writing of my ballerina card to Dr. Ulid. "The plaintiff ended this letter saying, 'Thank you again for your honesty. Thank you so much for trying to stop Dr. Allgood from cutting the bone wrong.' Now that's a statement that capsules what he told her. If she'd misunderstood, would he not have responded immediately and said, 'Janet, you misunderstood,' and everything would have gone away. If you write a letter like that don't you expect a reply? Don't you? Wouldn't you expect Dr. Ulid to grab that letter and pick up the phone, or write a letter and say, 'I didn't mean that we made a mistake, I didn't mean that we concealed it, I didn't mean that you weren't supposed to tell Dr. Allgood that I told you. No, no, no, you misunderstood. This is what happened,' and you know, Janet was a pretty trusting gal, and she probably would have accepted that. I'll paraphrase one of the instructions from the court that you will receive: When someone makes a statement against your interests and you don't respond to correct it, and you had time to respond, presumably then the statement may be considered true. Remember—Dr. Ulid did not respond to Janet's note!

"Now, I guess the first question that you'll ask yourselves is what is material information? Well it's material when a young girl places her faith, life, hopes, and dreams in the care of her doctor. Do you think, under such circumstances, that the doctor should tell her, 'I've never done this before'? Do you think that's material? I do. She wasn't told that, and her parents weren't told that—and they had a right to be told the qualifications. They believed these doctors were experienced surgeons. I have a daughter. I don't think I would have allowed her to go under the knife if somebody hadn't done it before. I don't care how many sport injuries Dr. Allgood cured; if he hadn't performed this particular type of operation before—I wouldn't want him and I don't think a reasonable mother would! A doctor has the duty to disclose who is going to be performing a surgery and what he is going to do. They also have a duty to disclose their qualification and background for doing it…We're entitled to that, as patients we're entitled, and I don't care what they say!

"Now, let me write this down," Marjorie said as she walked away from the podium over to the larger chart board standing next to the jury. "Material fact number one," she scrawled. From there she began creating a list of material facts for the jury to see. "Lastly," Marjorie proclaimed, "they concealed the mistake; they blamed it on God! These doctors had numerous opportunities to help Janet, but what did they do? They tried to perform a cover-up operation. I think that's contemptible. Why didn't they send her to Dr. Hughston, to some-body who knew what they were doing? Dr. Ulid said in this court that he himself had never performed a reconstruction like that ever! And Dr. Allgood should have never attempted such a complicated sur-gery—he had only been in practice for four years! But instead, they tried to cover it up. And that's a lie! And when you lie and someone is harmed by it, I think that you would have to take responsibility for that lie, and that's what we're asking for in your answer to the question, 'Did Dr. Albert Allgood and/or Dr. Ryan Ulid intentionally conceal from plaintiff material information concerning her medical care and treatment?' You have been a marvelous jury and we thank you."

Marjorie gathered her notes and returned to her seat. "Thank you, Counsel," Judge Fragassi said. "Mr. Wiley, you're closing?"

Within a minute Mr. Wiley had moved to the podium. "Good afternoon, ladies and gentlemen. This is my opportunity, as you know, to provide you with my thoughts, our thoughts as to what we believe the evidence has shown in this case. The question that you're now presented with during this phase of the trial deals with the issue of intentional concealment. It's one thing to accuse a physician of malpractice and it's quite another thing to accuse someone of intentional misconduct. Basically what they're saying is that not only are Drs. Ulid and Allgood bad surgeons, but also they're essentially bad, morally bankrupt individuals. And I believe the evidence has shown that is the furthest thing from the truth.

"There was no intentional concealment here. Did Dr. Ulid wrongly jump to a conclusion in 1992 when he saw Ms. Mitchell in his office and told her certain things? Certainly. Yes. He admits it! He got up on the stand and admitted that he told Ms. Mitchell some things he knows were wrong. Did he say the things that Ms. Mitchell has ascribed to him? I think he probably said a lot of it. Yet, I think it's probably been embellished a little bit, maybe spiced up a little bit for the purpose of this litigation. But I don't think that it really matters in this case. The reason I say this is because the medical evidence, if you look at just the medical evidence, there is only one conclusion that you can reach—the cut did not enter the joint space of Ms. Mitchell's knee. Tell me, how can you conceal something that did not happen? You can't! It's pretty simple. If there is no cut up to the joint space—there is no concealment. Now, when Dr. Ulid told plaintiff that he felt that the ligaments had been damaged, Ms. Mitchell thought—lawsuit! I don't think there's any question that she was thinking about a lawsuit.

"So you're probably asking yourself, well what did happen? How did Ms. Mitchell end up with this poor result? And there's no question this was a poor outcome. This is something that no one expected, something nobody wanted. So what happened was that after the surgery, for whatever the reason, when Ms. Mitchell began walking, the pressure on her knee started to loosen those ligaments and her knee became unstable. Ms. Mitchell did have a bad outcome, that's for certain, but it doesn't mean that anything was done wrong.

"Now, if one were to believe that the osteotomy cut was cut on the angle that has been theorized and cut the ligaments and damaged Ms. Mitchell's knee, then one would have to believe that there had been a joint conspiracy, not just amongst these defendants but amongst all kinds of doctors; essentially every doctor that's seen the plaintiff since 1977 has been involved in a conspiracy to cover this up and hide the truth from Ms. Mitchell as to what really happened. If you believe this cover-up, then Dr. Allgood would have to be lying; Dr. Ulid would have to be lying; Dr. Kent, my expert, would have to be lying; Dr. Borst, who read the films, would have to be lying; and Dr. Hughston the national expert who saw her for several years has had to be involved, trying to cover this up and not tell plaintiff what happened. Does this make sense to you? Doesn't make sense to me. I think the reason is because it didn't happen! Why would all those doctors risk so much over this? The answer is that they wouldn't."

Mr. Wiley continued his statement and the jury listened intently. With few facial expressions, it was difficult to read what they might be thinking. My heart raced. *How dare you! It was a conspiracy, if that's what you want to call it, but leave Dr. Hughston out of this.* I shut my eyes and listened to every word he said. "The evidence is that Dr. Ulid has always been honest with Ms. Mitchell. Even when he jumped to the wrong conclusion in 1992, he was honest enough to tell her what he thought happened. He must have known at that point that 'Boy, this could get me in trouble. My friend Dr. Allgood could get in trouble for this too.' Why did he tell her this? Because he was being honest with her and that's his personality. Maybe he tends to be a little direct, maybe a little blunt, maybe a little opinionated. Yet that's his personality, that's the way he is.

"Ladies and Gentlemen, the plaintiff has the burden of proof in this case, and I would suggest to you to look just at the medical evidence presented. The overwhelming medical evidence is that the cut did not damage the ligaments. I think that we all sympathize with the plaintiff's plight, but you have to decide this case on the evidence, not the feeling of sympathy or passion. The evidence that has been presented to you brings you to the only conclusion that makes any sense. That is that Dr. Ulid and Dr. Allgood did not hide anything. Number one, there was nothing to hide; and number two, more important is that these doctors would *never, never, ever* consider doing such. To do so would be unethical and morally wrong and that's not something that either one of them would ever do. Thank you for listening."

Mr. Wiley flipped the pages back from his yellow pad and walked behind me on his way to his seat. I felt his suit jacket brush against my back as he passed. I reminded myself that God's power is not diminished by lack of fair play.

"Thank you, Counsel," Judge Fragassi said. "Ladies and gentlemen, I'll recess at this time. Tomorrow Dr. Allgood will argue, closing his case. Then the plaintiff will have an opportunity to do closing arguments; then the matter will be submitted to you. Recall my admonishment. Don't discuss the case among yourselves. Don't form an opinion on the case. You're dismissed."

That night I lay in bed trying to imagine what it would feel like once this ordeal was behind me. I prayed that God would strengthen my parents and Marty and continue to bless Marjorie and Bridget with wisdom.

After a good night's sleep, my dad drove my mother and me to the courthouse because Marty had to conduct an important meeting at work. Family members met us, all eager to hear Dr. Allgood's closing statement.

"Good morning, Ladies and Gentlemen," Judge Fragassi said. "Let the record reflect that the jury is impaneled. All are present. Dr. Allgood, your closing, sir?"

"Thank you, Your Honor," Dr. Allgood said as he pulled out a notepad from his gym bag. "I wanted to go over each of the important points that we should touch on and find out if there was any voluntary concealment."

For the next hour the jury sat and listened to Dr. Allgood's story of "what really happened," and then he concluded his closing statement. "I don't feel there was any reason for any concealment. There has been not been a time when a person sat down and said, 'Hey man, we really did a botched job. We need concealment.' Now, first of all, as Mr. Wiley said yesterday, this concealment would have to include us all. And I've never heard of that in a million years in medicine, that doctors would say, 'This is a really nice guy. Let's protect him.' Now, there is no doubt we did not get the results we wanted, but through all of this there was no attempt or any reason to have voluntary concealment. If I had ten wishes in the world, I would give Janet one to say, 'I wish you had two great knees,' but I can't do that. Thank you."

Dr. Allgood briskly walked back to his seat as Marjorie was called to begin her final closing statement. "Well, we've heard the testimony about what was intended and what wasn't and that there was no concealment. Very interesting! There was a full record in 1992 and less than a year later those records were purged. Remember those were Dr. Allgood's words, *purged*. Why purge records? Now Dr. Ulid will now tell you that he had a 'synapse.' And I think a synapse is a gap, an interruption—a brain interruption. I hope Dr. Ulid doesn't have those when he does surgery. But some strange thought entered his mind—all of a sudden after fifteen years! If Dr. Ulid truly had a synapse, it was a synapse—a flaring up of his conscience—and he thought, 'I've got to tell her, she deserves to know.' That's what that wee small voice said to him and that's what he did, he told her.

"Now, a best defense is a good offense, and I've been accused of tampering with evidence, which is kind of silly when you think about it because the worst thing you can do is try to change an exhibit. What I tried to do when I removed Janet's writing from that exhibit was to restore it to its pristine state, exactly as Dr. Ulid had drawn it. So I put Wite-Out® on what she had written, "posterior cruciate," and photocopied it so I could say, 'Did you draw this?' which, of course, he did. But that's not manufacturing evidence, nor is it concealing anything. Janet testified that she wrote on it.

"And to call it a conspiracy, well, I don't have any doubt there was at least a tacit or silent agreement between these doctors. I think that because Dr. Ulid said to Janet, 'You're not going to find any records from Dr. Allgood, but go to him and tell him you know, that you have found out, but don't tell him who told you!' Yeah, there was an agreement or a conspiracy, if you want to call it that. But to drag poor Dr. Borst, who is an outstanding radiologist, and say he had to be in on it, that's silly. Dr. Borst was told that there were two osteotomy cuts. Did you ever hear him mention three? Out of forty x-rays and three MRIs, they gave him the June '92 x-rays and one MRI.

"They cut the bone wrong and they knew they cut it because Dr. Kent, their expert, insisted that you had to know. He said everybody in the room would know. Who's right? Certainly Dr. Kent was not in on this conspiracy; he simply believed what he was told. Dr. Kent is a good guy. He testifies a lot for the defense and I am on the other side and so I meet him a lot. And I think he's truthful, he's truthful to what he's asked. I said it would be below the standard of care to cut that and he said, 'Yes.' He didn't go any further, he didn't volunteer, but he tells the truth and he said everybody in that room would have known it.

"If this was a conspiracy, it was a very limited one. Poor Dr. Borst is now being tarred and feathered because he was given very, very limited information. Absurd! I haven't accused him. I haven't accused Dr. Kent and I certainly haven't accused anyone else. Nobody has set the doctors up. A seventeen-year-old girl doesn't set anybody up. She didn't plan this!

"The defendants are real proud of saying, 'You should look at our records.' But what I think what you ought to do is look at the records while you're looking for what *isn't* in the records. Dr. Ulid, you remember, operated on Janet's other leg just weeks after the first right-leg surgery. Dr. Ulid then followed the patient and you'll find all through his comments when he looks at the left leg, but he doesn't mention the progress on her right leg until months later—June.

"Ladies and Gentlemen of the jury, this is the last chance I have to talk with you before you answer the big question: Did they willfully conceal from Janet Hepp Mitchell? There are two statements that it happened. We now have total denials. They not only concealed it from Janet, they're trying to conceal it from you. So what's your answer? Did they conceal? Can you see what I wrote? It's 'Yes. Yes. Yes!' You've been a wonderful jury, thank you."

"Thank you, Counsel," Judge Fragassi said while leaning forward, appearing to be stretching. "Ladies and gentlemen of the jury, it is your duty to discuss this case in order to reach agreement...Each of you must decide for yourselves, but you should do so only after considering the views of each juror...Remember, you're not partisans or advocates in this matter; you must be impartial judges of the facts...As soon as nine or more jurors have agreed on the answer, have the verdict signed and dated by your foreperson and return it to this room." Judge Fragassi's instructions continued on and soon concluded.

I sat frozen as I watched the jurors rise and walk out the door, heading for deliberation.

We all left the courtroom and went to the cafeteria to get some lunch. I wasn't hungry. Instead of eating, I watched the clock and listened for *Mitchell v. Allgood* to be called on the intercom to let us know that a verdict had been reached. I called Marty at work. He assured me he'd leave work the moment a verdict had been reached.

The past six-plus years had been incredible. I now knew for certain that I was in the care of a loving God who is not an indifferent observer. The first two weeks of my trial were over. I knew that if the jury came back with a verdict of concealment, I would have won the statute-of-limitation phase of my trial and would then continue on for two more weeks of trial to determine damages. But if no concealment was found, I would hold my head high and walk out through the courtroom doors and head home—knowing I had walked a road that I believed God had asked me to walk.

Just two hours later, a voice came across the intercom: "*Mitchell v. Allgood.*"

"It's time."

"You're right, Janet, it's time," Marjorie said as she stood. "Janet, I'm proud of you," she added with a sparkle in her eye. "Now, let's go hear what the jury has to say."

In minutes we took our seats in the courtroom. This time I was granted permission to sit between my parents instead of at the counsel table. The judge called the court to order, and my dad took my hand in his. I took a deep breath as the clerk read the verdict: "We, the jury in the above entitled action, find the following special verdict on the question submitted to us: Did Dr. Albert Allgood and/or Dr. Ryan Ulid intentionally conceal from plaintiff material information concerning her medical care or treatment? Answer: YES."

Tears streamed down my face. For the first time, I turned and looked at the jurors face to face. I nodded, trying to find a way to thank them for their dedication. I knew their lives had been placed on hold for the past two weeks and that we had the damages phase of the trial yet to come. While the individual members were polled, I noted their names and thanked God for each person.

Judge Fragassi released the jury for the day and ordered them to be back in court Monday morning to proceed with the case.

My doctors exposed and truth prevailing, my family and I walked out through the courtroom doors. Marty was running down the hall to join us.

"We won!" I cried as he threw his arms around me.

Taking my face into his hands, he kissed me on my cheek and whispered, "Honey, I won the day we met."

And so did I.

*Epilogue*

# FOR RICHER OR POORER

NO ONE TRULY WINS in a medical malpractice case. Those who sue and win still have the medical disasters that brought them to trial. No judgment has changed the physical status of my knee. Those who sue and lose, lose much more than any hoped-for financial gain. Ironically, they struggle to meet financial, medical, and legal obligations while their trust in the medical profession and our legal system remains challenged.

For the past century, doctors have been regarded as gods. Rarely questioned, their imperfections have been tolerated and accepted as fate, or, in my case, as "God's will." Doctors are human. They have to use their fallible skills and knowledge to bring about wholeness and health. Maybe the pressure of needing to appear perfect added to the collapse of Dr. Allgood's and Dr. Ulid's character and judgment. Perhaps trying to live up to the roles they chose led to their greatest downfall.

Seven months after winning my lawsuit, I was told that the "explosives" found near my home and removed by the bomb squad were not in any way related to my litigation. This brought great relief as I again found myself in federal court fighting Dr. Allgood's bankruptcy. I believe Dr. Allgood had carefully calculated his strategy of not paying into a medical malpractice insurance plan for the sake of his personal financial gain. I believe he planned all along that, if sued, he'd simply file for bankruptcy. Without hesitation, I carried on, this time through the federal court system with Matthew K. Ross,

Esq., and Lisa Neal, Esq. After winning a seven-year battle in state court, I wasn't giving up.

On March 8, 1999, a U.S. bankruptcy judge ruled that Dr. Allgood could not discharge his debt owed to me. The judge concluded that Dr. Allgood's judgment was based on intentional concealment—a form of fraud. Dr. Allgood's judgment was ruled nondischargeable since it was based on willful, intentional, and malicious conduct. Yet even with a court ruling, Dr. Allgood refused to pay, and my legal fees for fighting his bankruptcy were well over $40,000.

Shortly after my verdict, the Medical Board of California received information regarding my judgment. This governing agency, whose purpose and design is to monitor and regulate doctors and protect the people of California, regretfully informed me that they were unable to investigate Dr. Allgood and Dr. Ulid because of the existing statute laws. Under existing law, only occurrences that had taken place within the previous seven years could be investigated. This statute of limitations held no provision for cases where fraud and/or concealment were issues.

After I had fought so hard to expose the lies and deceit of my doctors—trying to prevent other patients from becoming victims— the California Statute of Limitations shielded my doctors from any accountability or investigation by the medical board. For the law established that once the seven-year statute of limitations had expired, a doctor was home free. My doctors had beaten the system.

Per the suggestion of the California Medical Board, in January of 2000, I wrote Assemblyman Bill Campbell of California, explaining my story. I shared with him the inadequacies I saw in our existing law regarding the Medical Board's abilities to investigate. On February 29, 2000, Bill Campbell sent a letter informing me that just days earlier he had introduced legislation born out of my medical disaster, which, if signed into law, would eliminate California Business

Profession Code section 2230.5 and the existing seven year statute for investigations. Assembly Bill AB2571 was my hope in changing the future for others. Without the provisions of this bill, doctors had found a way to hide from their responsibilities.

Despite knowing that any change of existing law would not alter the medical board's ability to investigate Drs. Allgood and Ulid, I again stepped out of my comfort zone. At the request of Bill Campbell, Marty and I traveled to Sacramento to speak on the bill's behalf. Jillian, Dr. Ulid's patient who had lost her leg, offered her support. On the steps of the capitol building, Jillian and I met in person for the first time. Within months, Assembly Bill AB2571 passed both houses without a single no vote.

Regardless, this new law was not retroactive. Even though my doctors had been exposed, they remained unscarred and uninvestigated, continuing to practice—treating unsuspecting, trusting patients, all the while my leg shows a road map, scars for a lifetime, from two men who chose to deceive. Within the year, Dr. Allgood moved out of state to work as a medical expert offering court testimony on behalf of doctors and the Social Security Hearing and Appeals. He then unexpectedly passed away in 2004.

Up until 2005, Dr. Ulid held a medical license, and the California Medical Board's Website reflected no complaints, judgments, or disciplinary actions pertaining to him. He has since retired.

Today, I have moved on. No more detective work or courtrooms, yet I continue to speak on behalf of legislation to help prevent medical malpractice. I hold no resentment or unforgiveness—I am not living in a prison of my past. My life is proof positive that God fits even mistakes into his plans.

I often think back over the past few years and realize how my life has been richly blessed by so many people who stood by my side. I always thought there were incredible people in this world, and now I am privileged to know more of them. I have great peace knowing that I walked a road that I was destined to walk, and I walked it to the best of my ability—I gave my all!

Through my experiences, I am reminded that God cares greatly about each one of us. I'm in awe of the way he has answered my prayers. One of the greatest lessons I've learned is that it just takes one. One set of hands or one letter written or one person willing to say, "Yes, I'm willing to take a stand." One life can be used to bless and change the lives of many. My life has been blessed.

I don't know what the future holds for my knee, but God has assured me that walking or not, I will be okay. When I think about the surgeries ahead and the possibilities of losing my leg, I return to my "flip book" of affirmations. I turn to the last page inscribed with a quote from Patrick Overton. I pause, take a deep breath, and draw on my faith, and then I am reminded that all is well.

*When you walk to the edge of all the light you have,*
*and take that first step into the darkness of the unknown,*
*you must believe that one of two things will happen:*
*There will be something solid for you to stand upon,*
*or, you will be taught how to fly.*[9]

*—Patrick Overton*

*Appendix*

# TIPS FOR MANAGING
# YOUR OWN HEALTHCARE

Through my medical nightmare and journey, I've met several great physicians. Many have reminded me that physicians are not infallible, but still, most are knowledgeable, skilled human beings with a desire to heal.

In November of 1999, the National Academy of Science Institute of Medicine issued a report called "To Err Is Human," concluding that medical mistakes kill between 44,000 and 98,000 hospitalized Americans each year.[10] Thousands more are injured, gaining permanent disabilities, many not even knowing their doctors are at fault. It's shocking but true: Medical malpractice and/or negligence is the eighth most common cause of death in America. These preventable deaths exceed the deaths attributed to car accidents, breast cancer, or AIDS.

With these stunning facts and with the dramatic number of cases proven each year to be attributable to medical negligence, we, the patients, must assume responsibility and learn how we can keep from becoming dreaded statistics. We can take an active role in combating the odds that face us. We can remind, support, question, and pray for our physicians who come to our rescue.

In the past few years, I've had the privilege of speaking with many victims of medical negligence and fraud. Listening to horror stories, I have, as Carl Kirby suggested, "Made a castle out of a pile of rubble." I've compiled their ideas and suggestions, things they now say they wish they had known. These tips are our gift to you to help you develop a healthy doctor/patient relationship.

## 1. Select your own doctor.

Selecting your doctor is one of the most important consumer decisions you will ever make. Before choosing your doctor, research—get recommendations from friends, family, and other trusted physicians. If your medical insurance plan is "managed care," request the list of prospective doctors and learn all you can about these physicians so that *you* can make an *educated choice*. Strange but true, most people spend more time and energy in selecting a new car than they do in selecting a physician. When choosing a doctor, interview him or her. Ask:

- What are your areas of expertise?
- How long have you been practicing medicine?
- Where and when did you attend medical school?
- Do you have special training in managing my preexisting condition?
- Who is on call for you when you're off duty?
- In what hospitals do you have staff privileges?

Will the doctor take time to answer these questions? Are you comfortable when talking with him or her? When selecting a physician, you may also want to consider factors such as the gender and age of the physician and what languages he or she speaks.

## 2. Prepare before your appointment.

Before your appointment make a *written* list of *all* concerns and questions you have pertaining to your health. Include a list of *all* medications you're taking. Include all vitamins, herbs, and over-the-counter medications. At the appointment, provide your doctor with a dated copy of these questions and medications. Keep a copy of this list for your personal records.

## 3. Be assertive.

Ask your doctor the questions on your prepared list. *No* question you may have is stupid or inappropriate. Explain to your physician your health-care concerns. *Do not* expect your doctor to read your mind or have the time to play the game of "Guess doctor…I'm too embarrassed to ask." Do ask to be referred to a specialist if the need arises. Despite the sense of loyalty you may feel for your doctor, it is *not* an act of betrayal to seek out a specialist or second opinion. No doctor can be an expert in all areas!

Be patient with your doctor if he is running late. This shows that he is not afraid of providing the time needed to care for his patients. If your doctor does not listen to your concerns and take the time to answer your questions, your doctor could be hazardous to your health.

## 4. Inform your physician of your past medical history.

Make sure that your doctor is aware of your medical history. This includes all surgeries, serious illnesses, medication allergies, or sensitivities you may have. Ask your physician to request your medical records from all doctors you have seen. Obtain a copy for yourself as well.

## 5. You must feel comfortable!

Unless you're unconscious or heavily medicated, a doctor can only perform a procedure, a surgery, or an exam that you allow. If you are not comfortable, say so and walk out. You, the patient, have ultimate control of your medical care. A physician should *never* perform a gynecological exam without a nurse or third party present. One who does is not acting in your best interest nor protecting his or her career.

## 6. Bring an advocate with you to the doctor appointment.

The emotional stress that accompanies illness can be overwhelming. This stress sometimes prevents a patient from asking important questions or hearing what the doctor has to say. Ask a family member or friend to accompany you to your appointment, someone who will listen with you to what your doctor says. This is especially helpful if you have a chronic illness; it can be life-saving if you're hospitalized.

## 7. Don't be afraid to ask questions.

Make sure you ask about all new medications prescribed. If your doctor writes a prescription, ask him or her the name of the drug prescribed, as prescriptions are not always legible. Make sure you understand the dosage, how and when to take it, and what to do if you miss a dose. Ask about possible side effects and what you should do if they occur. Be sure to find out if this new medication is compatible with your other medication. You could be putting your heath at risk by not asking the questions that you have.

If your medication has not changed, and a pill prescribed looks different from your last prescription, you could be getting the wrong medication. If you're seeing more than one doctor, make sure each doctor knows all medications you are taking. Try to be consistent in your use of a pharmacy. Pharmacists often maintain records of all medications you purchase. These records help prevent disastrous medication interactions!

Whenever receiving an injection, always ask what the medication is and what it is for. This is especially important when hospitalized.

Contact your physician if you have problems or concerns. Medication errors occur when the patient is given the wrong medication or an incorrect dosage. Some medication mix-ups can actually result in death. The 1999 National Academy of Science Institute of Medicine report "To Err Is Human" states, "Medication errors account for one out of 131 outpatient deaths and one out of 854 inpatient deaths."[11]

## 8. Remember that you are the consumer.

If you do not support and agree with your doctor's philosophy and approach to your health care, it's time to make a change. You may need to contact your insurance company to do this, but most policies state that the insured is assured "appropriate care." This care includes seeing a doctor with whom you can communicate and feel confident that he or she listens and understands your health concerns. Write letters, if needed, to promote this change. In 1994, Richard Frankel and Howard Beckman conducted a study of malpractice depositions.[12] They concluded "71 percent of the litigating patients stated that they had a poor relationship with their physician, and 32 percent felt their doctor deserted them after something went wrong."[13]

## 9. Appeal if you've been denied treatment.

If your medical insurance denies a treatment that you and your doctor feel is necessary, file an appeal with your insurance company requesting an independent review. If this review is denied, contact the Insurance Commissioner of your state. Jamie Court, coauthor of *Making a Killing: HMOs and the Threat to Your Health,* states:

> In HMOs and other managed-care plans, doctors are often given a fixed budget for each patient. The result of this reimbursement system—known as capitation—is that the less they do for you, the more money they make. If you suspect a doctor is committing *financial medical malpractice,*

keeping his costs low by not ordering tests or making refer-rals, call the state Medical Board and report that doctor.[14]

## 10. Keep a journal.

Keep a journal of your pain and activity level. Note patterns and in-form your physician about them. Write down the dates of all medical appointments, results of medical tests, and important conversations you have with your health-care provider. When you have surgery, obtain a copy of the hospital surgical report to add to your personal records. Remember that an entire year of my medical records had been removed from Dr. Ulid's medical chart. If I had asked for a copy of these records throughout my care, I may have realized something was amiss.

In the state of California, medical records and x-rays are the property of the health-care provider. But all medical records must be made available to the patient within "a reasonable time period." In California, this is within fifteen days of a written request. Check with the medical board of your state regarding the procedure you must follow.

## 11. Research your doctor's standing with the medical board.

Call your state medical board or check your doctor's standing on your state medical board's Website. Most medical boards disclose "disciplinary actions" against physicians. Find out what information your state medical board offers and what it does not disclose. A mal-practice judgment does not necessarily mean a "bad" doctor. Yet you need to be aware that most medical boards do not inform the public of complaints or investigations concerning a physician, and most do not disclose malpractice settlements, so they remain hidden. As of January 1, 2003, the Medical Board of California discloses the facts of out-of-court settlements once a doctor has had three or four settlements (depending on his or her specialty).

Statistics show that 90 percent of medical malpractice cases filed are settled out of court. Most of these settlements accompany a confidentiality agreement that prevents the injured from filing a grievance and/or cooperating with their medical board, thus preventing the medical board from investigating and protecting future victims of their state. It is clear why doctors and their insurance companies only allow 10 percent (the cases they truly believe they can win) of medical malpractice cases to go to court. The benefits of settling, and not tarnishing their professional reputation and "scoreboard" with the medical board, is incentive enough. "Settle quietly, and nobody will ever know!" is one of the best-kept secrets in the United States.

## 12. Discover alternative treatment plans.

Most surgeries are not emergency procedures. Therefore, do not rush into them. Before agreeing to a surgical procedure, ask your doctor and surgeon if they are aware of any alternative procedures that may aid in your diagnosis and treatment. When appropriate, check with an alternative health-care provider such as a nutritionist, chiropractor, or podiatrist. Dr. Hughston says, "There's no knee that surgery can't make worse!"

## 13. Get a second opinion.

*Never* accept one laboratory result or one doctor's diagnosis as fact. Never, ever accept one doctor's surgical recommendation as the only way of regaining your health. *Always, always,* get a second opinion regarding advised surgery and/or extensive medical treatment. If possible, seek a second opinion in a different laboratory and/or medical community than your existing doctor. Some doctors remain silent regarding mistakes and misdiagnoses made by their peers.

A doctor or laboratory from a different community might be more comfortable and willing to expose the mistakes or misdiagnoses of their colleagues.

## 14. Before surgery, weigh the pros and cons and donate blood.

Ask your surgeon if he or she is board-certified to perform the needed procedure. Ask your surgeon how many times he or she has performed your prescribed surgery and what his or her success and mortality rates have been. Question your physician about any possible complications or side effects that may occur as a result of the surgery. Weigh the possible complications with the option of not having the surgery, and then decide if the surgery is really necessary. And believe it or not, you need to ask your surgeon if he or she will be conducting your operation.

When preparing for surgery, ask your doctor if you are a candidate to donate your own blood. This involves giving a few units of blood prior to surgery. Your donated blood is then stored and given back to you after surgery if the need arises. Self-donating reduces problems relating to blood matching and/or transmitting infection.

## 15. Personally check up on your doctor.

Before you or a family member has surgery, *you* do the checking! Make sure the surgeon has medical malpractice insurance coverage. Call the appropriate hospital and ask for this information. *Don't assume!* Accidents do indeed happen. While you have the hospital on the phone, ask them when their last inspection was by the Joint Commission on the Accreditation of Healthcare Organizations (JCAHO). You may also want to review your selected hospital's historical report at www.jointcommission.org.

Remember for over twenty years Dr. Allgood practiced medicine and performed surgery without carrying medical malpractice insurance. The hospitals in which he practiced medicine either did not require their physicians to carry malpractice insurance, were negligent in validating Dr. Allgood's malpractice insurance, or allowed him to be an exception to their own rule. It is my opinion that Dr. Allgood depended upon using the bankruptcy system to avoid paying any possible judgments against him.

## 16. Read about past litigation involving your chosen physician.

Before having surgery, make a trip to the county clerk's office at your local courthouse. Look up any and all medical malpractice cases. Note any additional cases stating concealment, fraud, and misdemeanor or criminal offenses pertaining to your doctor, as these may reflect upon his or her integrity and character. It usually takes years between the initial malpractice injury and the conclusion of a court case. This trip to the courthouse will aid you in discovering:

- The cases that have gone to trial that may be reflected with the each state's medical board.
- What cases have been filed and settled out of court. (In California, due to government code 68152, these court files may be disposed of within two years of a settlement.)
- What cases have been filed and are currently in the court system. One or two cases filed against a medical professional may be reasonable as doctors are human *and* some patients have accused inappropriately, thus abusing the court system. However, if your medical professional has a history of negligence, malpractice, fraud, and/or concealment—run!

## 17. Understand what you are signing.

Before signing any hospital form, make sure you understand what you're signing. If you do not understand, ask. Most hospital admission forms include a place to initial, waiving your rights to a jury trial if a medical error occurs. This binds you to arbitration. You have the right and option *not* to sign on this dotted line.

## 18. Surgeon or resident, it's your choice.

When signing a surgery consent form, note who the consent authorizes to perform the surgery. Many teaching hospitals allow residents (also known as house doctors) or physicians learning surgical techniques to perform surgery or practice their anesthesia skills while the patient's doctor and anesthesiologist stand by and offer guidance. Remember Dr. Allgood's words, "The patient could come in for surgery, and even though my name [Dr. Allgood] is on the informed consent form, a resident could have done the surgery. That's what can happen in a teaching hospital!" With the knowledge of this, you, the patient, have the choice to say, "I'd rather not take this risk."

## 19. Make sure you are informed.

Ask questions! Before signing the informed consent form, make sure you understand and agree to the surgery foretold. Make sure that you have been informed of the side effects or results that you may experience as a result of the suggested procedure.

## 20. When planning for surgery, find out who your anesthesiologist will be.

The anesthesiologist is responsible for maintaining your life while your surgeon is performing your needed procedure. Ask your doctor if he or she knows the assigned anesthesiologist. Check the courthouse and medical board of your state for any history of medical negligence and/or related matters.

## 21. *Question your doctor regarding poor results a surgery or treatment.*

Remember, medical professionals are not required by law to inform patients of medical blunders or misdiagnoses. If something seems wrong or your health is not improving, *be assertive!* Ask, "Doctor, why did I have that reaction to the medication? Why am I feeling this way? Why am I still in pain? Did something go wrong in my surgery?"[15] Learn from Carl Kirby, "Listen to your gut feeling."

Before considering a medical malpractice lawsuit, take a friend or family member with you and go talk to your doctor. Try to resolve your situation without legal intervention. Do not accuse your physician of wrongdoing until you are certain this accusation is correct. Pray and seek counsel. The Christian Medical and Dental Association Website says, "A malpractice lawsuit can wreak havoc on a doctor's family, career and emotional and spiritual well-being. The effects can be devastating."[16] We as patients must remember that a malpractice suit affects many.

## 22. *Be the patient that your physician will never forget.*

One out of every four orthopedic surgeons have cut or will operate on the wrong limb at some point in his or her career. In 1998, the American Academy of Orthopedic Surgeons launched a "Sign Your Site" campaign, encouraging surgeons to sign their names directly on the patient's skin, marking the spot intended for surgery, thus hoping to prevent these recurring mistakes.[17] These types of mistakes can be prevented. Be assertive—hand your doctor a pen!

## 23. When hospitalized, get well and get out.

The *People's Medical Society* has suggested that patients spend the least time possible in a hospital. Hospitals are an infection waiting to happen. The longer you stay, the greater your chances of picking up a hospital-acquired infection. Hospitals are not a resting place or vacation just to "get away." According to the Center of Disease Control and Prevention, "In [U.S.] hospitals alone, hospital-acquired infections account for an estimated 2 million infections, 90,000 deaths, and $4.5 billion excess health care costs annually."[18]

## 24. Know that great doctors make mistakes.

Medical errors are not usually the fault of a "bad" doctor, but are made by good—yet imperfect—physicians, using their human skills to bring wholeness and healing. Doctors and medical professionals *do* make mistakes, they *do* at times forget, and in no way can they know everything. Expect excellence, but not perfection. Remember, God is responsible for all miracles.

## 25. Be appreciative of your doctor.

Show your doctor respect by keeping your appointments. Follow his or her prescribed plan for your health care. And once in a while, drop him or her a note of thanks, sealed with a prayer.

# Endnotes

1. Corrie ten Boom with Jamie Buckingham, *Tramp for the Lord* (New York: Jove Books, Berkley Publishing Group, 1978), 97.

2. Deborah DeFord, *Quotable Quotes* (The Reader's Digest Association, 1997), 66.

3. John Dryden, *The Great American Bathroom Book*, vol. 1 (Salt Lake City: Compact Classics, Inc., 1992), 3-C2.

4. Kyle McCammon, "The Medical Liability Crisis," Association of American Physicians and Surgeons, *Medical Sentinel*, 2002; 7(3): 79-89, 104.

5. A.W. Wu, S. Folkman, S.J. McPhee, and B. Lo, "Do House Officers Learn from Their Mistakes?" *JAMA Report*, vol. 265, no. 16, April 24, 1991.

6. Doug Wojcieskak, personal e-mail dated February 25, 2005.

7. A.B. Witman, D.M. Park, and S.B. Hardin, "How Do Patients Want Physicians to Handle Mistakes? A Survey of Internal Medicine Patients in an Academic Setting," *Archives of Internal Medicine,* vol. 156, no. 22, December 9, 1996.

8. "Dead Man's Survivors Sue Doctors' Hospital," *The Orange County Register*, February 17, 1996.

9. Patrick Overton, *Rebuilding the Front Porch of America* (San Francisco: Columbia Publishers, 1977), 20.

10. Linda Kohn, Janet Corrigan, and Molla Donaldson, eds., *To Err Is Human: Building a Safer Health System,* Committee on Quality of Health Care in America (Washington, D.C.: National Academy Press Institute of Medicine, 1999), 22.

11. Ibid, 23.

12. *Archives of Internal Medicine,* vol. 154, no. 12, June 27, 1994.

13. H.B. Beckman, K.M. Markakis, A.L. Suchman, and R.M. Frankel, Department of Medicine, Highland Hospital, Rochester, NY 14620.

14. Jamie Court, personal e-mail dated February 18, 2006.

15. Christian Medical and Dental Associations, "Medical Malpractice Ministry," http://www.cmdahome.org (accessed Sept. 17, 2006).

16. William C. Watters III, "SMaX (Sign, Mark & X-ray program): Early Data and Practical Applications," *Spineline,* May/June 2003.

17. "'Sign Your Site' Gets Strong Support From Academy Members," *The American Academy of Orthopaedic Surgeons' Bulletin,* vol. 47, no. 1. www.aaos.org (accessed March 8, 2004).

18. "Birth and Deaths: Preliminary Data for 1998," *National Vital Statistics Reports,* Center for Disease Control and Prevention (National Center for Health Statistics, 1999, 47(25); 6).